ENGINEERING & COMPUTER GRAPHICS WORKBOOK

Using SolidWorks 2006

Ronald E. Barr, Ph.D.
Professor

Thomas J. Krueger, Ph.D.
Teaching Specialist

Theodore A. Aanstoos, MSE
Senior Lecturer

Davor Juricic, D.Sc.
Professor Emeritus

Mechanical Engineering Department
The University of Texas at Austin

ISBN: 1-58503-281-6

SDC
PUBLICATIONS

Schroff Development Corporation

www.schroff.com
www.schroff-europe.com

The instructions in this Engineering and Computer Graphics Workbook are based on the following release of SolidWorks:

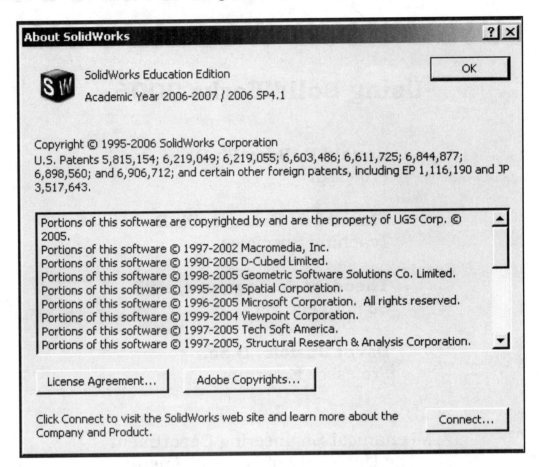

Copyright

Examination Copies:

Electronic Files:

Table of Contents

Notes:

Computer Graphics Lab 1:
2-D Computer Sketching I

INTRODUCTION TO SOLIDWORKS

SolidWorks® is a parametric solid modeling package that is used to build solid computer models. The designer starts with a 2-D sketch that at first is loosely defined. Dimensions and other constraints are applied to the 2-D sketch to fully define its geometry. The sketch is turned into a 3-D solid model using an extrusion or revolution. If the base part is not correct, the designer can simply change the dimensions of the original sketch or definition of the base feature, and then re-build the part with a click of the mouse. Once the base part is defined, new sketches can be defined on planes around the base part, and they can then be extruded to form bosses and cuts on the part. Also, special design features can be easily added to the part, such as fillets, chamfers, and counter bores. This is called feature-based modeling and it is the latest approach to 3-D computer modeling. In this first computer graphics lab, you will concentrate on 2-D computer sketching methods, and will extrude or revolve simple parts. Four different, short exercises are provided.

SOLIDWORKS TOOLBARS SETUP

Your instructor will show you how to launch SolidWorks on your computer. Then your first task is to set up your SolidWorks screen layout to have a common appearance that will be referenced throughout this workbook. To accomplish this, follow these instructions. Go to the **View** pull-down menu on the top of screen, select **Toolbars** and activate the following toolbars: **Features, Sketch, Standard, Standard Views,** and **View**, as shown in Figure 1-1. This will arrange the common toolbars around your screen for easy access during your exercises. Note that, until you activate a part, these toolbars are all faint in appearance, meaning you cannot yet access them.

STARTING A NEW PART

To start your session with SolidWorks, you need to pull down the **File** main menu and click on the **New** command. This will invoke an on-screen menu, as shown in Figure 1.2. You have three options: Part, Assembly, and Drawing. To start a new model, click **Part** and then **OK.** Once you have clicked the OK button, the screen changes into the SolidWorks computer working space with all the previously checked toolbars ready to be used. Your first step is to study this initial screen layout as depicted in Figure 1-3.

Figure 1-1. Setting the Proper Screen Toolbars During Setup.

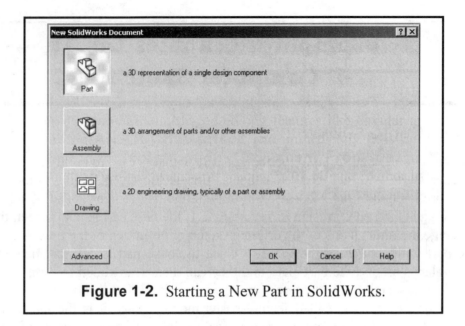

Figure 1-2. Starting a New Part in SolidWorks.

THE SOLIDWORKS SCREEN LAYOUT

The SolidWorks screen layout when you start a part uses the top, left, and right side of the screen to arrange various menus and toolbars. The center of the screen is the computer sketching area for your design work. Study Figure 1-3 to become familiar with this standard screen layout. Each of these menus and toolbars will be described in the subsequent paragraphs.

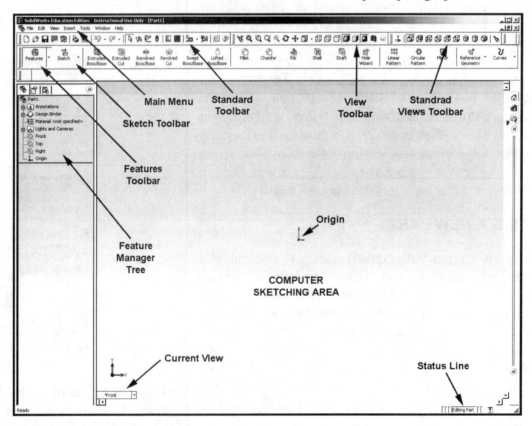

Figure 1.3. The SolidWorks Screen Layout with Major Menus and Toolbars Identified.

MAIN MENU

File is where you can create New files and Open, Save, Print Preview, and Print existing files. You also can set up your Page on this menu.

Edit is where you can Undo the last command, and Cut, Copy, and Paste Entities. It also has the Rebuild command that you may find convenient when you make changes to your model.

View is where you Redraw and set Display parameters. You can set the View Orientation, and select View commands like Zoom, Rotate, and Pan.

Insert is where the major feature creation commands are located. Here you can create the Base part, Cut the part, and invoke many of the parametric features.

Tools has an assortment of helpful commands. It has Sketching Tools, Dimensioning Tools, and Relations Tools. It also has analysis tools like Mass Properties.

Window is where you can set some window properties like vertical and horizontal tiling.

Help is where you can access on screen listings of the command functions and other information that will help you navigate and learn SolidWorks.

FEATURE MANAGER TREE

SolidWorks has a special "Feature Manager Tree" capability that keeps track of the solid modeling process. It relates each feature with the appropriate sketch in a tree diagram and allows you to edit your feature later if needed. The "Feature Manager" is located in the upper left part of the screen. Figure 1-4 shows an example of the Feature Manager.

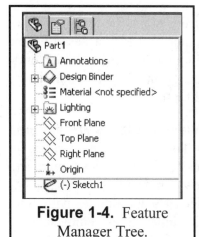

Figure 1-4. Feature Manager Tree.

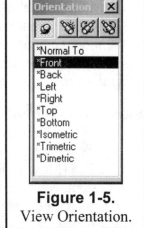

Figure 1-5. View Orientation.

VIEW ORIENTATION

The "View Orientation Menu" (Figure 1-5) is a special on-screen window that is used to easily change your view of the modeling space. The "View Orientation Window" is accessed in the **View** pull-down selection from the Main Menu, and then select **Modify** and **Orientation**. It will then appear on the screen, where you can move it in position and can attach it to the area of the computer screen using the "pushpin" box option. **You may also use the view orientation toolbar as shown in Figure 1-7.**

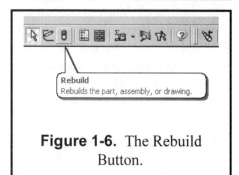

Figure 1-6. The Rebuild Button.

THE REBUILD BUTTON

The "Rebuild Button" is located on the Standard Toolbar and looks like a red/green traffic light, as shown in Figure 1-6. When you press it with the mouse button, it will rebuild your model and update any changes that have been made.

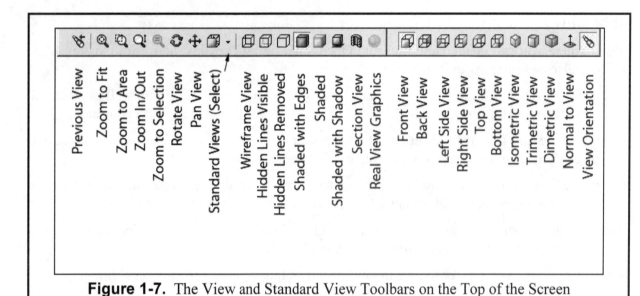

Figure 1-7. The View and Standard View Toolbars on the Top of the Screen

TOOLBARS

Toolbars are clickable icons along the top and side of the screen that permit quick and easy access to some of the more common commands used in SolidWorks. You can see the toolbars, grouped by function, in the general screen layout of Figure 1.3

View and **Standard View Toolbars** are shown in Figure 1-7. The View Toolbar contains buttons for several Zoom commands, the Rotate View command, and the Pan (Move) View command. It also has icons to represent your model as a wireframe, with light gray hidden lines, with hidden lines removed, as a shaded image, and as a shaded image with a shadow. The Standard View Toolbar allows you to select Front, Back, Left, Right, Top, Bottom, Isometric, and Normal Views. As such, it is an alternative to using the "View Orientation" menu (Figure 1-5).

Sketch Toolbar is shown in Figure 1-8. It can be divided into sketch entities, relations, and dimension tools. To start, you click on the **Sketch** icon. As you establish 2-D sketch entities, you can use **Dimension** and **Add Relation** buttons to fix the geometric parameters of your design. To aid you in your sketching, numerous 2-D entity icons are available, such as Line, Arc, Circle, and Rectangle. To edit your sketch, several common commands like Trim, Mirror, Fillet, and Offset are available.

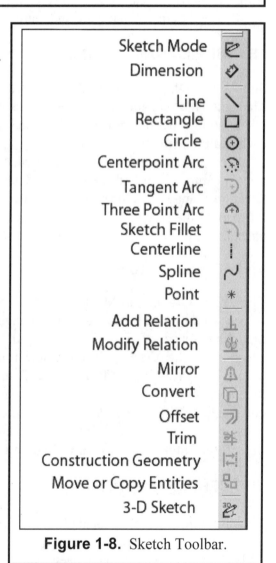

Figure 1-8. Sketch Toolbar.

SKETCHING PLANES

Before you start a 2-D sketch with SolidWorks, you must define (highlight) a sketch plane. The three default orthogonal sketch planes are the three standard orthographic view planes: **Front**, **Top**, and **Right**, as shown in Figure 1-9. Later, you can also pick any plane or flat surface on a base part that has been created. The surface does not necessarily have to be parallel to one of these three principal planes.

LINE COLORS

SolidWorks has several ways to feedback information to the user. One of these ways is to use different line colors. When sketching 2-D profiles, the following color codes prevail.

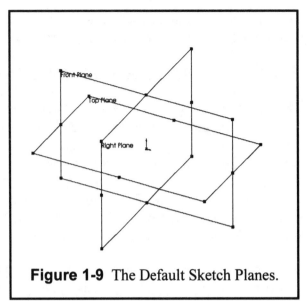

Figure 1-9 The Default Sketch Planes.

Green lines mean that the entities are **Selected**.
Blue lines mean that the dimensions of the geometry are **Under Defined**.
Black lines mean that the dimensions of the geometry are **Fully Defined**.
Red lines mean that the dimensions of the geometry are **Over Defined** (undesirable).

STANDARD TEMPLATES

Before you start any exercises in SolidWorks, it is a good idea to establish some standard drawing templates and title blocks to reflect the two styles of engineering measurements. One set will be for the American National Standards Institute (ANSI) for Inches and the other for Metric.

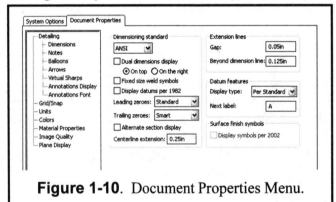

Figure 1-10. Document Properties Menu.

To start, go to **File**, select **New**, then **Part** and **OK** this selection. Go to the **Tools** pull-down menu. Select **Options**. Under the **Document Properties** tab, make sure that the **Dimensioning Standard** is set for **ANSI** (see Figure 1-10). Next select **Units** in the left hand column of the menu. In the window that appears, activate **IPS (Inch, Pound, Second)**. You should also increase the Decimal Places to four **(4)**. Close the "Document Properties" menu with the **OK** button. Go to **View, Toolbars** and select the **Dimensions/Relations** toolbar and the **Standard Views** toolbar. Now go to **File** and select **Save As**. First select the FOLDER you wish to save this template in, then title your part as **ANSI-INCHES**, select **Save as Type** and select **Part Templates (*.prtdot)**. Then save it in your folder.

Repeat the above process, only this time, the **Units** you select will be **MMGS (Millimeter, Gram, Second)**. Two decimals should be sufficient for metric measurements. Save this template also in your FOLDER, but change your title to **ANSI-METRIC** and select the **Save as Type** and select **Part Templates (*.prtdot).**

STANDARD TITLE BLOCK DRAWING SHEETS

The next process is to set up a Title Block to reflect the two measurement styles. You may have to draw a title block (see Figure 1-12) if one has not been provided. An example of a title block, with suggested dimensions and style, is available in **Appendix A**. If a Title Block has been provided, go to **File** and **Open** that drawing file. Go to the **Tools** pull-down menu and select **Options**. Under the **Document Properties** tab make sure that the **Dimensioning Standard** is set for **ANSI**. Next select **Units** in the left hand column. In the window that appears, activate **IPS (Inch, Pound, Second)**. Three **(3)** decimal places will be all you should use here unless you are doing very high tolerance drawings.

Right mouse click (**RMB**) on **SHEET FORMAT** in the Feature Manager, and select the **Properties** option. The "Sheet Properties" on-screen menu now appears, as shown in Figure 1-11. Here you can setup the "Scale" and "Type of projection" to be used for the drawing. Use a "**Scale**" of **1:1**. Also, the U.S. standard is *third angle projection*. So, check the dot (•) on the "**Third angle**" menu item as shown in Figure 1-11. Then click **OK** to close the menu.

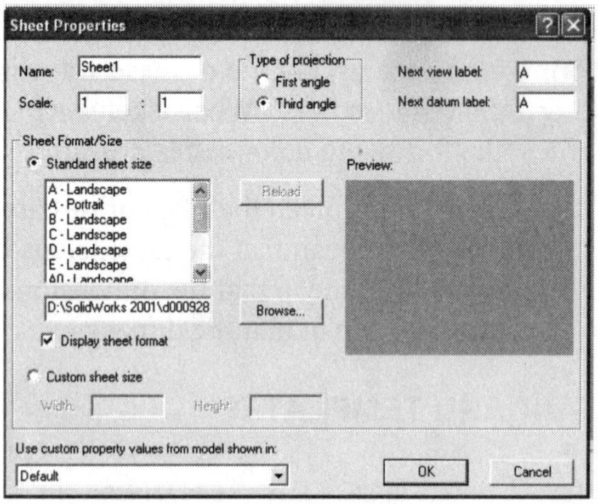

Figure 1-11 The Sheet Setup Menu.

Add your personal information, such as name, desk number, and section number. In the **Feature Manager Tree**, right click on **Sheet 1** and select **Edit Sheet**. Now that this is done, go to **File** and **Save As**. First select the FOLDER you wish to save this template in, then title your part as **TITLEBLOCK-INCHES** and select the **Save as Type** and select **Drawing Template (*.drwdot).**

Repeat the above process, only this time, the **Units** you select will be **MMGS (Millimeter, Gram, Second)**. Two **(2)** decimals should be sufficient for metric measurements. Add your personal information such as name, desk number, and section number. In the **Feature Manager Tree**, right click on **Sheet 1** and select **Edit Sheet**. Save this template in the same way, but change your title to **TITLEBLOCK-METRIC** and select the **Save as Type** and select **Drawing Template (*.drwdot).**

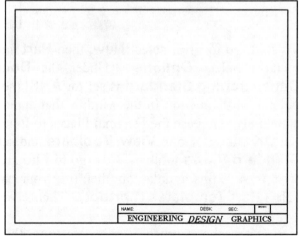

Figure 1-12. An Example of a Student Title Block Sheet.

INSERTING A PART (RENDERED PICTORIAL) ONTO A TITLE BLOCK SHEET

For each of the assignments you will be asked to submit a printed copy of the part that you built in SolidWorks. The following will be the procedure to accomplish this requirement.

A. Build the solid model according to instructions and save that part in your folder with the file extension of **.sldprt**.

B. Open the appropriate Title Block drawing sheet (see Figure 1-11 for example). The Title Block drawing sheet that you open should have the same units as the solid part (metric or inches).

C. Pull down **Windows** and then select **Tile Vertically**. This allows you to see all the windows that you have open at the same time.

D. Select the Part Name in the **Feature Manager Tree** and while holding down the left mouse button, drag it onto the Title Block drawing sheet. You will see three views of the object that you inserted onto the Title Block. If you do not see the three views, right click on **Sheet 1** in the **Feature Manager Tree** and select **Edit Sheet**.

E. Select two of the views and delete them. Activate the box around the remaining view, go to the pull-down menu **Insert**, select **Drawing View** and then **Model.** Left Click on the blue arrow pointing toward the right, (This is the **"Next"** button). You are now given the option of which view you wish to select (normally you will select **"Isometric").** After you have selected the pictorial view you desire, go to **Display Style** and select the far right hand yellow box. Next bring your cursor onto the Title Block sheet and you will see a box following the cursor. When it is in the position desired, press the left mouse button to place it.

F. Select the third view that was activated in the previous step and delete it.

G. Pick the window around the pictorial view. You get a menu window that lets you adjust the scale of the image to better fill the sheet.

H. In the drawing area of the Title Block Sheet insert the title of the object and also provide the exercise number in the upper right hand box of the Title Block. Your Title should be a larger font size, i.e. **0.18** or **0.20**. Your name, desk, Sec and exercise number should be font size **0.125 or 12pt**.

Exercise 1.1: METAL GASKET

In this first exercise, you will build a metal gasket part. This part is primarily a 2-D object with a thin depth that will be extruded. The gasket features can be drawn with many of the 2-D sketching entities and editing features using the sketch toolbars. Go to your folder and **Open** the file **ANSI-INCHES.prtdot.** In order to avoid corrupting the **ANSI-INCHES.prtdot template** go to **File - Save as:** under **File Name**, type **METAL GASKET**, and under **Save as type**, Select **.sldprt** and select **SAVE**.

First set up the sketching grid and units. Pull down the **Tools** menu and select **Options**. Under the **Document Properties** tab, click the **Grid/Snap** tab and set the "Major grid spacing" to **0.25** and "Minor lines per major" to **1**. Also click **on** (√) all the "Grid" boxes and set "Snap points per minor" to **1**, as shown in Figure 1-13. Click on the **Go To System Snaps** and make sure that the **Grid** and **Snap only when grid is displayed** boxes are checked. Also make sure the **Units** are in **Inches** to **2** decimal places. Then click **OK** to close the menu.

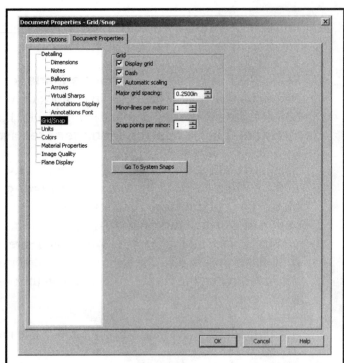

Figure 1-13. Setting Grids and Units for the Sketch.

You will design the gasket in the front view, so click on the **Front** plane in the Feature Manager tree. The front plane should highlight in green. Next click on the **Sketch** icon (drawing pencil) on the right side toolbar. The sketching grid will now appear on the screen with grids spaced every 0.25 inches. Also make sure you are viewing this from the **Front View** orientation (see Figure 1-5).

Now study the outline of the gasket shown in Figure 1-14. You will sketch this outline on the quarter-inch grids using the line tool. Click the **Line** icon on the right side toolbar. Now draw five lines according to the specifications in Figure 1-14 and detailed below. All **(X,Y)** coordinates are relative to the sketch "origin" seen in the middle of the screen.

The *top line* starts at **(-2.75, 1.25)** and ends at **(2.75, 1.25)**.
The *right side line* starts at **(2.75, 1.25)** and ends at **(2.75, -1.25)**.
The *bottom right diagonal line* starts at **(2.75, -1.25**) and ends at **(0.00, -2.75)**.
The *bottom left diagonal line* starts at **(0.00, -2.75)** and ends at **(-2.75, -1.25)**.
The *left side line* starts at **(-2.75, -1.25)** and ends at **(-2.75, 1.25)**.

The 2-D outline of the gasket should now be finished and completely enclosed.

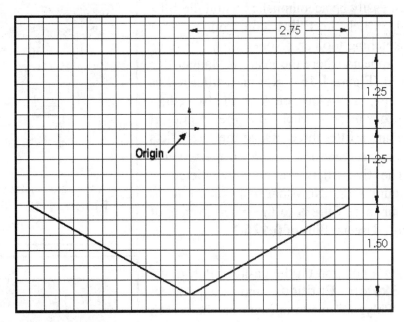

Figure 1-14. The Beginning Outline for the Metal Gasket.

Using the **Rectangle** sketching tool, draw a rectangular slot **3.00** inches wide by **0.50** inches high, and completely centered on the origin, as shown in Figure 1-15. Next select the **Circle** sketching tool, and create the five circles along the corners of the outline. All circles have the same diameter of **0.50** inches and are positioned as indicated in Figure 1-15. *Note:* While you are sketching the lines, rectangle, or circles, the end of the cursor pencil shows a small icon that indicates the current type of sketch entity that you are using. This is called a "smart cursor."

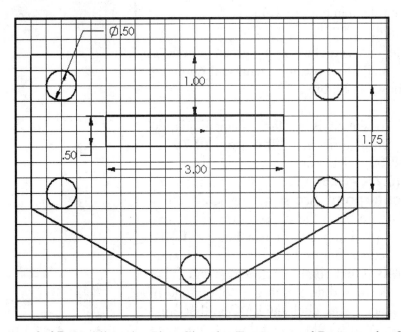

Figure 1-15. Adding the Five Circular Features and Rectangular Slot.

The five corners of the gasket are sharp and need to be rounded. This can easily be accomplished using the fillet editing command. Click the **Fillet** icon (round corner symbol) on the sketching toolbar. Notice that a "Sketch Fillet" menu now appears where the Feature Manger tree usually is displayed (Figure 1-16). Key in a fillet radius of **0.50** inches. Now, one by one, click on the two edges of the corners (or merely click on the point of intersection) to create a fillet there. Once the five fillets are added, click on the green (√) button on the "Sketch Fillet" menu. The five fillets are now completed as shown later in Figure 1-18. Now that you know how to add fillets, add four more **Fillets** to the inner corners of the rectangular slot. Use a radius of **0.125**.

Figure 1-16. Sketch Fillet Menu.

Now you will draw a polygon on the gasket. Pull down **Tools**, select **Sketch Entities**, and then select **Polygon.** The "Polygon" menu appears on the screen where the previous fillet menu appeared. First draw the polygon on the gasket in its approximate place. Now study the actual parameters needed for the polygon and then set them as shown in Figure 1-17.

> Number of sides = **6**
> Inscribed circle **dot**
> X-origin = **0.00**
> Y-origin = **-1.00**
> Inscribed circle diameter = **1.00**
> Rotation angle = **120°**

Once the parameters are set, click on the green (√) button on the "Polygon" menu to close the menu and complete the polygon, as shown in Figure 1-18.

The next feature to sketch is a "fan" shaped quarter-circle. First, sketch a horizontal **Line** from **(0.75, -0.50)** to **(1.50, -0.50)**. Then draw a vertical **Line** from **(0.75, -0.50)** to **(0.75, -1.25)**. To add the quarter circle arc, select the **Centerpoint Arc** sketching icon. Click the center of the arc to be at the intersection of the two lines just drawn. Hold the left mouse button (**LMB**) down and drag the cursor out to the end of the horizontal line. Click the **LMB** at that point to define one end of the arc. Then hold it down and drag it to the bottom end of the vertical line. Once again, click the **LMB** at that point to complete the arc. You should have a drawn arc feature as shown in Figure 1-18.

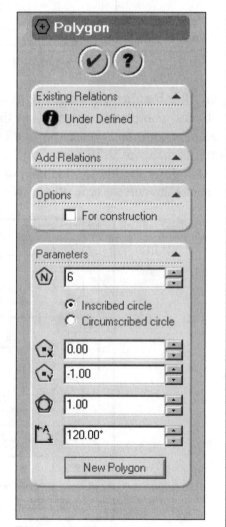

Figure 1-17. Polygon Menu.

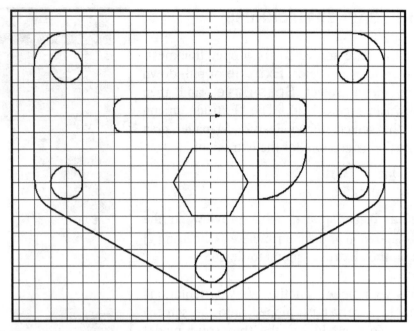

Figure 1-18. Sketching the Polygon and Right Side Fan-Shaped Arc.

You now need to finish the gasket by creating a symmetric arc feature on the left side of the polygon. SolidWorks offers many tools for sketching and editing. One of these tools is the "Mirror" sketch feature about a centerline. So, select the **Centerline** sketch icon and draw a centerline vertically from top to bottom, and through the origin, as shown in Figure 1-18 above. Click the **Select** button. Now hold down the Control (**Ctrl**) key and select the following: the centerline, horizontal line of the arc, vertical line of the arc, and the arc itself. Now click the **Mirror** (bell-shaped) icon. The fan-shaped arc feature will now mirror to the left side. The gasket outline is now complete as shown in Figure 1-19.

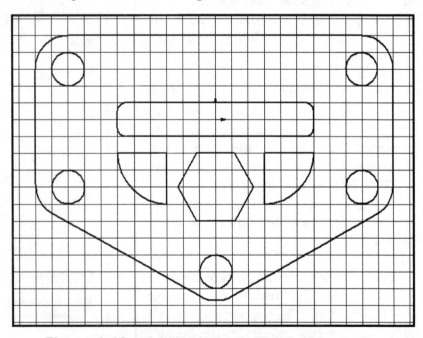

Figure 1-19. The Finished 2-D Sketch of the Gasket.

EXTRUDING THE GASKET THICKNESS

The gasket can now be extruded to its proper thickness. Select the **Features** icon and select **Extrude** or pull down the **Insert** main menu, select **Boss/Base**, and then **Extrude**, as shown in Figure 1-20. The "Extrude" menu then appears on the screen in the Feature Manager area (Figure 1-21). Set the parameters for the extrusion:

Direction One = **Blind**
Distance1 = **0.125** inches

Notice that the extrusion appears as a preview in the computer sketching area in an Isometric view. Click on (√) the green button on the "Extrude" menu to finish.

Now you can view your model. On the "View Orientation" window (you should have it push-pinned onto the screen) click **Trimetric**. You should see the thin solid model appear as a trimetric view (see Figure 1-22). Also try **Isometric**, **Dimetric**, and **Front** view orientations. You can experiment with some of the viewing operations in SolidWorks. Click the **Rotate View** icon (it appears as circular arrows on the top toolbars). Now rotate your model into different configurations. Also try several **Zoom** commands and the **Pan** command.

You should save your model. Now save your model. Pull down the **File** menu and select **Save As**. On the "Save As" menu, select your appropriate file folder, type in the part name **METAL GASKET**, and the file type as **sldprt**, then click **Save**.

Before you finish this exercise, you should print a hard copy for submission to your instructor. *Check with your instructor first for any special printing instructions.* You may need to use a special sheet like the Title Sheet shown in Figure 1-12. You can insert the rendered Metal Gasket image into your **Title Block** drawing sheet that was created in the introduction to this chapter, as shown in Figure 1-22. To put this object on a Title Sheet, follow the instructions on **Page 1-7**.

Conversely, you can place your name and class data on the printed drawing. Pull down the **Insert** menu, select **Annotations,** then **Note**. A note box appears at the end of the cursor and a "Note" menu appears in the Feature Manager area. Type in your name and class data in the

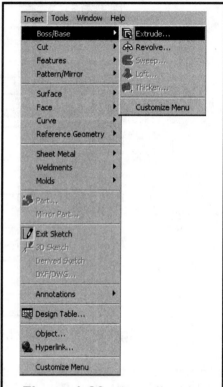

Figure 1-20. Extruding the Gasket Thickness.

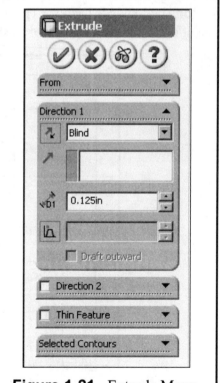

Figure 1-21. Extrude Menu.

note box. If you check (√) **off** the "Use documents Font" in the menu, you can change the font, for example to:

> Font = **Arial**
> Font Style = **Regular**
> Points = **12**

Now **SAVE** your drawing sheet to your directory as **METAL GASKET.slddrw**. Take note that the title of the part and the drawing are the same but the extension has changed. The solid model and the drawing are linked, meaning that any changes made to the solid model will automatically be updated on the drawing.

Before you print your copy, make sure you have set the **File**, **Page Setup** to **Landscape** mode. Now pull down the **File** and **Print Preview** commands from the top main menu, then the **Print** button to send it to the default printer.

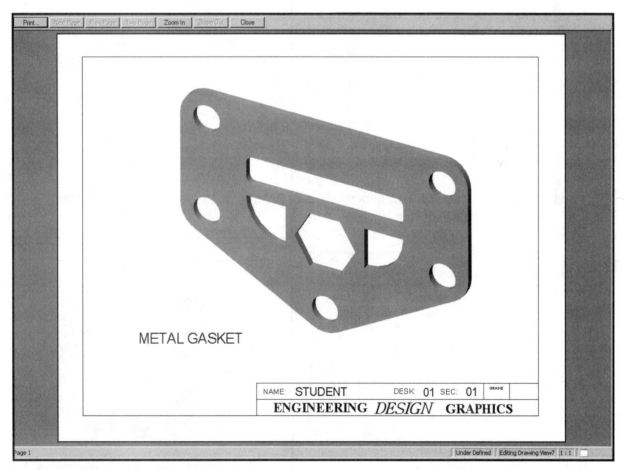

Figure 1-22. Metal Gasket Model Inserted into the Title Block Drawing Sheet.

Exercise 1.2: COVER PLATE

There are many different approaches to creating a 2-D computer sketch using SolidWorks. The approach will depend on the design intent and also on the designer's own preferences and choices. In the previous exercise 1.1, geometry was constructed on a frontal plane using X-Y coordinate geometry and a grid system. In this exercise 1.2, you will construct the 2-D geometry on a horizontal (top) plane since this is the normal orientation of the cover plate. Also, instead of using a grid coordinate system for laying out the design, you will use simple dimensions related to the geometry and to the computer space origin.

Go to your folder and **Open** the file **ANSI-INCHES.prtdot**. In order to avoid corrupting the **ANSI-INCHES.prtdot template** go to **File - Save as:** Under **File Name**, type **COVER PLATE**, and under **Save as type**, select **.sldprt** and select **SAVE.** Click the **Top** plane in the "Feature Manager." Also click **Top** view in the "View Orientation" window to see the top plane in *green* on the screen. Now click the **Sketch** icon on the right toolbar, then click the **Circle** icon. Draw a large circle that is centered at the origin. For now, the diameter is unimportant because you will dimension it. Click the **Dimension** icon (slanted dimension line) on the right toolbar. Pick a point on the circumference of the circle and drag the dimension out to the upper right side of the circle. The dimension is not likely to be correct, so double click on it to edit it (see Figure 1-23). The small "Modify" box appears. Key in **10.00** inches and click the green (√) check box. The diameter of the circle changes to the new value. If the circle gets too big, use **Zoom** to see it better.

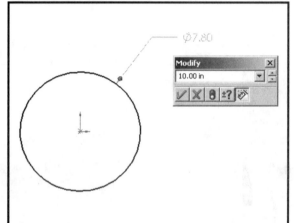

Figure 1-23 Setting the Circle Diameter.

Now you will extrude the circle into the solid base part of the cover plate. Select the **Features** icon and select **Extrude**; or pull down **Insert**, select **Boss/Base**, and then **Extrude.** Set the parameters for the extrude to be:

> Direction One = **Blind**
> Distance1 = **0.50** inches

Click the green (√) button on the "Extrude" menu to finish. View the cover plate as an **Isometric** (Figure 1-24).

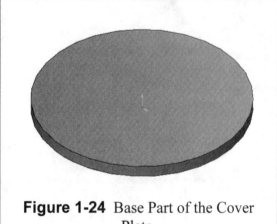

Figure 1-24 Base Part of the Cover Plate.

You will now draw the geometry for the indentation part of the cover plate. Click on the top surface of the cover plate model and it should turn *green*. This will be the next sketch surface. Also select **Top** on "View Orientation" for better viewing of the sketch plane. Click the **Sketch** icon to start the next sketch. Select **Circle** and draw a circle centered at the origin. Now draw a second bigger circle centered at the origin, but not as big as the 10.00 inch diameter of the base plate. Now, using the **Dimension** icon, set the diameter of the smaller new circle to **4.00** inches and the diameter of the bigger new circle to **8.00** inches.

Using the **Line** sketching tool, draw two parallel lines across the plate. One line should be slightly above the origin, and the other should be below. Both should span across the two circles as shown in Figure 1-25. Next **Dimension** them so that one line is **0.50** inches above the origin, and the other is **0.50** inches below the origin. This places the parallel lines 1.00 inch apart, as indicated in Figure 1-25.

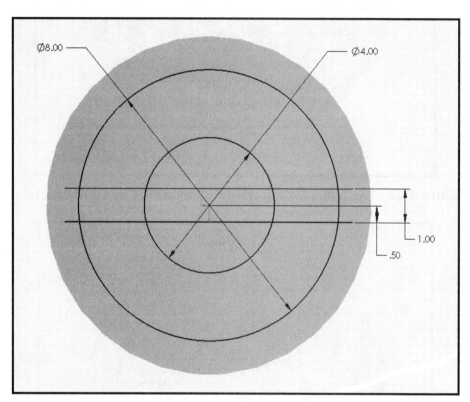

Figure 1-25 The Beginning Geometry for the Indentation.

Now you will trim these lines. Now select the **Trim** icon on the sketch editing toolbar. A scissors icon now appears on the end of the cursor indicating that you are in the trim mode. Trim the line portions (four places) that extend beyond the big circle by just clicking on them with the **LMB**. Next trim the two line pieces inside the small circle. Finally trim the portions of the circles that cross between the two parallel lines (four places). You should now have a pattern like in Figure 1-26. Now repeat the above process (**Line**, **Dimension**, **Trim**) to create identical patterns in the vertical direction. This final pattern for the indentation is shown in Figure 1-27.

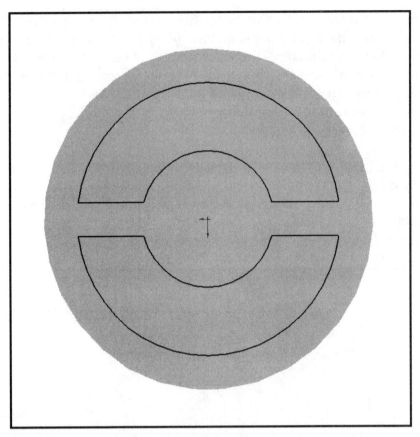

Figure 1-26. The Initial Pattern after Trimming the Lines and the Circles.

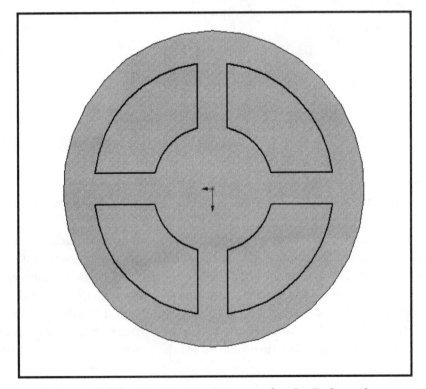

Figure 1-27. The Finished Pattern for the Indentation.

Now you will cut the indentation pattern into the cover plate. Select the **Features** icon and select **Extrude**; or pull down **Insert**, select **Cut**, and then **Extrude**. The "Cut Extrude" menu appears in the Feature Manager area. Key in these parameters:

Direction One = **Blind**
Distance1 = **0.25** inches

Click the green (√) button to finish. View the cover plate as a rotated **Isometric** (Figure 1-28).

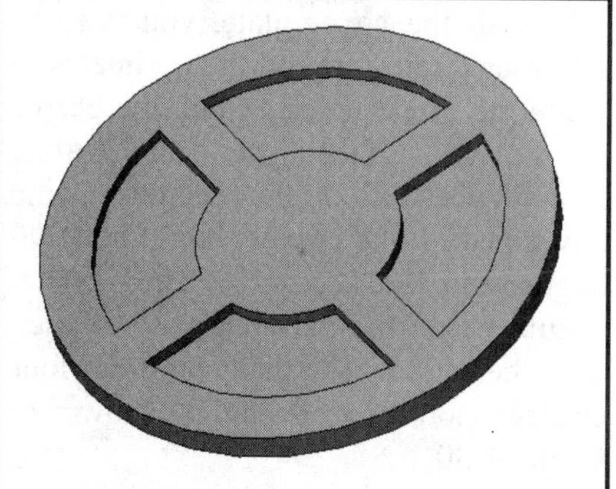

Now create the lift hole in the middle of the plate. Click the cursor on the top center surface of the cover plate (it should turn *green*). Also, select a **Top** view orientation. You might also need to **Zoom** in to see

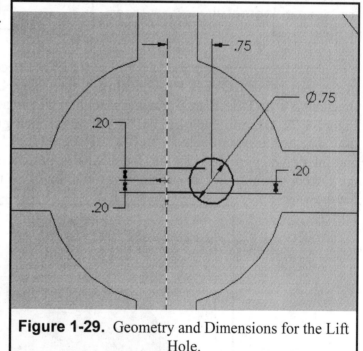

Figure 1-28. The Indentation Pattern Cut into the Plate.

the center portion better. Click the **Sketch** icon to get into the sketching mode. Since the lift hole is symmetric about the origin, you can use a mirror function. So start by drawing a vertical **Centerline** (CL) through the origin. Draw a small **Circle** to the right side of the centerline.

Then draw two parallel **Lines** that start at the centerline and go through part of the circle, as indicated in Figure 1-29. Now apply the following inch **Dimensions** to the sketch geometry.

Circle Diameter = **0.75**
Lateral Dist. from CL = **0.75**
Line1 from origin = **0.20** (above)
Line2 from origin = **0.20** (below)
Circle center = **0.20** (above Line2)

Now **Trim** the two line pieces that overhang the circle, and then trim the part of the circle between the two parallel lines. If you get a warning from SolidWorks about eliminating associated dimensions while you are trimming, just ignore it and answer **Yes** to proceed with the trim.

Figure 1-29. Geometry and Dimensions for the Lift Hole.

To mirror the feature to the left side of the centerline, click the **Select** button. Now hold down the Control (**Ctrl**) key and select the following: the centerline, the top line, the circle, and the bottom line. Then click the **Mirror** icon. The feature should mirror to the left and the lift hole sketch is complete. Now cut the lift hole pattern through the cover plate. Select the **Features** icon and select **Extrude**; or pull down **Insert**, select **Cut**, and then **Extrude**. The "Cut Extrude" menu appears in the Feature Manager area. For Direction1, just select **Through All**. Click the green (√) button to finish this extrude-cut operation and view the lift hole in Figure 1-30.

To finish the cover plate, you need to add four circles around the perimeter to make the guide holes. Click the cursor on the top surface again and **Sketch** four **Circles** around the perimeter of the cover plate. The circles should be at 90 degrees to each other. The centers should be on the perimeter and aligned with the origin. The diameter of all four circles should be **0.75**, as shown in Figure 1-30.

Now pull down **Insert**, select **Cut**, and then **Extrude**. The "Cut Extrude" menu appears in the Feature Manager area. For Direction1, just select **Through All,** and click the green (√) button to finish the part. Now view your model in an **Isometric** view, as shown in Figure 1-31.

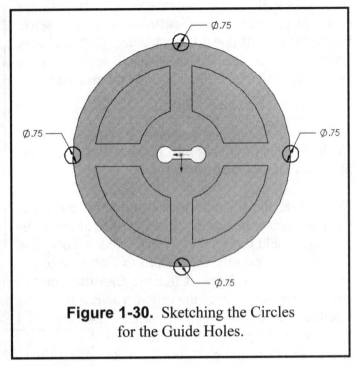

Figure 1-30. Sketching the Circles for the Guide Holes.

You should now save your model. Pull down **File,** select your file folder, select **Save As,** type in the part name **COVER PLATE.sldprt**, then click **Save**. Insert the rendered Cover Plate image into your **Title Block** drawing sheet that was created in the introduction to Chapter 1 (See Figure 1-22 as an example). Follow the instruction given on **Page 1-7**. Now **SAVE** your drawing sheet to your directory as **COVER PLATE.slddrw**. Take note that the title of the part and the drawing are the same but the extension has changed. The solid model and the drawing are linked, meaning that any changes made to the solid model will automatically be updated on the drawing.

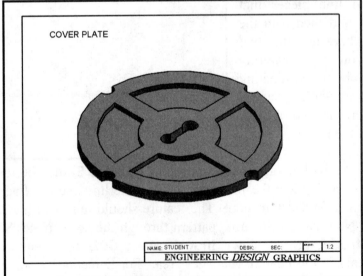

COVER PLATE

| NAME: STUDENT | | DESK: | SEC: | DRAW. | 1.2 |
| ENGINEERING *DESIGN* GRAPHICS | | | | | |

Figure 1-31. The Finished Cover Plate Part.

Exercise 1.3: WALL BRACKET

The sketch geometry used in Exercises 1.1 and 1.2, like line, circle, rectangle, and arc, are sufficient for designing many different kinds of parts. Sometimes more advanced 2-D geometry, like an irregular curve, may be needed to complete a design. In the case of the Wall Bracket for this Exercise 1.3, you will learn how to use a spline.

Go to your folder and **Open** the file **ANSI-INCHES.prtdot**. In order to avoid corrupting the **ANSI-INCHES.prtdot template** go to **File - Save as:** Under **File Name**, type **WALL BRACKET**, and under **Save as type**; select **.sldprt** and select **SAVE**. Click the **Front** plane in the "Feature Manager." Also click **Front** view in the "View Orientation" window to see the front plane in *green* on the screen. Now click the **Sketch** icon on the right toolbar. First sketch the straight line segments of the Wall Bracket outline using the **Line** tool. Refer to Figure 1-32 for the proper **Dimension** for each line segment. Units are in inches and the upper left corner is at the origin.

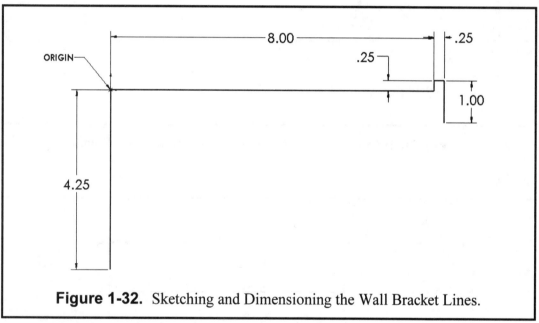

Figure 1-32. Sketching and Dimensioning the Wall Bracket Lines.

Now you will draw a spline from the bottom of the 4.25 inch line to the bottom of the 1.00 inch line. Click the **Spline** sketch icon (it looks like a sine wave). Click the **LMB** at the first bottom point. Then with the mouse pressed down, drag the spline over to the first intermediate point about one third of the way up and about one third of the way to the right. Release the **LMB** there, then press it down again and drag the spline to the second intermediate point about two thirds of the way up and over. Again release the **LMB** there, then press it down again and drag the spline to the final point, where you end the spline by double clicking the **LMB**. Refer to Figure 1-33 for these four points' positions.

The two intermediate points are used to control the shape of the spline. With the **Select** cursor, pick the spline (it should highlight *green* with its four points identified). Now pick intermediate point 1 and drag it out and down a little to create a slight bulge. Next pick intermediate point 2 and pull it up a little to create a slight inflection (see Figure 1-34). *Note*: There are *no exact* X-Y coordinates for you to drag these intermediate points to. Just try it a few times until you achieve a shape that pleases you (for example the shape in Figure 1-34 is acceptable).

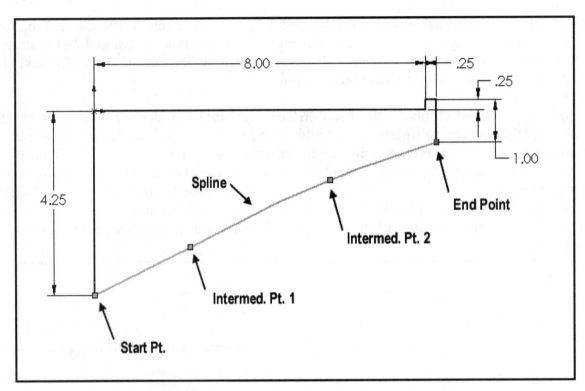

Figure 1-33. Sketching the Spline Through Its Four Points.

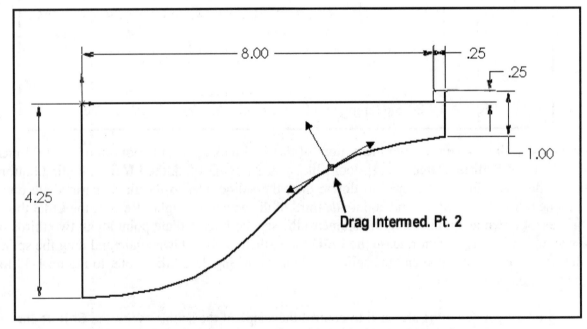

Figure 1-34. Dragging the Intermediate Points to Shape the Spline.

Now you will complete the left end of the Wall Bracket by adding the wall hooks. On the left side edge, add the two wall hooks using the **Line** tool and the **Dimension** values given in Figure 1-35. You will have to **Trim** two places on the left edge to make the wall hooks contiguous with the rest of the profile. *Note:* The bottom wall hook has the same dimensions as the top one.

You will finish the Wall Bracket by adding a fillet to the sharp bottom corner on the right end. Since it was earlier associated with the *1.00 inch* dimension, SolidWorks will give you a warning if you try to fillet it. So it is best to just first **Delete** that dimension. Now click the **Fillet** sketch icon. Key in a radius of **0.25** inches (refer back to Figure 1-16). Next pick the vertical 1.00 inch right edge of the bracket and pick the spline close to its end point, and then click the green (√) check to execute the fillet command. The 2-D profile is now complete and ready to be extruded. Pull down

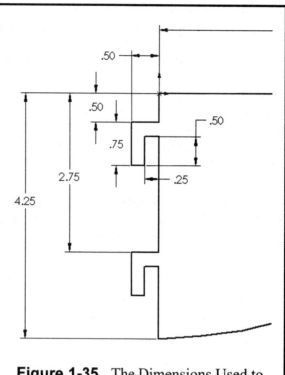

Figure 1-35. The Dimensions Used to Create the Wall Hooks on the Left Side.

Insert, **Boss/Base**, and **Extrude**. Key in a **Blind** distance of **0.125** and click the green (√) check to complete the Wall Bracket, as shown in Figure 1-36 in a **Trimetric** view.

Now **Save** the part as **WALL BRACKET.sldprt**. Insert the Wall Bracket onto a Title Block drawing sheet (see earlier Figure 1-22). Save as **WALL BRACKET.slddrw** and **Print** a hard copy for your instructor. See Page 1-7 for instructions.

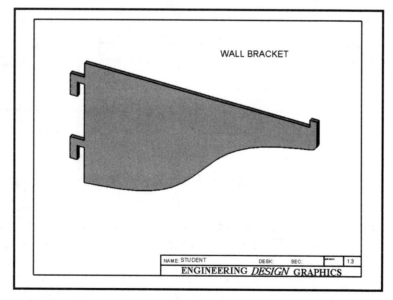

Figure 1-36. The Completed Wall Bracket in a Trimetric View.

Exercise 1.4: MACHINE HANDLE

In the previous exercises, the parts were designed using English units (inches). Metric, or System International (SI), units are also common in engineering practice. In this exercise 1.4, the Machine Handle will be designed using millimeters as the basic units (see Figure 1-36). In addition, because of the round symmetry of the machine handle, you will create a base revolve using the 2-D sketch rather than a base extrude.

Go to your folder and **Open** the file **ANSI-METRIC.prtdot**. In order to avoid corrupting the **ANSI-INCHES.prtdot template** go to **File - Save as:** Under **File Name**, type **MACHINE HANDLE**, and under **Save as type**; select **.sldprt** and select **SAVE**.

Next click the "Grid/Snap" tab. Make the following settings on this menu:

"Major grid spacing" = **5 mm**
"Minor lines per major" = **0**

Also make sure "Display Grid" and the "Snap" functions are checked (√) on, then click the **OK** button.

Pick a **Front** plane and click the **Sketch** icon to start your sketch. The screen area should show a metric grid with spacing every 5 millimeters. You may need to **Zoom** in. Using the **Centerline, Line**, and **Centerpoint Arc** tools, sketch the enclosed 2-D profile shown in Figure 1-37.

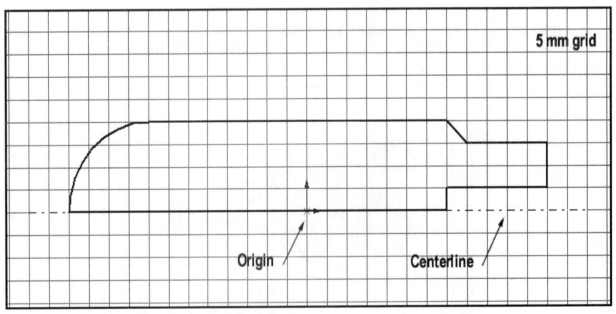

Figure 1-37. The 2-D Sketch for the Machine Handle.

Now you will revolve this simple sketch into a solid model. Pull down **Insert**, select **Boss/Base**, and this time select **Revolve**. The "Base Revolve" menu appears in the Feature Manager area as shown in Figure 1-38. The main choice you have here is the degrees of revolution about the centerline. Set it to a full revolution of **360°** and then click the green (√) check to close it. Your part should now appear as shown in Figure 1-39 with an **Isometric** view.

There are many different designs for a Machine Handle, and the one here is quite typical. After studying it, however, you notice that the sharp outer edge on the right side poses a concern. SolidWorks allows you to easily fix these design changes after the solid model has been built. One way is to simply go back and edit the original sketch.

Notice in the Feature Manager that SolidWorks keeps a running tabulation of the features you used to build the part. One of them should read "Base Revolve," which is the operation you just completed. Left of this "Base Revolve" is a plus (+) sign. Click on this (+) sign and down comes the name of "Sketch1." Right mouse click on this Sketch1 label and a short pull-down menu appears as shown in Figure 1-40. Left mouse click on the **Edit Sketch** option and the sketch appears again, with grids, on the screen. Select the **Front** view orientation to better see the sketch.

There are different ways to eliminate the sharp edge. One way is to use a chamfer; however you probably cannot find a chamfer icon on the sketch editing toolbars. Nonetheless, SolidWorks provides this sketching capability. Pull down **Tools**, select **Sketch Tools**, and then find **Chamfer**. The "Sketch Chamfer" menu now appears. Set the "Chamfer parameters" as shown in Figure 1-41, including the chamfer distance of **3 mm**. Now click on the two lines that form the sharp edge corner, and then click the green (√) check to complete this chamfer operation.

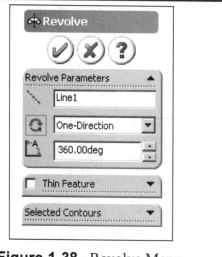

Figure 1-38. Revolve Menu.

Figure 1-39. The Part After the Sketch is Revolved.

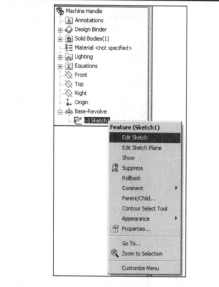

Figure 1-40. Editing the Sketch.

The new feature is created, but the new model is not displayed yet. You need to rebuild the model first. Pull down **Edit**, and select the **Rebuild** option (it may be in the *customize menu* section of the pull-down menu). <u>Note:</u> There is also a small icon for the rebuild command. It appears on the top toolbar and looks like a green traffic light. The model is rebuilt now with a chamfer, as shown in the final picture (Figure 1-42) in an **Isometric** view with the **Shadows in Shaded** icon clicked **on**. Now you see how easy it is to make design changes to a solid model that is already built. You just simply edit the sketch that created the model in the first place.

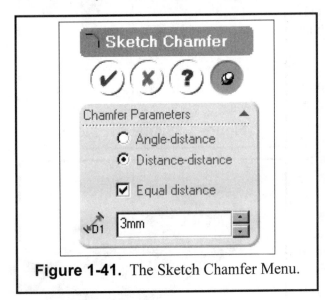

Figure 1-41. The Sketch Chamfer Menu.

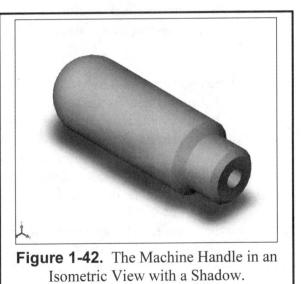

Figure 1-42. The Machine Handle in an Isometric View with a Shadow.

You should now save your model. Pull down **File,** select **Save As,** type in the part name **MACHINE HANDLE.sldprt**, and then click **Save**. Insert the rendered Machine Handle image into your **Title Block** drawing sheet, as shown in Figure 1-43. Now **SAVE** your drawing sheet to your directory as **MACHINE HANDLE.slddrw**. Take note that the title of the part and the drawing are the same but the extension has changed. The solid model and the drawing are linked, meaning that any changes made to the solid model will automatically be updated on the drawing.

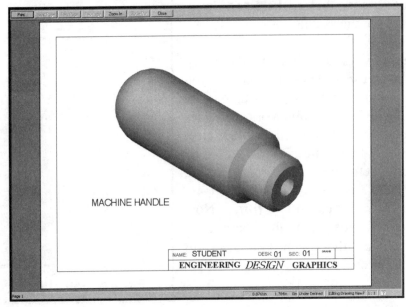

Figure 1-43. A Print Preview of the Machine Handle On the Title Block Drawing Sheet.

Supplementary Exercise 1-5 SLOTTED BASE

Make a full size sketch of the figure below in the **Top Plane** and extrude it for **0.50** inches. Insert it on a Title Block and title it **"SLOTTED BASE."**

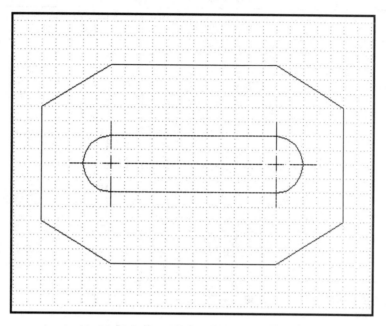

ASSUME THE GRID DIVISIONS TO BE 0.25 INCHES.

Supplementary Exercise 1-6 TRANSITION LINK

Make a full size sketch of the figure below in the **Front Plane**. Extrude it **0.375"**. Insert it onto a Title Block and title it **TRANSITION LINK**.

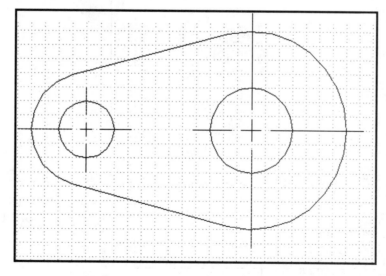

ASSUME THE GRID DIVISIONS TO BE 0.25 INCHES.

Supplementary Exercise 1-7 TEE BRACKET

Make a full size sketch of the figure below in the **Top Plane** and extrude it to the height indicated. Insert it on a Title Block and title it **"TEE BRACKET."**

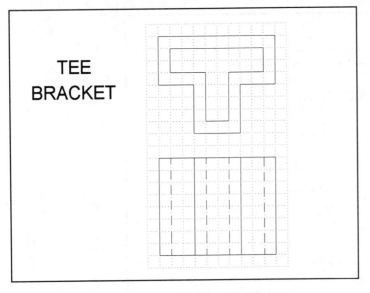

TEE
BRACKET

ASSUME THE GRID DIVISIONS TO BE 5 MM

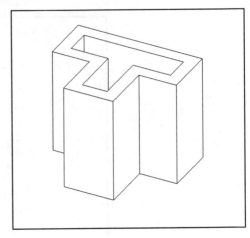

**PICTORIAL OF THE TEE
BRACKET**

Supplementary Exercise 1-8 CABLE SPOOL

Make a full size sketch of the **PROFILE** below in the **Front Plane** and do an **INSERT – BASE - REVOLVE**. Insert it on a Title Block and title it **"CABLE SPOOL."**

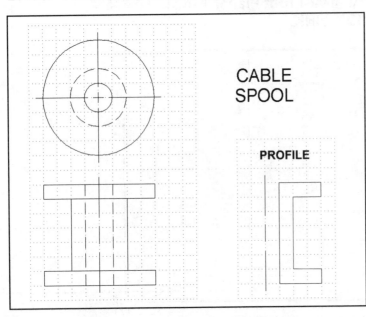

CABLE
SPOOL

PROFILE

ASSUME THE GRID DIVISIONS TO BE 1.00 INCH.

**PICTORIAL OF THE CABLE
SPOOL**

Computer Graphics Lab 2: 2-D Computer Sketching II

ADVANCED 2-D SKETCHING

In the first Computer Graphics Lab 1, you used some of the basic 2-D sketching capabilities of SolidWorks. These first exercises concentrated on using items that were available on the sketching toolbars. You learned how to draw a Line, Circle, Rectangle, Arc, Polygon, Centerline, and Spline. You also learned how to edit the 2-D sketch using Dimensions, Trim, Mirror, Fillet, and Chamfer functions. In this Computer Graphics Lab 2, you will learn some more advanced 2-D sketching and editing features that are available in the vast SolidWorks menu structure.

SKETCH ENTITY MENU

The sketch entities on the right side toolbar are not the only ones available. From the **Tools** pull-down menu, you can find all of them under the **Sketch Entities** selection menu as Shown in Figure 2-1. Here you can find the following 2-D sketch entities:

> **Line**
> **Rectangle**
> **Parallelogram**
> **Polygon**
> **Circle**
> **Perimeter Circle**
> **Centerpoint Arc**
> **Tangent Arc**
> **3 Point Arc**
> **Ellipse**
> **Partial Ellipse**
> **Parabola**
> **Spline**
> **Point**
> **Centerline**
> **Text**

Some of these 2-D entities are more common in engineering design than others, but hopefully you will have a chance to use each of them somewhere in one of your exercises.

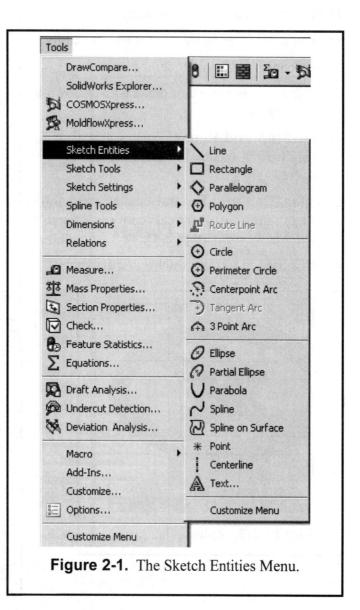

Figure 2-1. The Sketch Entities Menu.

SKETCH TOOLS MENU

All of the 2-D sketch editing functions are found under the **Tools**, **Sketch Tools** pull down menu. On this menu you will find the following common editing functions:

Fillet is used to round a corner with a radius.

Chamfer is used to cut a corner at an angle.

Offset Entities is used to create another exact copy at a linear distance away.

Convert Entities converts an entity from an earlier feature to the current sketch.

Trim cuts away a piece of the entity.

Extend extends an entity to meet another entity.

Mirror copies a pattern around a centerline.

Jog Line moves a piece of the line up or down in a rectangular shape.

Linear Step and Repeat creates a rectangular array (row X column) of identical entities (see Figure 2-3).

Circular Step and Repeat creates a radial (or polar) array of identical entities around a center point (see Figure 2-4).

Align is used to align a sketch and a grid point.

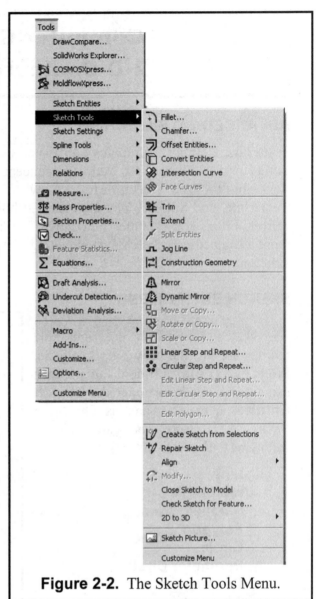

Figure 2-2. The Sketch Tools Menu.

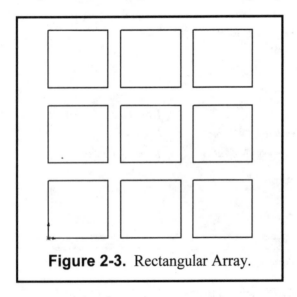

Figure 2-3. Rectangular Array.

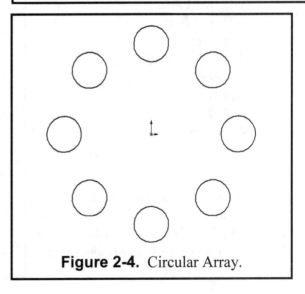

Figure 2-4. Circular Array.

Exercise 2.1: METAL GRATE

In this Exercise 2.1, you will design a Metal Grate. The function of a metal grate is such that many identical slots are cut through it. Instead of drawing each slot separately, you will use an advanced sketching feature of SolidWorks and create a rectangular array of these slots. Then you can simply extrude a base to create the beginning grate feature.

Start by going to your folder and **Open** the file **ANSI-METRIC.prtdot** because the dimensions of the Metal Grate are in Metric units. Immediately **SAVE AS – METAL GRATE.sldprt**. You will not need a grid for this exercise, so click the **Grid/Snap** tab and make sure the "Display Grid" function is <u>not</u> checked (√) on, then click the **OK** button. Now click the **Front** plane in the Feature Manager for the sketch plane.

Now click the **Sketch** (pencil) icon to start your sketch. You will first draw two **Rectangle**s. The first one is the large outline of the grate and the second one is the initial small rectangular slot that eventually will be arrayed. Refer to Figure 2-5 below for applying each **Dimension**. The overall size of the grate is **260** mm by **191** mm, and it is centered about the origin with its other two dimensions (**130** and **95.5**). The small slot is **20** mm by **37** mm, and is **20** mm below the top and **20** mm to the right of the upper left corner. <u>Note:</u> After all the dimensions are applied, the lines turn black. This means that the geometry is completely fixed and constrained.

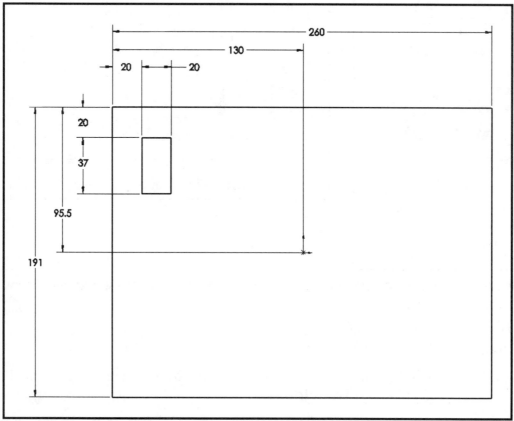

Figure 2-5. The Beginning Dimensions for the Metal Grate Centered at the Origin.

Now select the **Linear Repeat** icon in the sketch entities toolbar; or pull down **Tools**, select **Sketch Tools** and then pick the **Linear Step and Repeat** option. The "Linear Sketch Step and Repeat" menu pops onto the screen. The Entities to Pattern box at the bottom of the menu is prompting you to select the lines of the small rectangle. The settings for this rectangular array operation are shown in Figure 2-6 below. "Direction 1" is horizontal and will have **6** repeats. The horizontal spacing is **40** mm and the angle is **0** degrees. "Direction 2" is vertical and will have **3** repeats. The vertical spacing is **57** mm and the angle is **270** degrees. Notice that as you make adjustments to the linear table a **Preview** of the operation is shown before it is officially executed. If it is correct, click the **OK** button to complete the array. You should have a 6 x 3 array of slots that now can be extruded. You will have to click on the arrows to the left of the Y-axis button under Direction 2 to make the boxes drop below and onto the metal grate. Your pattern preview should look like the image in Figure 2-7.

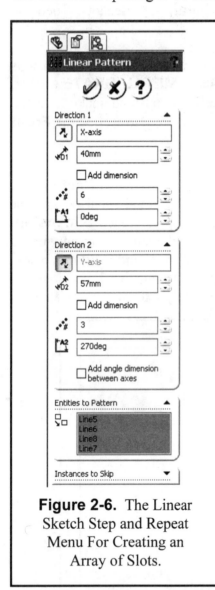

Figure 2-6. The Linear Sketch Step and Repeat Menu For Creating an Array of Slots.

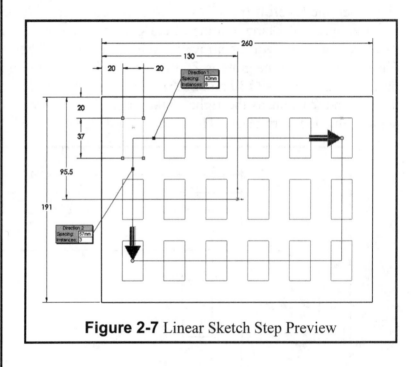

Figure 2-7 Linear Sketch Step Preview

Pull down **Insert**, select **Boss/Base**, and then **Extrude**. On the "Base Extrude" menu, key in the following parameters:

> Type of Extrusion = **Blind**
> Distance 1 = **3** mm

Then click the green (√) check to close the menu. You will now have the base solid model of the grate, as shown in Figure 2-8 in a **Trimetric** view.

Now you need to add four attachment holes to the corners of the grate. **Select** the front face of the part (it should turn *green*). Also pick the **Front** view orientation. Enter the **Sketch** mode and draw a **Circle** in the upper left corner. Use the **Dimension** values supplied in Figure 2-9 for the circle diameter (**8** mm) and position from the corner (**10** mm x **10** mm).

Now draw three more **Circle**s in the other three corners. **Dimension** them to have the same diameter (**8**) and same relative position (**10** x **10**) from each corner. *Or*, now that you are an expert with a rectangular array, use the **Linear Step and Repeat** operation instead. If you use this function, then the horizontal distance of the **2** items is **240** mm and the angle is **0** degrees. The vertical distance of the **2** items is **171** mm and the angle is **270** degrees. *Either way*, when you are finished you should have circles at the four corners.

Pull down **Insert** menu, select **Cut**, and then **Extrude**. Select the extrude type to be **Through all** and click the green (√) check to execute the cut. The four corner attachment holes are now created on the grate.

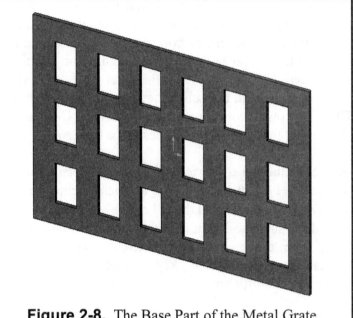

Figure 2-8. The Base Part of the Metal Grate.

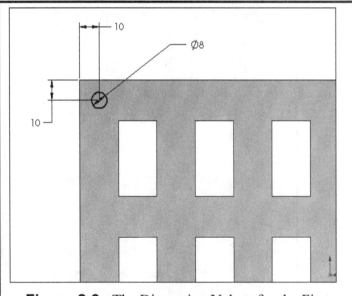

Figure 2-9. The Dimension Values for the First Small Hole.

If you look on the Feature Manager tree, you will see that you have created a "Base Extrude" and a "Cut Extrude1" feature. They were done using a Sketch1 and a Sketch2. You might ask, why not create the four small holes also on Sketch1 instead of waiting until later? That also would have been an acceptable (and maybe more efficient) way to create the grate. This is just an example of the many choices and different pathways you have to design a part that ends up with the same final geometry.

The final design step for the Metal Grate is to add a small lip to the metal grate in order to provide a small relief when attached to the wall air duct. So first, select a **Front** view orientation of the grate. Click on this front surface and it should highlight *green*. Then click on the **Sketch** icon to add another sketch to the design. You have already drawn the outer rectangular profile. So you will borrow from it for the outer edge of the lip. Click one of the outer edges of the grate (it turns *green*) and then click the **Convert** sketch edit icon (it looks like a cube with a red edge). That line now becomes part of your sketch. **Convert** the other three edges in a similar manner. Notice that they are all black lines since the geometry is already fixed.

Now click the top converted line (it turns *green*) and then click the **Offset** icon (it looks like two bent parallel lines). The "Offset Entities" menu appears in the Feature Manager area. Key in the offset value of **3** mm and then click the green (√) check to create the offset, as shown in Figure 2-10. Make sure the 3 mm offset is on the ***inside***. Also, notice that the offset command places a small 3 mm dimension on your sketch to indicate the offset value. You could now simply click on that dimension directly, key in a new dimension value, and instantly change the offset to a new value. But for now leave it at 3 mm.

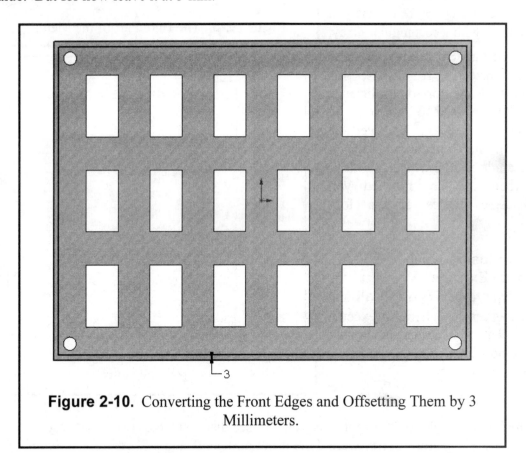

Figure 2-10. Converting the Front Edges and Offsetting Them by 3 Millimeters.

Now pull down **Insert**, **Boss/Base**, and **Extrude**. Select the type as **Blind** and key in the distance as **3** mm, and then click the green (√) check to complete the boss. The part is now complete and you can view the lip feature more clearly by using the **Rotate View** icon as shown in Figure 2-11.

Return to a nice **Trimetric** View of your part as shown in Figure 2-12. You should now save your model. Pull down **File,** select **Save As,** type in the part name **METAL GRATE.sldprt**, and then click **Save**. Open your copy of **TITLE BLOCK – METRIC.drwdot** and immediately **SAVE AS – METAL GRATE.slddrw**. Now insert the rendered Metal Grate image into your **Title Block** drawing sheet that was created in Chapter 1 and **Print** it on this sheet (see Figure 2-13).

Conversely, using the **Insert, Annotations**, and **Note** menu, add your name and class data to the image. **Print** a hard copy to submit to your lab instructor.

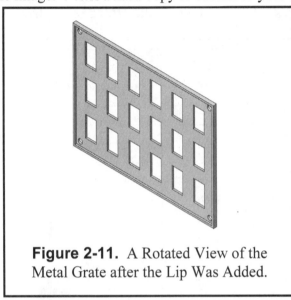

Figure 2-11. A Rotated View of the Metal Grate after the Lip Was Added.

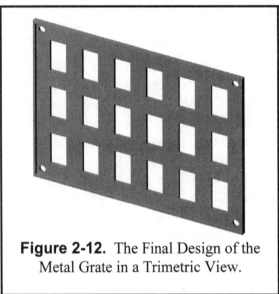

Figure 2-12. The Final Design of the Metal Grate in a Trimetric View.

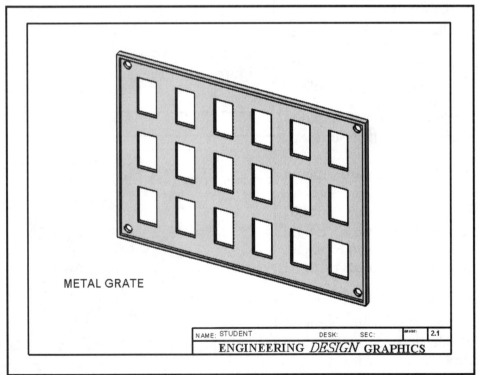

METAL GRATE

| NAME: STUDENT | | DESK: | SEC: | GRADE: | 2.1 |
| ENGINEERING *DESIGN* GRAPHICS | | | | | |

Figure 2-13. The Metal Grate Rendered Image on a Title Block Drawing Sheet.

Exercise 2.2: TORQUE SENSOR

In Exercise 2.2 you will design a Torque Sensor casing. Since it is a circularly symmetrical object, you will employ some of the advanced editing features like circular array. Go to your folder and **Open** the file **ANSI-INCHES.prtdot.** and immediately **SAVE AS – TORQUE SENSOR.sldprt** Select the **Tools, Options, Document Properties** menus. With the **Grid/Snap** tab highlighted, set the "Major grid spacing" to **1.00** and "Minor lines per major" to **4.** Also click on (√) the "Grid" and "Snap" boxes. Also, make sure the **Units** are in **Inches.** Then click **OK.**

The circular features of the Torque Sensor are on the top and bottom surfaces. But the main body is also round and can be created by a 360 degrees revolution of a profile that has been drawn on a frontal plane. So click on the **Front** plane in the Feature Manager tree. Click the **Sketch** icon and the sketching grid appears with minor grids spaced every 0.25 inches. Also make sure you are viewing this from the **Front** view orientation.

First draw a **Centerline** vertically through the origin. Next use the **Line** tool to sketch the completely enclosed profile that is depicted in Figure 2-14. Note that the "Minor Grid" spacing is 0.25 inches. This design will yield a part that is 2.50 inches tall and 4.00 inches in diameter on the top and bottom surfaces.

Now pull down **Insert**, select **Boss/Base**, and then select **Revolve.** Key in the full revolution value of **360°** and click the green (√) check to perform the revolution. The circular base part appears as shown in Figure 2-15 in an **Isometric** view.

The next design step is to create a circular array of eight holes around a bolt circle on the top surface of the part.

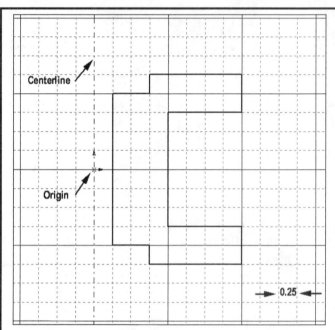

Figure 2-14. The Initial Lines to Revolve for the Base Part.

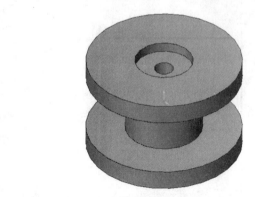

Figure 2-15. The Base Part After the Revolution.

Click on the *top* surface of the base part and it should highlight *green*. Also select a **Top** view orientation. Then select the **Sketch** icon. The diameter of the bolt circle that defines the center of the eight holes is 3.25 inches, thus resulting in a radius of 1.625. To better locate the center of the first hole, return to the **Document Properties** menu and on the **Grid/Snap** tab change the "Minor lines per major" value to **8**, thus resulting in a one-eighth inch grid. Also on the **Units** tab change the decimal places to **3**. Click **OK** and the grid should now be updated to the new values. Now locate the center of the first **Circle** on the grid and draw it with a diameter of **0.25**. Use Figure 2-16 to aid you. To help you better see the grid, you can **Zoom** in and also change the model display mode to **Wireframe**.

With the **Select** icon, pick the first circle (it should highlight *green*). Pull down **Tools**, select **Sketch Tools**, then select the **Circular Step and Repeat** command. The "Circular Sketch Step and Repeat" menu appears on the screen. Referring to Figure 2-17, set the parameters for this circular array. The "Radius" is **1.625** from the center (**0,0**). The "Step Number" is **8** for a "Total angle" of **360°**. The spacing is "Equal" checked (√) on. Click **Preview** to see if everything is correct, and then click the **OK** button. You now have a bolt circle of 8 holes as previewed earlier in Figure 2-16. You are now ready to cut these holes through the entire base part.

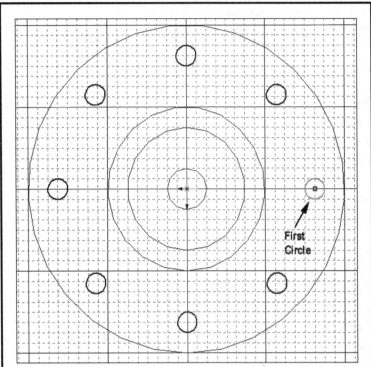

Figure 2-16. Sketching the First Circle and Executing a Circular Array of Eight Holes.

Figure 2-17. The "Circular Sketch Step and Repeat" Menu for Creating the Bolt Circle Holes.

Switch to the **Shaded** model mode and to an **Isometric** view to better see the next operation. Pull down **Insert**, select **Cut**, and then pick **Extrude**. On the "Cut Extrude" menu select **Through all** for the direction and click the green (√) check to execute the extrusion all the way through the model. Use the **Rotate View** icon to see that the holes are indeed all the way through the bottom of the model. If so, then the model is complete as shown in Figure 2-18.

You should now save your model. Pull down **File,** select **Save As,** type in the part name **TORQUE-SENSOR.sldprt**, and then click **Save**. Open your **TITLE BLOCK – INCHES.drwdot** and immediately **SAVE AS – TORQUE SENSOR.slddrw**. Now insert the rendered Torque Sensor image into your **Title Block** drawing sheet that was created in Chapter 1 and **Print** it on this sheet (see Figure 2-19).

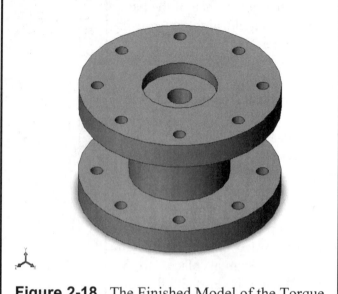

Figure 2-18. The Finished Model of the Torque Sensor in an Isometric View.

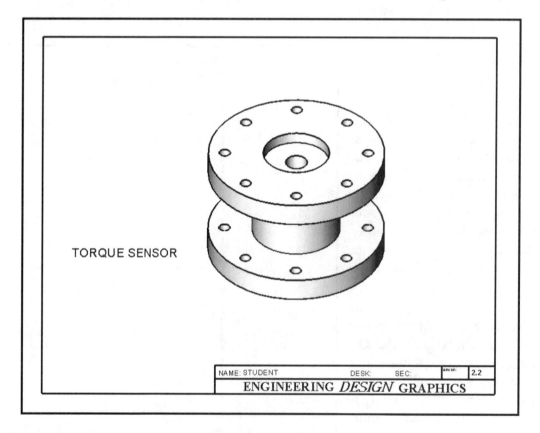

Figure 2-19. The Torque Sensor Rendered Image on a Title Block Drawing Sheet.

Exercise 2.3: SCALLOPED KNOB

In Exercise 2.3, you will design a Scalloped Knob that has some complicated geometry around its edges. This particular knob design will be a hexagon type. Since the hexagonal features are equally spaced around the center of the knob, you can use a circular array function.

Start by going to your folder and **Open** the file **ANSI-INCHES.prtdot** and immediately **SAVE AS – SCALLOPED KNOB.sldprt**. Select the **Front** plane for the sketch. Then start a new **Sketch**. Complete the initial geometry of the sketch according to Figure 2-20. Using the **Line** tool, draw two vertical lines and cap them off with a horizontal line that touches their top ends. **Fillet** the top two corners with a **0.10** radius. Use the **Dimension** tool to completely fix the geometry by applying the dimensions shown in Figure 2-20. Include dimensions that relate to the origin. When the geometry is fixed, all lines turn *black*.

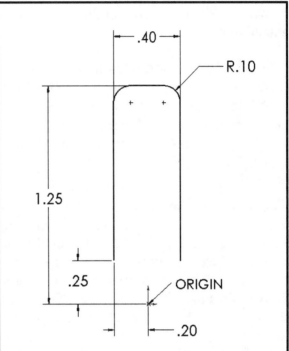

Figure 2-20. The Initial Knob Geometry.

Now array this pattern in a circle to form a hexagonal layout. Press the **Cntrl** key down and hold it. With the **Select** cursor, one-by-one pick the two arcs and three lines pieces that define the pattern (you can also pick all of them with a rubber-band window). Pull down **Tools**, select **Sketch Tools**, then select the **Circular Step and Repeat** command. The "Circular Sketch Step and Repeat" menu appears on the screen. Set the "Step Number" to **6** for a "Total angle" of **360°**. The spacing is "Equal" checked (√) on. Click **Preview** to see if everything is correct, and then click **OK**. You now have an array that is the beginning of the sketch for the knob outline. Notice that some of the lines overlap in the middle. You will trim them, but first **Delete** the Dimension values so SolidWorks will not give you a warning. Next pick the **Trim** icon and trim the pieces of the lines that cross over each other, to complete it as shown in Figure 2-21.

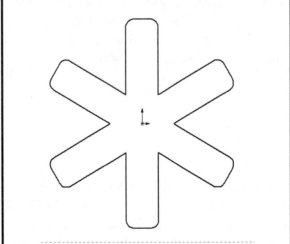

Figure 2-21. The Sketch After Arraying the Pattern and Trimming.

Next you will fillet the six sharp inner corners to create the scallop effect. Pick the **Fillet** sketch icon and key in a fillet radius of **0.45** in the "Sketch Fillet" parameter box. Now pick one of the sharp corners to fillet it. A large 0.45 radius is made and a small dimension is attached to show the fillet value. Repeat this filleting process on the remaining five sharp inner corners. When you are finished, your sketch should look like Figure 2-22.

Now pull down **Insert**, **Boss/Base**, and select **Extrude**. Extrude the sketch to a **Blind** depth of **0.375** inches. Click the green check (√) to close the operation. When finished, view the part in a **Trimetric** orientation as shown in Figure 2-23.

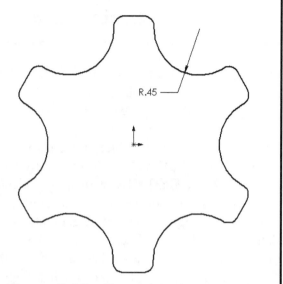

Figure 2-22. The Finished Sketch After Filleting Six Sharp Inner Corners.

You now can finish the part by adding the attachment base. Set your view orientation to **Front**. Click the front surface to highlight it in *green*. Click the **Sketch** icon and draw two concentric **Circles**, centered at the origin. **Dimension** the outer circle to be **1.00** inches in diameter, and the inner circle to be **0.50** inches in diameter. Now pull down **Insert**, **Boss/Base**, and select **Extrude**. Extrude the sketch to a **Blind** depth of **1.00** inches.

Select the **Rotate View** icon to better see the extruded attachment base and the hole for the scalloped Knob, as shown in Figure 2-24. Then return to an **Isometric** view, and click the **Shadows in Shaded** icon to see the finished part as shown in Figure 2-25.

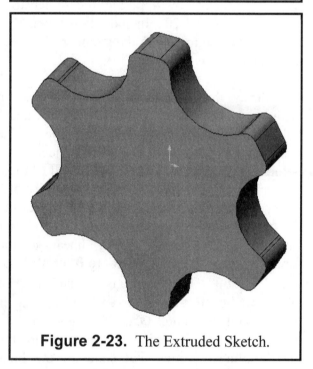

Figure 2-23. The Extruded Sketch.

Now save your model to your designated folder. Pull down **File**, select **Save As**, type in the part name **SCALLOPED KNOB.sldprt**, and then click **Save**. Open your **TITLE BLOCK – INCHES.drwdot** and immediately **SAVE AS – SCALLOPED KNOB.slddrw**. Now insert the rendered Scalloped Knob image onto your **Title Block** drawing sheet that was created in Chapter 1 and **Print** it on this sheet (see Figure 2-26).

Conversely, using the **Insert**, **Annotations**, and **Note** menu, add your name and class data to the image. **Print** a hard copy to submit to your lab instructor.

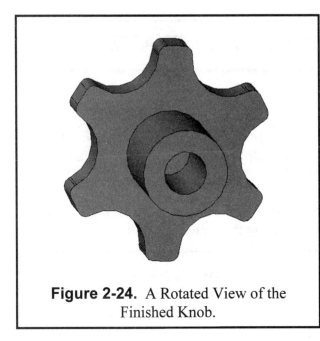

Figure 2-24. A Rotated View of the Finished Knob.

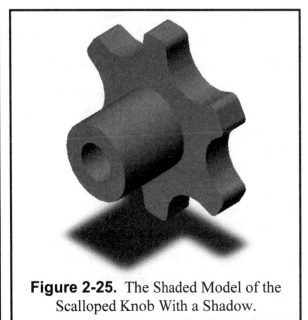

Figure 2-25. The Shaded Model of the Scalloped Knob With a Shadow.

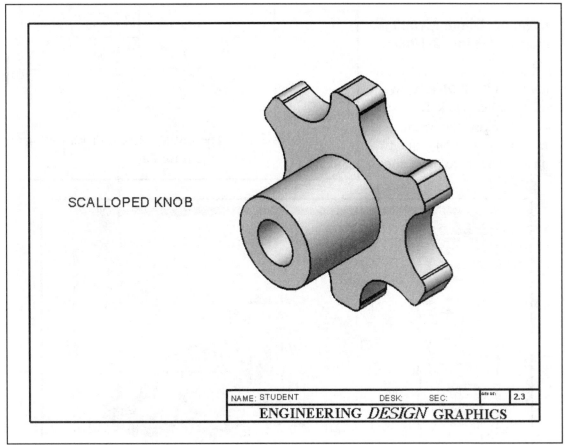

SCALLOPED KNOB

NAME: STUDENT	DESK:	SEC:		2.3
ENGINEERING *DESIGN* GRAPHICS				

Figure 2-26. The Scalloped Knob Rendered Image on a Title Block Drawing Sheet.

Exercise 2.4: LINEAR STEP PLATE

In Exercise 2.4, you will design a Linear Step Plate used for linear motion control in machinery. There are a lot of holes on this plate, and you will find the linear array and mirror functions to be quite helpful. Start by going to your folder and **Open** the file **ANSI-INCHES.prtdot**, immediately **SAVE AS – LINEAR STEP PLATE.sldprt**. Select the **Right** plane as the drawing plane and the **Right** view orientation to see it head on. Then start a new **Sketch**. Complete the initial geometry of the part according to Figure 2-27. Use the **Line** tool to draw the outline using horizontal and vertical lines. Use the **Dimension** tool to set the geometry by applying the dimensions shown in the Figure 2-26, including the dimension to the origin.

Now pull down **Insert**, **Boss/Base**, and select **Extrude**. On the "Base Extrude" menu, set the extrude parameters as shown in Figure 2-28:

> *Direction 1:* **Blind, 2.1000** in.
> *Direction 2*: **Blind, 2.1000** in.

Notice that you can preview this operation in an **Isometric** view on the screen. Then click the green (√) check to close the menu and execute the extrusion in two directions. The base part looks like Figure 2-29.

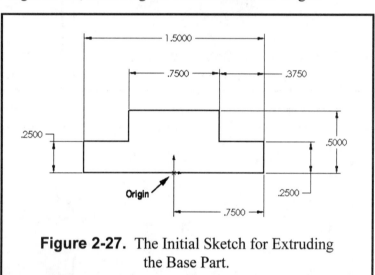

Figure 2-27. The Initial Sketch for Extruding the Base Part.

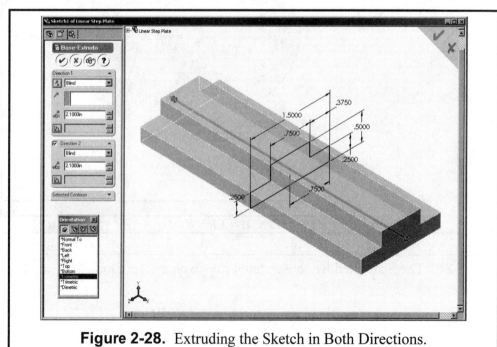

Figure 2-28. Extruding the Sketch in Both Directions.

Now you will create some linear holes. Pick the top surface of the small step on the front side (see Figure 2-29). It should highlight *green*. In a **Top** view, click **Sketch** and draw a small **Circle** on the surface as shown in Figure 2-30. Use the **Dimension** tool to add the three dimensions given to fix it:

Diameter = **0.1625**
From center origin = **0.5625**
From center origin = **1.5000**

Now you will linearly repeat that circle. **Select** the circle (it should turn *green*). Pull down **Tools**, select **Sketch Tools**, then select the **Linear Step and Repeat** command. The "Linear Sketch Step and Repeat" menu pops onto the screen. Key in the following parameters:

Direction 1:
Number = **6**
Spacing = **0.6000**
Angle = repeat to right side

Direction 2:
Number = 1

Click the **Preview** button to see if it is correct and then click **OK**. You now should have six circles on the front step surface. You need to add six more circles to the back step surface. You can quickly mirror them.

Draw a horizontal **Centerline** across the origin (Note the "—" symbol on your cursor means horizontal). Hold down the **Ctrl** key and **Select** the six circles on the front step that were just created, and also pick the centerline you just sketched. Now click the **Mirror** sketch icon and the selected items will get mirrored about the centerline, as shown in Figure 2-32.

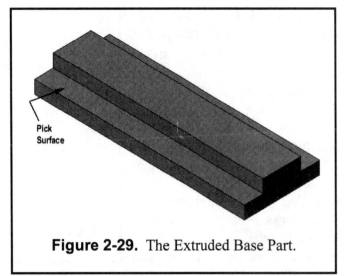

Figure 2-29. The Extruded Base Part.

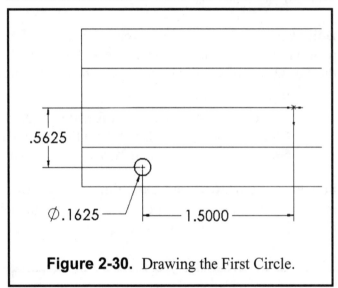

Figure 2-30. Drawing the First Circle.

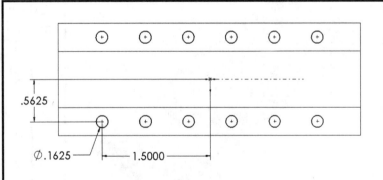

Figure 2-31 Linearly Repeating and Mirroring the Circles.

Pull down **Insert**, **Cut**, and **Extrude**. Use the **Through All** option and click the green (√) check to close the menu. You now drilled the small holes all the way through the plate's steps. You now need to drill some counter holes a quarter of the way down the small through holes. _Note:_ This design feature is called a "Counterbore" and SolidWorks has a special "Wizard" that can create it. However, we will leave that "Wizard" for a later lab.

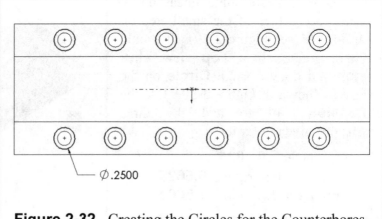

Figure 2-32. Creating the Circles for the Counterbores.

Select the top surface of the front step again. **Sketch** a **Circle** on that surface. Then add a relation to make the circle concentric with the hole beneath it (The diameter is **.25**). Now repeat the exact same process as before to get the twelve circles for the counterbore holes.

- o **Select** the new circle
- o Execute a **Linear Step and Repeat** to get the front **6** circles at **0.6000** inches apart.
- o **Sketch** a horizontal **Centerline** through the origin.
- o **Select** the six circles and **Mirror** them about the centerline.

Pull down **Insert**, **Cut**, and **Extrude**. Use the **Blind** option to a depth of **0.0625** inches into the material. Click the green (√) check to close the menu. You now drilled the counterbores into the plate's two steps, as shown in Figure 2-33 in a **Rotated View**.

Note: Sometimes you might make a mistake with a "Cut-Extrude" operation like this one. You can simply right mouse click on its name in the Feature Manager and select the **Edit Feature** option on the menu.

Figure 2-33. The Model with Counterbores.

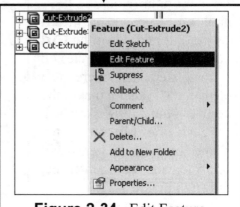

Figure 2-34. Edit Feature.

The final design requirement is to create four counterbore holes on the bottom of the plate. Pick a **Bottom** view and select the bottom surface to **Sketch** on. Draw a first **Circle** with the three **Dimension** values given in Figure 2-34. Use a **Linear Step and Repeat** operation to get a second circle **0.6000** inches from the first circle. Draw a vertical **Centerline** through the origin (a | appears on the cursor). Then **Mirror** the two circles. This results in four circles as shown in Figure 2-35.

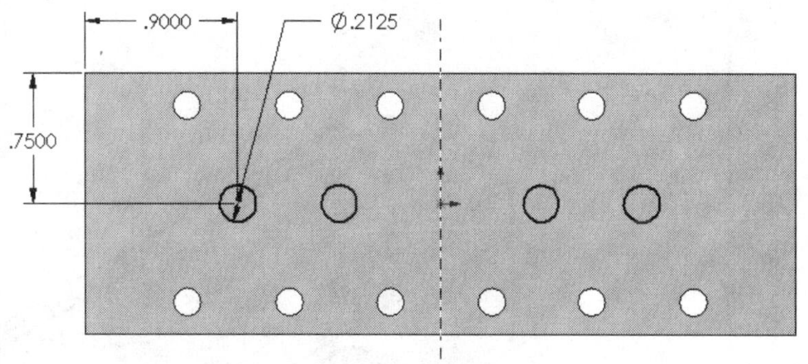

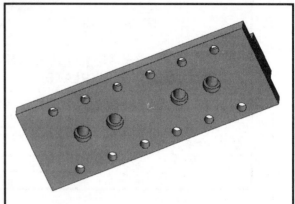

Figure 2-35. Creating the Bottom Holes.

Pull down **Insert, Cut, Extrude**. Use the **Through All** option and click the green (√) check to close the menu. You now drilled the small holes all the way through the thick part of the plate. Now **Sketch** four more bore **Circles** with a *diameter* of **0.3000** inches concentric with the four bottom circles. You can use an identical process as above. Then **Cut Extrude** them to a **Blind** depth of **0.1250**. These bottom counterbores are shown in Figure 2-36.

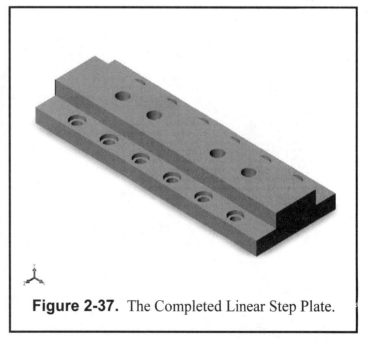

Figure 2-36. The Bottom Counterbores.

The part is now finished. Return to an **Isometric** view of the finished part as shown in Figure 2-37. Pull down **File,** select **Save As,** type in the part name **LINEAR STEP PLATE.sldprt**, and then click **Save**. Open your **TITLE BLOCK – INCHES.drwdot** and immediately **SAVE AS – LINEAR STEP PLATE.slddrw**. Now insert the rendered Linear Step Plate image onto your **Title Block** drawing sheet that was created in Chapter 1 and **Print** it on this sheet (see Figure 2-38).

Figure 2-37. The Completed Linear Step Plate.

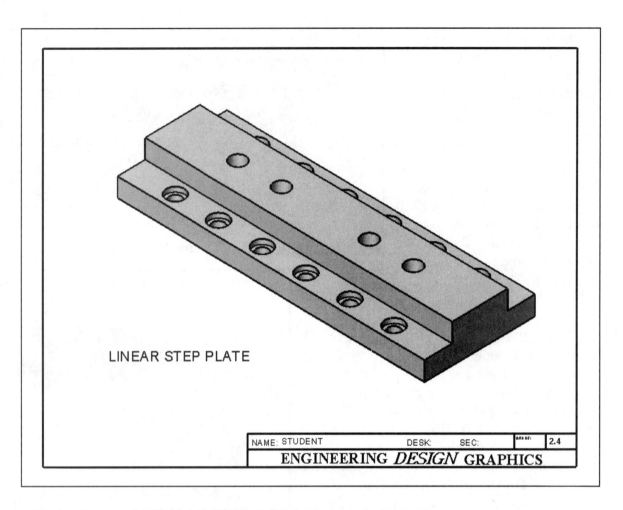

LINEAR STEP PLATE

Figure 2-38 Linear step Plate on the Title Sheet

SUPPLEMENTARY EXERCISE 2-5 FLANGE

Using the **Revolve** command in the **Front Plane**, the **Circular Step** and **Repeat** commands learned in Unit 2, in the **Top Plane** build the Flange and extrude it according to the grid divisions. Insert it on a Title Block and title it **"FLANGE."**

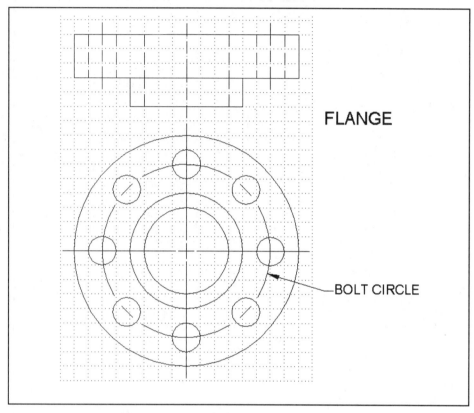

FLANGE

BOLT CIRCLE

ASSUME THE GRID DIVISIONS TO BE 0.50 INCHES.

SUPPLEMENTARY EXERCISE 2-6 STEEL VISE BASE

Make a full size model of the figure below using the commands learned in Unit 2. Insert it onto a Title Block and title it **STEEL VICE BASE**.

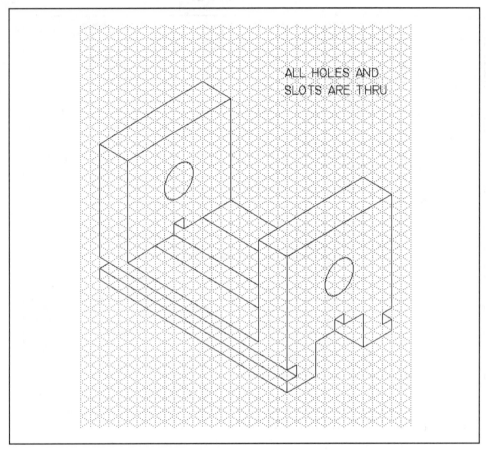

ALL HOLES AND
SLOTS ARE THRU

ASSUME THE GRID DIVISIONS TO BE 0.25 INCHES.

Computer Graphics Lab 3: 3-D Solid Modeling of Parts I

In your first two Computer Graphics Labs #1 and #2, you created some simple solid parts by using 2-D sketches. Almost all of the geometric size and shape data were defined in the 2-D sketch and you simply extruded or revolved the sketch to get the 3-D solid model. While this is the normal beginning procedure, SolidWorks contains a variety of advanced commands in which your geometric data can be created or edited directly in 3-D space. In this Computer Graphics Lab #3, you will start to create solid models using both 2-D sketches and 3-D features.

ADDING SKETCH RELATIONS

The 2-D sketch will continue to be the normal mode for initiating the construction of a solid model. You have already learned how to draw a variety of sketching entities, and how to edit and dimension them. One more capability in the 2-D sketching mode is to **Add Relations**. The Relations toolbar is shown in Figure 3-1 and can be placed on screen

Figure 3-1. The Relations Toolbar.

by going to View – Toolbars and select Dimension/Relations. Relations fix the characteristics of one or more sketch entities. The following are the common relations you may find useful in making a 2-D sketch.

Horizontal makes one or more lines horizontal.

Vertical makes one or more lines vertical.

Collinear makes two or more lines lie on the same infinite line.

Coradial makes two or more arcs share the same center point and radius.

Perpendicular makes two lines perpendicular to each other.

Parallel makes two or more lines parallel to each other.

Tangent makes an arc, ellipse, or spline, and a line or arc tangent to each other

Concentric makes two or more arcs, or a point and an arc to share the same center point.

Midpoint makes a point on a line to remain at the midpoint of the line.

Intersection makes two lines and one point to remain at the intersection of the lines.

Coincident makes a point and a line, arc, or ellipse to lie on the line, arc, or ellipse.

Equal makes two or more lines or two or more arcs have the same lengths or radii.

Symmetric makes a centerline and two points, lines, arcs, or ellipses to be equidistant from the centerline.

Fix makes the entity's size and location fixed.

THE FEATURES TOOLBAR

The "Features" toolbar is located on the top of your screen and is shown in Figure 3-2. These represent the main tools available in SolidWorks to create and edit parts in 3-D space. Below are descriptions of these features. <u>Note:</u> In SolidWorks, the first solid feature that you build is called a base, and after that they are called bosses for that part.

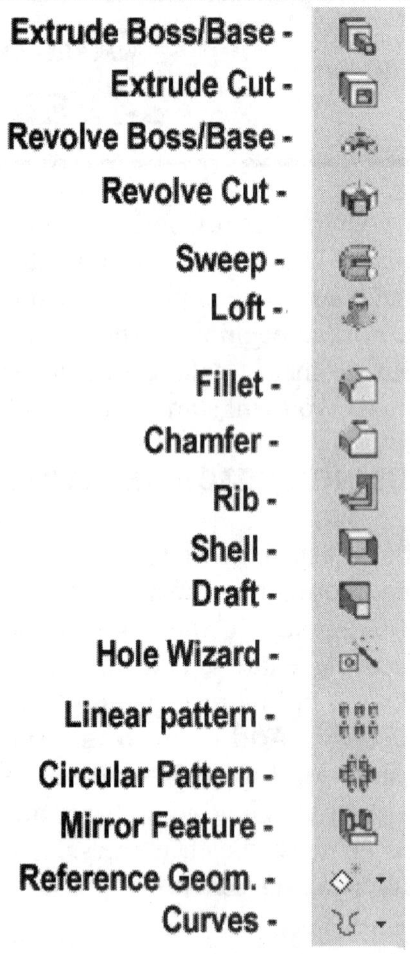

Extrude Boss/Base creates a base or boss by linearly extruding a sketch in an orthogonal direction.

Revolve Boss/Base creates a base or boss by revolving a sketch around a centerline. The default angle is 360 degrees.

Extrude Cut subtracts material from a solid body by linearly extruding a sketch through it.

Revolve Cut subtracts material from a solid body by revolving a sketch around a centerline.

Sweep creates a base, boss, cut, or surface by moving a profile (section) along a designated path.

Loft creates a feature by making transitions between profiles. A loft can be a base, boss, cut, or surface.

Fillet creates a rounded internal or external face on the part by picking an edge.

Extrude Boss/Base -	
Extrude Cut -	
Revolve Boss/Base -	
Revolve Cut -	
Sweep -	
Loft -	
Fillet -	
Chamfer -	
Rib -	
Shell -	
Draft -	
Hole Wizard -	
Linear pattern -	
Circular Pattern -	
Mirror Feature -	
Reference Geom. -	
Curves -	

Figure 3-2. The Features Toolbar.

Chamfer creates a beveled feature on selected edges or a vertex.

Rib adds material of a specified thickness determined by a contour and an existing part.

Shell hollows out the part, leaves open the faces you select, and creates thin-walled features on the remaining faces.

Draft tapers faces of a part using a specified angle.

Hole Wizard allows you to quickly add different types of common holes to your part.

Linear Pattern creates multiple instances of selected features along one or two linear paths.

Circular Pattern creates multiple instances of one or more features uniformly around an axis

Mirror Feature creates a copy of a feature (or multiple features) that is mirrored about a plane.

Reference Geometry creates reference geometry like planes, axis, coordinate system, and points.

Curves creates different types of curves including spiral and helix.

Exercise 3.1: CLEVIS MOUNTING BRACKET

In this Exercise 3.1, you will design a Clevis Mounting Bracket. You will start with a 2-D sketch of the main outline in a frontal view. Because of its design nature, certain features of the Bracket must remain fixed while other features and dimensions can be varied to accommodate design changes. For example, a hole must remain concentric with an outer arc, but the height of the hole from the bottom base could vary. So you will need to add some relations to the sketch that will fix or "constrain" the geometry. In addition, in this exercise you will use some 3-D editing functions, like "Mirror Feature," to complete the design

Go to your folder and **Open** the file **ANSI-INCHES.prtdot**. In order to avoid corrupting the **ANSI-INCHES.prtdot template** go to **File - Save as:** Under **File Name**, type **CLEVIS MOUNTING BRACKET**, and under **Save as type**, select **.sldprt** and select **SAVE**. Click the **Front** plane in the Feature Manager (it turns *green*). The Clevis Bracket is symmetric about the front plane in 3-D space. So the initial Sketch1 needs to be constructed on a plane that is parallel to the front plane, but a distance from it. To better see this operation, click to **Isometric** view orientation. Pull down **Insert**, select **Reference Geometry,** and then select **Plane**. The "Plane"

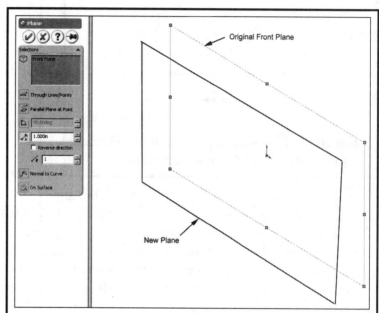

Figure 3-3. Inserting a New Plane Parallel to the Front Plane and 1.000 Inch in Front of It.

menu appears as shown in Figure 3-3. Indicate the distance, which should be **1.000** inch, then close the "Plane" menu with (√).

You now have a new plane in the Feature Manager tree called **Plane1**. Click on this new plane and then click the **Sketch** icon to start your 2-D sketch. Click to a **Front** view to better see your sketch plane. Use the **Line**, **Circle**, and **Arc** sketch tools to construct the rough 2-D profile shown in Figure 3-4. You do not have to be very accurate right now with your sketch because, in a minute, you will be defining relations and dimensions that will constrain the geometry. Just make sure the sketch is a little above the origin as shown in Figure 3-4.

Now click the **Add Relations** icon on the sketch toolbar (it is the icon with perpendicular symbol). Click the bottom base line and it turns *green*. Now also notice that the "Add Relations" menu appears in the Feature Manager area as shown in Figure 3-5. It has three menu boxes:

"Selected Entities" displays the currently selected entity(ies),

"Existing Relations" displays any pre-existing relations before you clicked the item(s),
"Add Relations" lists all the possible relations the item(s) can have.

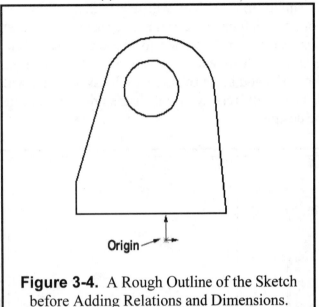

Figure 3-4. A Rough Outline of the Sketch before Adding Relations and Dimensions.

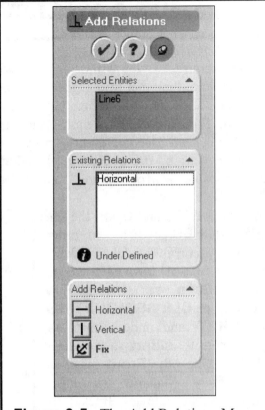

Figure 3-5. The Add Relations Menu

Add the **Horizontal** relation to this bottom line and click the green check mark (√) to close the menu. The bottom line is now horizontal. _Note:_ Depending on how you drew the first line, it may already be horizontal, because the smart cursor sometimes infers the intent of the designer.

Now study all the remaining relations to add to the sketch, as shown in Figure 3-6. Each time click the **Add Relations** icon, pick the entity(ies) to turn *green*, add the appropriate relation(s) in the "Add Relations" menu, and then click the green check mark (√). Repeat these steps to add the following as indicated in Figure 3-6.

- Origin and Bottom Horizontal Line are **Coincident** and **Midpoint**.

- Left Short Line and Bottom Line are **Perpendicular**.

- Right Side line and Top Arc are **Tangent**.

- Top Arc and Circle are **Concentric**.

- Top Arc and Left Angled Line are **Tangent**.

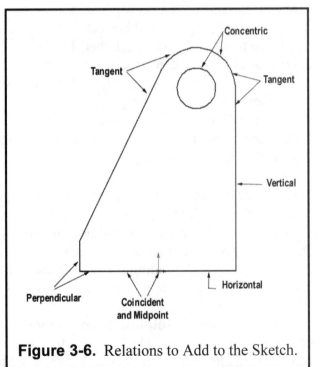

Figure 3-6. Relations to Add to the Sketch.

This completes all the relations for the sketch. However, your current sketch may not look like the final version. It may be too short or too tall or too wide. Also your lines are *blue* meaning the geometry is under-defined. Try something now. With the **Select** cursor, pick the center of the concentric circle and arc. Hold the **LMB** down and move it up, to the right, or to the left. See the sketch change shape, but the relations (like tangent, vertical, midpoint, and perpendicular) remain true and fixed. This is called constraint-based modeling. Now return the center point back to its original position.

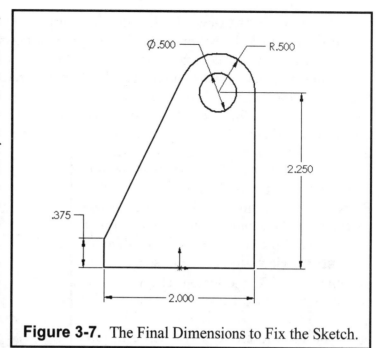

Figure 3-7. The Final Dimensions to Fix the Sketch.

You will now complete the geometry of your sketch by adding dimensions. Study the dimensions to add in Figure 3-7. With the **Dimension** tool, apply the dimensions (all in inches). Start with the **2.250** height of the center of the concentric circle and arc. Then apply equal **0.500** diameter and radius dimensions for the circular features. Finally, add the **2.000** length of the bottom line and the **0.375** height of the small vertical line on the left side. Now the sketch, with relations and dimensions added, is fixed and all lines turn *black*.

You can now try another thing. With the **Select** cursor, double click the **2.000** dimension of the bottom line and change it temporarily to **4.000**. Notice how wide the base becomes, but it is centered at the origin because of the "Midpoint" relation it possesses. Then change that same dimension to **1.000**. See how skinny it becomes, but the "Midpoint" and "Tangent" relations still hold true and standout in the design. Now return the dimension back to the original value of **2.000**. You are now ready to extrude the sketch to get some 3-D geometry for the Clevis Mounting Bracket.

Click the **Extrude Boss/Base** icon on the "Features" toolbar and the "Base-Extrude" menu appears. Give it a **Blind** extrusion distance of **0.375** inches in the direction of the "Original Front Plane" (see Figure 3-3). You can use the flip direction button if needed to get it pointed towards that *Front* plane **(away from your point of view)**. Use an **Isometric** view to aid in seeing this direction and then click the green mark (√). You should now have a solid piece of the Bracket as shown in Figure 3-8.

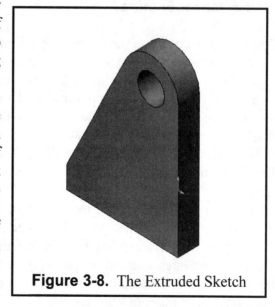

Figure 3-8. The Extruded Sketch

Now return to a **Front** view and click the front surface (it turns *green*) to sketch on it. Click the **Sketch** icon. Pick the bottom horizontal edge, hold down the **Ctrl** key and pick the left short vertical edge of the model (they turn *green*). Next click the **Convert** sketch icon to convert *those edges* into lines for the current sketch. They still retain the previous data so they are *black* lines. Now draw a **Line**, from the top of the converted vertical line, horizontally over to the right edge. Then draw a final **Line** vertically down to the bottom right corner. This essentially makes

a rectangular sketch that can be extruded to form the bottom of the Clevis Mounting Bracket. Click the **Extrude Boss/Base** icon on the "Features" toolbar. Give it a **Blind** extrusion distance of **2.000** inches <u>back</u> into the direction of the "Original Front Plane" (use flip direction if needed). Use an **Isometric** view to aid in seeing this direction. Click the green check (√) to complete this bottom base.

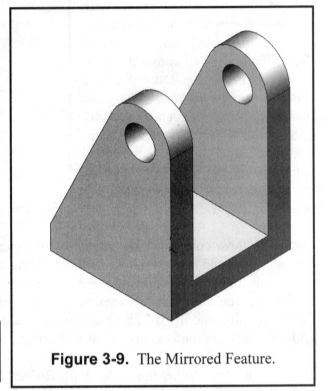

Now you need to create a symmetric feature like Figure 3-8 on the backside of the model. Hold down the **Ctrl** key, and on the Feature Manager tree, click both the **Front** plane label and the **Base-Extrude** label. Now click the **Mirror Feature** icon on the "Features" toolbar (see icon to right). The "Base-Extrude" upright feature is now mirrored about the front plane, as shown in Figure 3-9.

Mirror Feature

Figure 3-9. The Mirrored Feature.

Note: You can also access this operation by pulling down **Insert**, select **Pattern/Mirror**, and then **Mirror Feature**.

You will now complete the Bracket by adding some features to the bottom base. Refer to Figure 3-10 for this data. Select a **Top** view orientation. Click on the top surface of the bottom base to turn it *green* and then click the **Sketch** icon. Use the **Circle**, **Arc** and **Line** tools to draw the hole and slot outline. Use the **Dimension** tool to add the given dimensions. The slot on the right side can extend over the edge a little to make sure it cuts off the solid middle part of that edge. Notice that the center point position of the circle and arc area aligned horizontally with the origin. If it is correct, the lines should turn *black* once all dimensions are applied.

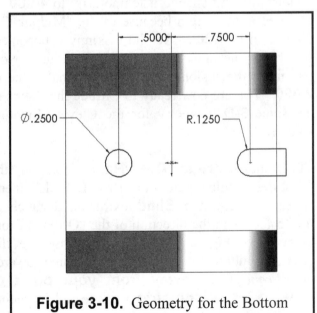

Figure 3-10. Geometry for the Bottom Holes.

Now click the **Extrude Cut** icon. In the "Extrude-Cut" menu, give it the **Through All** condition and make sure the cut direction is downward. Use an **Isometric** view to aid in visualizing this operation. Then click the green check mark (√). Your Clevis Mounting Bracket is now complete. You can use the **Rotate View** icon to see the thru holes on the bottom and any other feature that you wish. View your final model in an **Isometric** view orientation as shown in Figure 3-11.

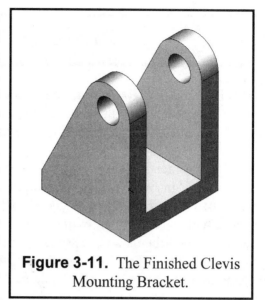

Figure 3-11. The Finished Clevis Mounting Bracket.

Pull down **File,** select **Save As,** select your proper folder, type in the part name **CLEVIS MOUNTING BRACKET.sldprt**, and then click **Save**. Insert the rendered Clevis Mounting Bracket image onto your **Title Block** drawing sheet, as shown in Figure 3-12. Now **SAVE** your drawing sheet to your directory as **CLEVIS MOUNTING BRACKET.slddrw**. Take note that the title of the part and the drawing are the same but the extension has changed. The solid model and the drawing are linked, meaning that any changes made to the solid model will automatically be updated on the drawing. (see Figure 3-12).

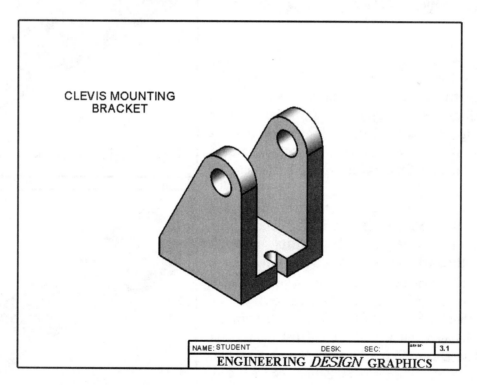

CLEVIS MOUNTING
BRACKET

NAME: STUDENT   DESK: SEC: | 3.1
ENGINEERING *DESIGN* GRAPHICS

Figure 3-12. The Clevis Mounting Bracket Rendered Image on a Title Block Drawing Sheet.

Exercise 3.2: MANIFOLD

In this Exercise 3.1, you will design a Manifold. The Manifold is designed to allow air or fluid to flow in many directions through its ports. There will be many similar flow ports, so you will use some 3-D editing commands in SolidWorks to replicate them.

Go to your folder and **Open** the file **ANSI-METRIC.prtdot** since the Manifold is designed in metric units. In order to avoid corrupting the **ANSI-METRIC.prtdot template** go to **File - Save as:** Under **File Name**, type **MANIFOLD**, and under **Save as type**, select **.sldprt** and select **SAVE**. Click the **Right** plane icon in the Feature Manager, select a **Right** view orientation, and then start a **Sketch**. Draw two **Circles** that are concentric and centered at the origin, with one circle a little larger. **Dimension** the larger circle to be **60** mm in diameter and the smaller circle to have a **45** mm diameter. These two dimensions should fix your geometry.

Click the **Extrude Boss/Base** icon on the left toolbar. In the "Base-Extrude" menu, pick **Direction 1** to be **Mid Plane** at **300 mm**, then click the green check mark (√). You now have a long throat centered at the origin, as shown in Figure 3-13.

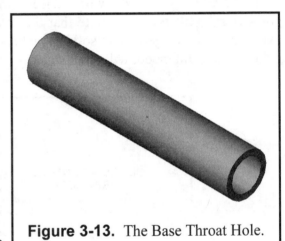

Figure 3-13. The Base Throat Hole.

Now add two collars on each end. Click on the right side surface of the throat hole (defined by the two concentric circles). The surface should turn *green*. Click **Sketch** and pick the smaller inner circular edge. Click the **Convert** icon to convert it to the new sketch. Now draw one **Circle**, centered at the origin, and **Dimension** it with a diameter of **75** mm.

Now click the **Extrude Boss/Base** icon. In the "Base-Extrude" menu, pick **Direction 1 (back over the throat)** to be **Blind** at **50** mm then click the green check mark (√). You now have a small collar on one end of the throat. You can easily copy it to the other side. Hold down the **Ctrl** key. In the Feature Manager, click both the **Right** plane icon and the last **Boss-Extrude 1**. They both should turn *green* in the computer modeling space. Now simply click the **Mirror** feature icon on the features toolbar. Click the green check mark (√) in the "Mirror Feature" menu to execute the operation. You now have a collar on each end of the throat, as shown in Figure 3-14.

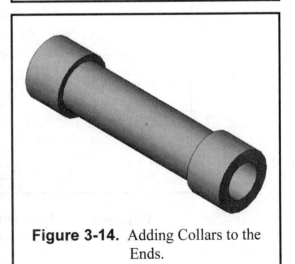

Figure 3-14. Adding Collars to the Ends.

You will design the first port hole. Click the **Top** plane in the Feature Manager. Now Pull down **Insert**, select **Reference Geometry,** and then select **Plane**. The "Plane" menu appears. Indicate the distance to be **42.5** mm above the top plane, then click the green check mark (√) to add the plane to the working space. **Plane 1** is added to the Feature Manager, so click on it (it turns *green*) and start another **Sketch**. Click a **Top** view orientation to better see this new sketching plane.

Now draw a small **Circle** on the plane just inside the collar on the left side of the throat. Click the **Add Relations** icon, and click both the <u>center</u> of the circle and the origin. Under the "Add Relations" menu, select the **Horizontal** relation to add to these two entities. Click the green check mark (√) to add this relation to make then align horizontally. Next **Dimension** the circle to have a diameter of **35** mm and to be **75** mm to the left of the origin, as shown in Figure 3-15.

Now click the **Extrude Boss/Base** icon in the features toolbar on the left side of the screen. In the "Base-Extrude" menu, pick Direction 1 to be **Up to Surface**. Pick the outer throat surface on the model (it turns *green*), then click the green check mark (√). You now have a boss extruded down from Plane 1 to the outer throat surface.

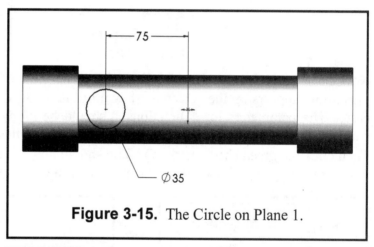

Figure 3-15. The Circle on Plane 1.

Now repeat a **Sketch** on **Plane 1**, and draw a smaller **Circle** that is concentric with the boss (**Add Relations**, **Concentric**) and has a diameter of **17.5** mm.

Return to an **Isometric** view orientation. Click the **Extrude Cut** icon on the left side toolbar. In the "Cut-Extrude" menu, pick Direction 1 to be **Up to Surface**. Pick the *inner throat surface* on the model (it turns *green*) by clicking inside the throat hole on the right side. Click the green check mark (√). You now have a hole extruded down from Plane 1 into the inside of the throat as shown in Figure 3-16.

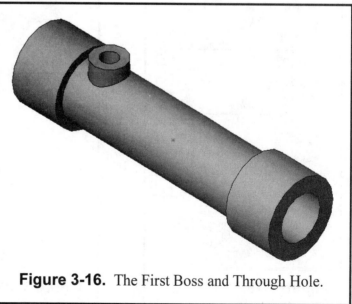

Figure 3-16. The First Boss and Through Hole.

To better see the through hole, use the **Rotate View** icon to rotate your model around the computer screen. Try to view the through hole by peering down the throat of the part. In a minute, you will cut a temporary section view to see things better on the inside.

Now that you have one boss and hole feature, it is easy to create a 3-D array of the other three that are needed. First you need an axis for the direction of the 3-D array. Pull down **Insert**, select **Reference Geometry,** and then select **Axis**. The "Reference Axis" menu appears on the screen as shown in Figure 3-17. Select the **Cylindrical/Conical Face** definition for the axis and then click the outer surface (**Face<1>**) of the throat. It gets added to the "Selections" list and then click the green check mark (√). You now have added an "Axis 1" to the Feature Manager tree that goes down the center of the throat. Press down the **Ctrl** key, and one-by-one select in the Feature Manager tree:

Axis 1
Boss-Extrude 2
Cut-Extrude 1

Figure 3-17. Adding a Reference Axis to the Model.

Now click on the **Linear Pattern** feature icon on the bottom left toolbar. The "Linear Pattern" menu now appears on the screen as shown in Figure 3-18. There is only one Direction for this case. The parameters for "Direction 1" should be along **Axis 1**, distance of **50** mm, and **4** patterns. Use you Isometric view to see the patterns replicate over the Manifold to the right side. Then click the green check mark (√). You should now have a pattern of four port holes as shown in Figure 3-19. Try viewing down the middle of the throat with the **Rotate View** icon.

Figure 3-18. The Linear Pattern Menu.

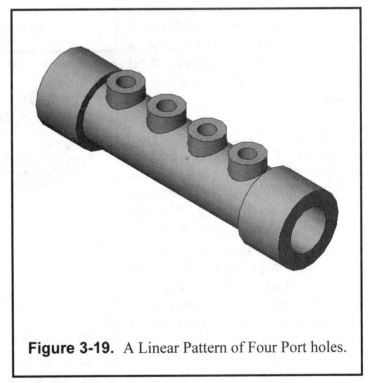

Figure 3-19. A Linear Pattern of Four Port holes.

There are two remaining port holes that need to be added to the bottom of the Manifold. They are identical in geometry to the top, so you can just mirror the in 3-D space. Hold down the **Ctrl** key and, in the Feature Manager tree, one-by-one select: **Top Plane**, **Boss-Extrude 2**, and

Cut-Extrude 1. Then click the **Mirror Feature** icon and click the green check mark (√) in the "Mirror Feature" menu to execute the operation. You now have one port hole on the bottom of the Manifold, which is named "Mirror 2." Repeat this 3-D **Mirror Feature** operation, this time using the **Right Plane** and **Mirror 2.** After you complete this operation, you will have a "Mirror 3" feature for the Manifold solid model, as shown in Figure 3-20.

Now add some final fillets to the edge where the portholes touch. Click the **Fillet** icon on the features toolbar. Enter the fillet radius of **6 mm** in the "Fillet" menu. One-by-one click on the edges (loops) of the six port holes where they touch the outer surface of the throat (they turn green). You can do this easily with a **Front** view orientation. Then click the green (√) to execute the fillet command (see the finished Figure 3-20 in **Trimetric** view).

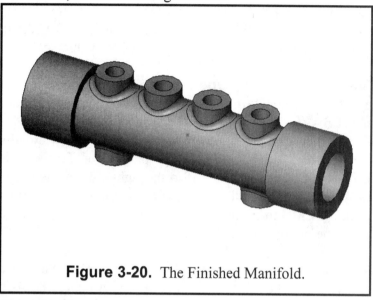

Figure 3-20. The Finished Manifold.

Earlier you rotated the model around to see through the long throat hole to see if the port holes went through to the middle. Now you will create a temporary section view to see internal features. Pull down **View**, select **Display**, and then pick **Section View**. A "Section View" menu appears on the screen. The section view parameters should be set to **0** mm distance and the **Front** plane is the default plane, as shown in Figure 3-21. Just press cancel (**X**) on the menu, after you have inspected the inside features of the manifold.

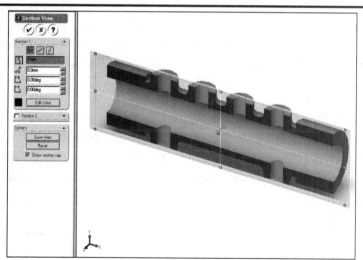

Figure 3-21. A Section View Display of the Inside of the Manifold.

Pull down **File,** select **Save As,** type in the part name **MANIFOLD.sldprt**, select your proper folder, and then click **Save**. , Insert the image into the **Title Block** drawing sheet like in previous labs (refer to page 1.7). *Conversely,* using the **Insert, Annotations,** and **Note** menu, add your name and class data to the image. **Print** a hard copy to submit to your lab instructor.

Exercise 3.3: HAND WHEEL

In this Exercise 3.3, you will design a Hand Wheel. The Hand Wheel has an elliptical cross-section that can be revolved 360 degrees. So you will learn how to sketch an ellipse. The four spokes for the hand wheel can be created using a 3-D circular pattern array. So you will employ some new SolidWorks commands in this lab exercise.

Go to your folder and **Open** the file **ANSI-INCHES.prtdot**. Immediately go to **File - Save as:** Under **File Name**, type **HAND WHEEL**, and under **Save as type**, select **.sldprt** and select **SAVE**. Click on the **Front** plane in the Feature Manager tree. Set the view orientation to **Front**, then start a new **Sketch**. You need to draw an ellipse, but notice that it does not have an icon on the sketch toolbars. So pull down **Tools**, select **Sketch Entity**, and then select **Ellipse**. Draw an ellipse off to the right side of the origin as shown in Figure 3-22. Click the **LMB** cursor to place the center of the ellipse off to the right side of the origin. Drag upward and click the **LMB** to set the major axis of the ellipse. Then drag rightward and click the **LMB** again to set the minor axis of the ellipse.

Right now the ellipse is somewhat randomly placed on the frontal sketch plane. The center of the ellipse should be aligned with the origin. So click the **Add Relations** icon. Pick the center of the ellipse and then pick the origin. Add the **Horizontal** relation to align them and then click the green check mark (√). Now **Dimension** the ellipse using Figure 3-22 as a guide. The major diameter is **1.000** inches, the minor diameter is **0.750** inches, and the center's distance from the origin is **4.500** inches. Also sketch a vertical **Centerline** (remember the I on the screen cursor) as shown in Figure 3-22. The ellipse is now ready to be revolved.

Click the **Revolve Boss/Base** icon on the left side features toolbar. In the "Base-Revolve" menu, set the menu parameters to **One Direction** and to **360** degrees, then click the green check mark (√). You now have the first feature for the Hand Wheel as shown in Figure 3-23.

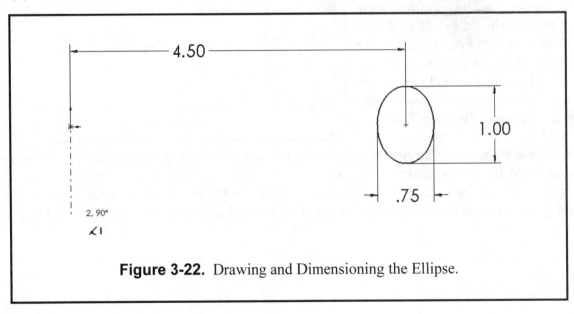

Figure 3-22. Drawing and Dimensioning the Ellipse.

You will now construct a spoke across the Hand Wheel. It also has an elliptical shape as shown in Figure 3-24. Click the **Right** Plane in the Feature Manager and select a **Right** view orientation. **Sketch** an **Ellipse** centered at the origin (recall that ellipse it is in the **Tools Sketch Entity** pull down menu). Next **Dimension** the ellipse according to Figure 3-24.

Switch to an **Isometric** view orientation to better see the next operation. Click the **Extrude Boss/Base** icon and select the **Up to Surface** end condition for Direction 1, and also **Up to Surface** end condition for Direction 2. Now **Select** the round tube surface of the Hand Wheel (Figure 3-23) for the surface for the end conditions for both directions. It should turn *green* and the extruded spoke should preview on the screen. If it looks correct, click the green check mark (√) and the operation is executed. You should now have one spoke as shown in Figure 3-25.

You can now add the remaining spokes using a circular pattern feature. But first you need to add an axis for the pattern function. Pull down **Insert**, **Reference Geometry**, and select **Axis**. The "Reference Axis" menu appears on the screen as shown in Figure 3-26. Select **Point and Face/Plane** as the axis option. Now carefully **Select** the origin as the "Point" and the surface of the spoke as the "Surface" in the axis definition. Both the origin and spoke surface should turn *green*. Then click **OK** to close the menu. You should now see an Axis 1 on your screen.

Hold down the **Ctrl** key and **Select** both the Axis 1 (you can click it in the Feature Manger area) and the spoke. They should highlight in *green*. Click on the **Circular Pattern** icon on the Features Toolbar and the "Circular Pattern" menu appears. Since they were pre-selected, **Axis 1** should appear in the "Parameters" box and **Boss-Extrude 1** should appear in the "Features to Pattern" box. Now set the "Angle" to **90** degrees and the number of patterns to **2**. Now click the green check mark (√) and the circular pattern with the spokes is created as, shown in Figure 3-27.

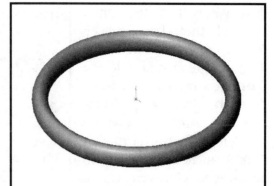

Figure 3-23. The First Feature of the Hand Wheel.

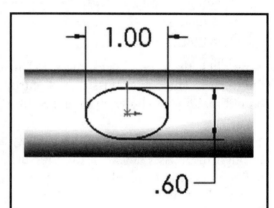

Figure 3-24. Dimensions for the Elliptical Spoke.

Figure 3-25. The Extruded Spoke.

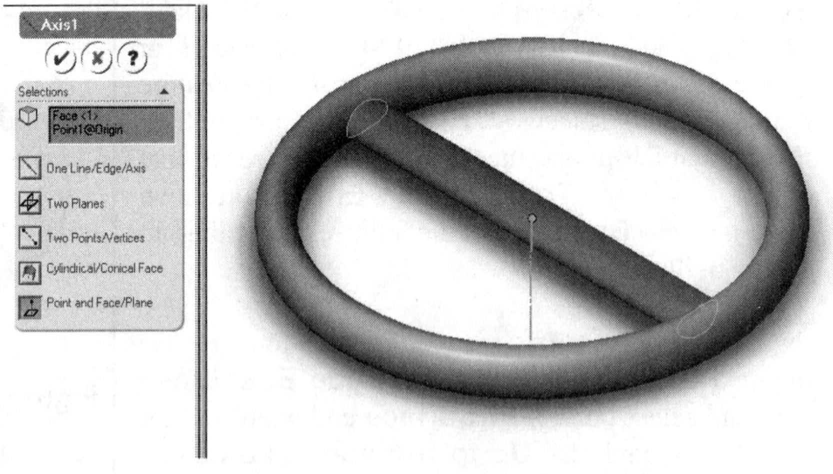

Now you will add the central hub of the Hand Wheel. Select the **Top** plane in the Feature Menu and select a **Top** view orientation. Click **Sketch** and draw a **Circle**, centered at the origin with a diameter **Dimension** of **2.000** inches. Switch to **Isometric** view orientation. Click **Extrude Boss/Base** features icon. On the "Extrude-Boss" menu, set the following parameters:

Figure 3-26. Inserting a Reference Axis.

Direction 1: **Mid Plane, 1.50** inches,
Direction 2: off.

Now click the green check mark (√) to close the menu. The center boss hub is extruded in both directions as shown in Figure 3-28.

You will now add the hole and keyway to go through the boss. Click on the top surface of the central boss to highlight it in *green*. Also select a **Top** view orientation. Now click the **Sketch** icon and draw a sketch similar to the one shown in Figure 3-29. You will need to draw a **Circle** and then either a few **Lines** or maybe a **Rectangle**. Use the **Trim** sketch editing capability to cut away the profile for the keyway. Then **Dimension** the sketch as shown in Figure 3-29:

Figure 3-27. Circular Pattern of Spokes.

Circle radius = **0.625** inches
Keyway width = **0.220** inches
Keyway height = **0.750** inches
Keyway distance = **0.1100** inches

If all is correct, your sketch should turn *black* meaning the geometry is fixed.

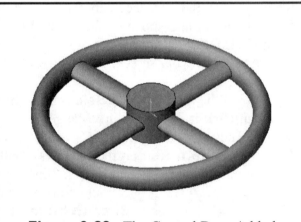

Now click the **Extrude Cut** icon and select the **Through All** end condition. Make sure

Figure 3-28. The Central Boss Added.

the direction for the "through all" condition is down, then click the green check mark (√). The cut is created through the hub as shown in Figure 3-30. The Hand Wheel is almost complete, you just need to add the fillets to the places where the spokes intersect the hub and wheel hub.

Now click the **Fillet** features icon on the left side toolbar (it looks like a block with a round corner). Key in a fillet radius of **0.125** inches. One-by-one, pick the four surfaces of the four spokes to fillet the edges. They turn *green* when picked and they get added to the "Items to Fillet" list in the menu. Then click the check mark (√) to execute the eight fillets. The finished Hand Wheel model is shown in Figure 3-30 in an **Isometric** view.

Pull down **File,** select **Save As,** type in the part name **HAND WHEEL.sldprt**, select your proper folder, and then click **Save.** Insert the image into the **Title Block** drawing sheet like in previous labs (see Figure 3-31). **Print** a hard copy to submit to your lab instructor. Save your drawing as **HAND WHEEL.slddrw.**

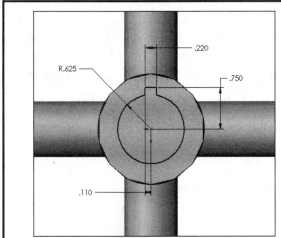

Figure 3-29. The Sketch Shape and Dimensions for the Through Hole and Keyway.

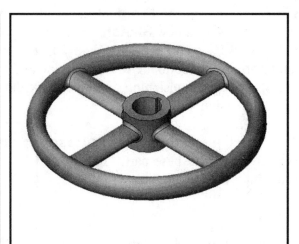

Figure 3-30. The Finished Hand Wheel Model Shown in Isometric.

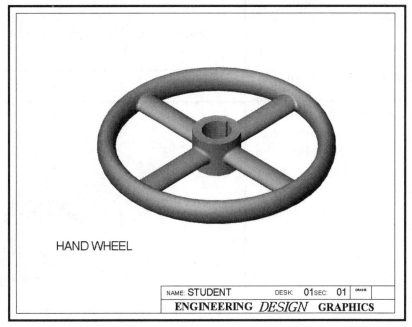

HAND WHEEL

NAME: STUDENT	DESK: 01	SEC: 01	GRADE
ENGINEERING *DESIGN* GRAPHICS			

Figure 3-31. The Hand Wheel Image on a Title Block Drawing Sheet.

Exercise 3.4: TOE CLAMP

In the previous lab exercise, you created sketches on planes that were orthogonal to the principal planes (Front, Top, or Right). In this simple Exercise 3.4, you will create features for the Toe Clamp by sketching on both orthogonal and inclined planes. The inclined plane is at a 45 degrees angle to the top surface, so you will also learn how to dimension angles.

Go to your folder and **Open** the file **ANSI-INCHES.prtdot**. Immediately go to **File - Save as:** Under **File Name**, type **TOE CLAMP**, and under **Save as type**, select **.sldprt** and select **SAVE**. Click on the **Front** plane in the Feature Manager tree. Set the view orientation to **Front**, then start a new **Sketch**. You need to draw the front outline of the Toe Clamp as shown in Figure 3-32. Use the **Line** and **Dimension** tools to create and fix the geometry. **Add Relations** to the bottom **Horizontal** line and make it both **Coincident** and **Midpoint** with the origin. When dimensioning an angle, pick the two lines that form the angle and then drag the angle dimension into place.

Now select the **Extrude Boss/Base** icon to create the base part. Enter the following parameters in the "Base-Extrude" menu:

Direction 1:
Mid Plane, **2.00** inches

Direction 2:
Off

Then click the green check mark (√) to execute the bi-directional extrude, as shown in Figure 3-33.

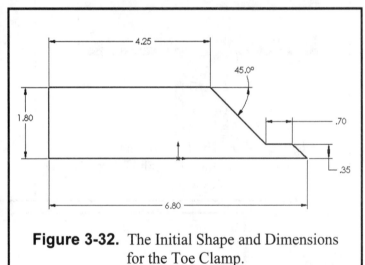

Figure 3-32. The Initial Shape and Dimensions for the Toe Clamp.

You will now cut the counterbore and hole on the inclined surface. Click on the inclined surface to highlight it *green*. Now you want to see this surface head on (ortho-directional).   So click the **Normal to** selection in the View Orientation box (or you can also click the **Normal to** icon on the top display toolbars as shown below).

Figure 3-33. The Base Part for the Toe Clamp.

Sketch a **Circle** on the inclined plane as shown in Figure 3-34. **Dimension** the diameter to be **0.50** inches. Center the circle **1.00** inches vertically and **1.00** inches horizontally from the lower left corner of the inclined plane. Click the **Extrude Cut** icon on the features toolbar and give it the **Through all** end condition. Make sure the hole is cut at an angled, downward direction and then click the green check mark (√). You can see it with the **Rotate View** icon.

Click on the inclined surface and return to a **Normal to** view of it, and then **Sketch** another larger **Circle** on it. **Dimension** it with a diameter of **0.80** inches. Next click **Add Relations** and make this new circle **Concentric** with the edge of the through hole. Click the **Extrude Cut** icon and give it a **Blind** end condition of **0.25** inches into the part. You now have a counterbore hole as seen in Figure 3-35.

You can now make the V-cut to add stress relief for the Toe Clamp. Click on the plateau horizontal surface just below the inclined surface. Click **Sketch** and with the **Line** tool draw a small triangle shape approximately over the beveled edge of the Toe Clamp, as suggested in Figure 3-36. Apply **Dimensions** as shown in the figure. If you apply them correctly, the sketch will turn *black*.

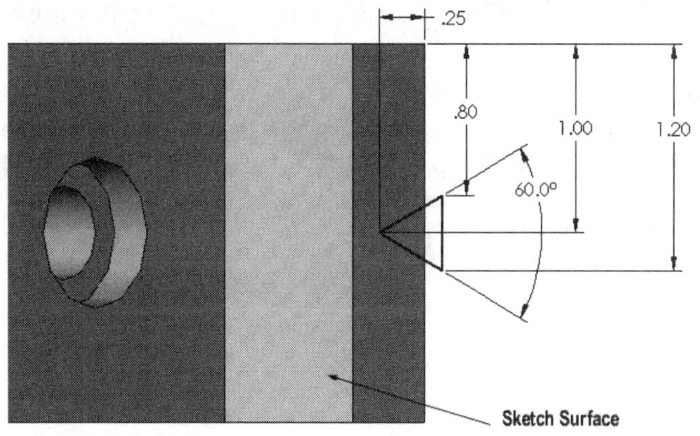

Now you can execute the V-Cut. Click the **Extrude Cut** icon on the features toolbar and give it the **Through all** end condition. Make sure the cut goes in the downward direction through the beveled end, and then click the green check mark (√). Use the **Rotate View** icon to see it.

The final feature to create is the large counter slot on the very top

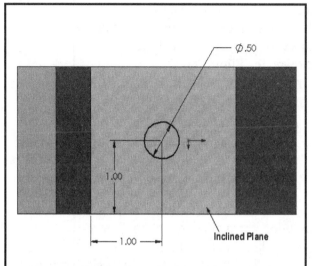

Figure 3-34. Creating the Circle on the Inclined Plane.

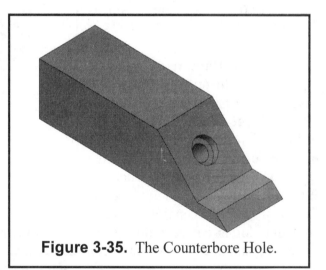

Figure 3-35. The Counterbore Hole.

Figure 3-36. The Dimensions for the V-Cut.

surface of the Toe Clamp. Click on the top surface (it turns *green*) and **Sketch** the outer slot shape as shown in Figure 3-37. Use two **Lines** and two **Arcs** to begin the sketch. **Add Relations** as follows:

Line (top) =**Horizontal** and **Tangent** to both arcs
Line (bottom) =**Horizontal** and **Tangent** to both arcs

Next **Dimension** the slot by applying the values given in Figure 3-37. The sketch should be fixed and turn *black*. Click the **Extrude Cut** icon and give it a **Blind** end condition of **0.25** inches into the part. The 0.25 deep counter slot is created.

Start the final **Sketch** on the same top surface. Identify the large slot edge you just drew, and **Convert** it. Next **Offset** it inward by **0.20** inches to create a smaller slot that has the identical shape. *Delete* the bigger slot on the sketch. Click the **Extrude Cut** icon and give it the **Through all** end condition. Make sure the slot is cut at a downward direction, and then click the green

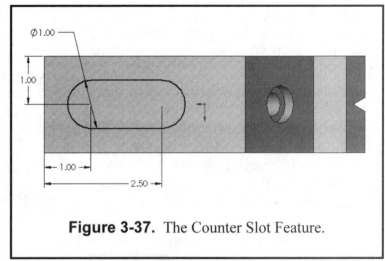

Figure 3-37. The Counter Slot Feature.

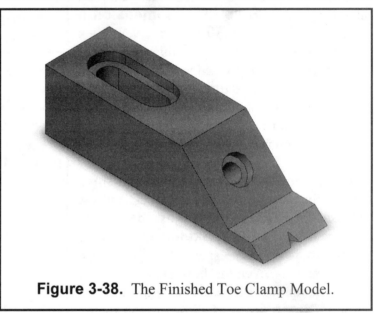

Figure 3-38. The Finished Toe Clamp Model.

check mark (√). You can now see it with the **Rotate View** icon. (*Note:* This process for creating the counter slot was the reverse of the counterbore process, but they both worked correctly.) The Toe Clamp model is now finished as shown in Figure 3-38 in an **Isometric** view.

Pull down **File,** select **Save As,** type in the part name **TOE CLAMP.sldprt**, select your proper folder, and then click **Save**. Insert the image into the **Title Block** drawing sheet like in previous labs. Save your drawing as **TOE CLAMP.slddrw**. **Print** a hard copy to submit to your lab instructor.

SUPPLEMENTARY EXERCISE 3-5 CONVEYOR RAMP GUIDE

Build a full size model of the figure below. Insert it on a Title Block and title it **"CONVEYOR RAMP GUIDE"**.

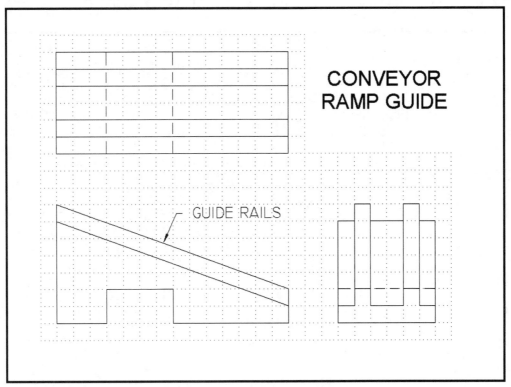

CONVEYOR
RAMP GUIDE

GUIDE RAILS

ASSUME THE GRID DIVISIONS TO BE 0.25 INCHES

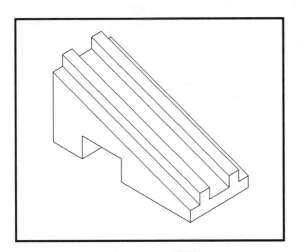

PICTORIAL VIEW

SUPPLEMENTARY EXERCISE 3-6 DOUBLE SHAFT HANGER

Using the commands learned during the last two Units, build a full size model of the figure below.   Insert it onto a Title Block and title it **DOUBLE SHAFT HANGER**.

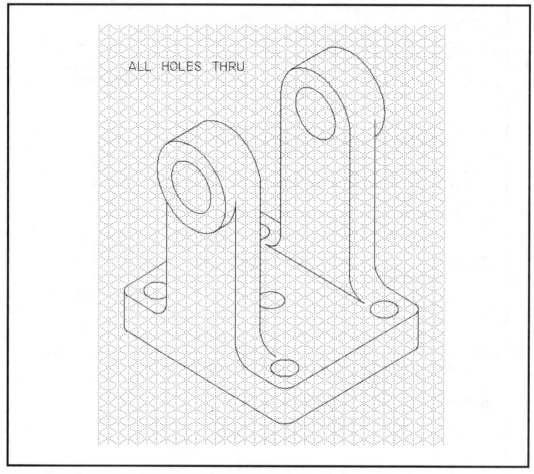

ALL HOLES THRU

ASSUME THE GRID DIVISIONS TO BE 0.25 INCHES

Computer Graphics Lab 4: 3-D Solid Modeling of Parts II

INTRODUCTION TO LAB 4

In this lab you will be using many of the design features that make building solid models more efficient. Commands you will be using:

Draft Creates a feature that tapers selected model faces by a specified angle, using either a neutral plane or a parting line. **NOTE:** You can also apply a draft angle as a part of an extruded base, boss, or cut.

Offset Plane You can create planes in part or assembly documents. You can use planes to sketch, to create a section view of a model, for a neutral plan in a draft feature, and so on.

Offset You can create sketch curves offset from one or more selected sketch entities, edges, loops, faces, curves, set of edges, or set of curves by a specified distance. The selected sketch entity can be construction geometry. The offset entities can be bi-directional.

Convert Entities You can create one or more curves in a sketch by projecting an edge, loop, face, curve, or external sketch contour, set of edges, or set of sketch curves onto the sketch plane. You can covert sketched entities into construction geometry to use in creating model geometry.

Fillet surfaces - Fillet/Round creates a rounded internal or external face on the part. You can fillet all edges of a face, selected sets of faces, selected edges, or edge loops.

Shell The shell tool hollows out the part, leaves open the faces you select, and creates thin-walled features on the remaining faces.

Loft - creates a feature by making transitions between profiles. A loft can be a base, boss, cut, or surface.

Dome – creates a loft type of feature that begins with the shape of the selected surface and lofts to a zero feature at a specified height.

Sweep - creates a base, boss, cut, or surface by moving a profile (section) along a path, according to these rules:
- The profile must be closed for a base or boss sweep feature; the profile may be open or closed for a surface sweep feature.
- The path may be open or closed.
- The path may be a set of sketched curves contained in one sketch, a curve, or a set of model edges.
- The start point of the path must lie on the plane of the profile.
- Neither the section, the path, nor the resulting solid can be self-intersecting.

Exercise 4.1: DRAWER TRAY

Go to your folder and open **ANSI-INCHES.prtdot**. A good practice is to immediately name your part and save the file in your folder. Pull down **File** again, select **Save As**, and then name it **DRAWER TRAY.sldprt**.

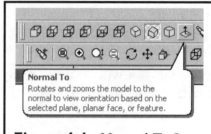

Figure 4-1. Normal To Icon.

Select the **Top Plane** in which to work, then click on the **Normal To** icon (Figure 4-1) which looks like a square plate with an arrow pointing upwards out of the center of the plate.

Select the **Sketch** icon and draw a **Rectangle** at the origin and toward the upper right.

Using the Dimension command constrain the rectangle to **4.5** inches high and **12** inches long. The resulting sketch should look like the object in Figure 4-2

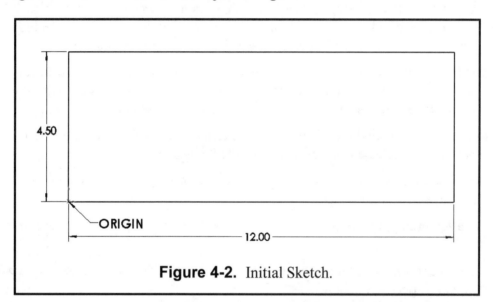

Figure 4-2. Initial Sketch.

Select the **Extrude** symbol (Figure 4-3) under Features.

Do a **Blind Extrude** downward for **3** inches, with a draft angle of **5 Degrees** (See Figure 4-4). If the upward-pointing arrow is highlighted, select it and pull it downward or click on the "Arrow" icon next to the "Blind" box. Click on the (√) button, which will produce an image similar to Figure 4-5.

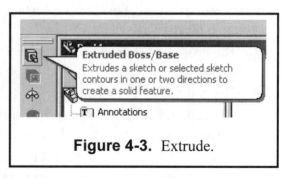

Figure 4-3. Extrude.

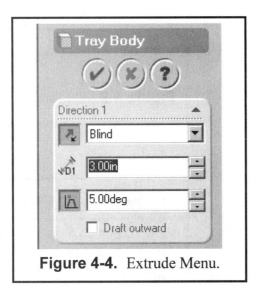

Figure 4-4. Extrude Menu.

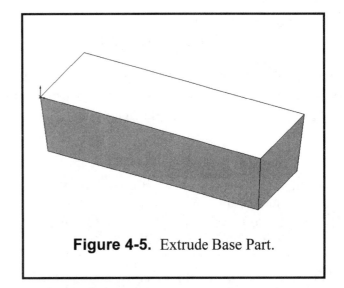

Figure 4-5. Extrude Base Part.

Click on the words "**Base Extrude**" in the Feature Manager twice (This is not a double click) and rename this feature as "**Tray Body**".

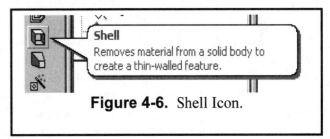

Figure 4-6. Shell Icon.

Click on the **Top** surface of the Tray Body and pick the **Shell** icon (Figure 4-6) in the left tool bar. Give the shell thickness of **0.10** in the parameters box and okay the selection. The model should now resemble the model in Figure 4-7.

Drawer Tray Rim: In order to strengthen the upper edge of the drawer tray you will now create a rim around the top edge of the tray.

You might have to **Zoom** in to select the top thin surface of the resulting tray. After you have selected the thin surface, select the **Sketch** icon and then select the **Convert Entities** icon (Figure 4-8). This converts the outer edges of that surface into new sketch entities that can be used for a new feature. Next select the **Offset Entities** icon (See Figure 4-9) and pick one of the black edges of the converted entities, enter the distance of **0.10**. If the orange preview line is on the outside of the pattern selected, then select the Reverse option (Figure 4-10) so the new offset pattern lies directly over

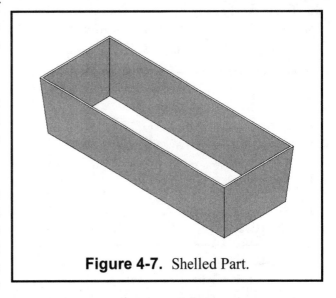

Figure 4-7. Shelled Part.

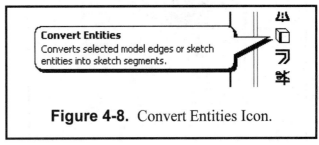

Figure 4-8. Convert Entities Icon.

the entire top edge surface of the Drawer Tray. Another option to create the inner lines is to hold down the Ctrl button while selecting all of the inner edges of the tray and then selecting the **Convert Entities** icon. Extrude this pattern downward by **0.625** inches. Make sure that the **Merge Result** box is checked. This creates a vertical rim around the upper edge of the tray.

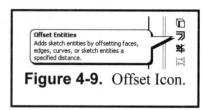

Figure 4-9. Offset Icon.

Now rotate  the tray so you can see the bottom surface. Select the bottom surface and pick the solid **Fillet** feature (Figure 4-11) in the left tool bar. Enter **0.3750** inches. The entire outline or loop of this surface will be filleted.

This causes a problem with the construction of the tray since the large fillet was applied after the shell command was used. If you go to the **Right** side view and turn it into a **Wire-Frame View** you will see that the interior wall is touching the exterior fillet (See Figure 4-12). This is caused because the last operation does not effect the previous shell operation. If you move the fillet operation above the shell operation the problem will be corrected. To correct this, go to the **Feature Manager Tree** and select the word **Fillet 1** (Figure 4-13) and drag it upward to the **Tray Body** (Figure 4-14) operation. Since the fillet is now applied before the shell operation, the shell wall will be uniform throughout the model (Figure 4-15).

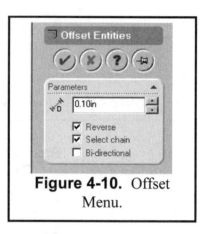

Figure 4-10. Offset Menu.

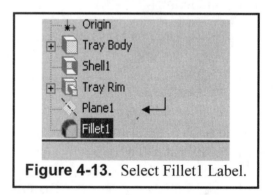

Figure 4-11. Fillet Icon

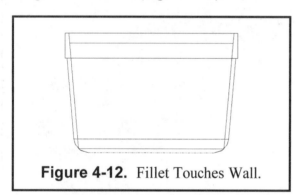

Figure 4-12. Fillet Touches Wall.

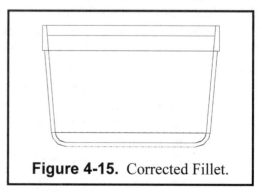

Figure 4-13. Select Fillet1 Label.

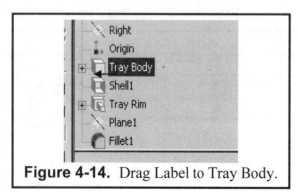

Figure 4-14. Drag Label to Tray Body.

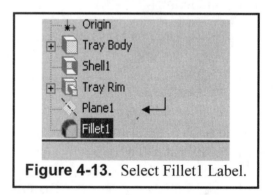

Figure 4-15. Corrected Fillet.

The next step of the construction is to place three equally spaced dividers on the inside of the tray. Select the **Top Plane** in the feature manager. Then select **Insert, Reference Geometry, Plane.** Enter the distance of **0.25** and make sure the **Reverse Direction** box is checked (Figure 4-16). Click on the green (**OK**) button. This establishes a new sketch plane that can now be used to draw the top view of the ribs. It might be advisable to rename this plane. Rename it **Dividers Plane**.

Select the **Dividers Plane** in the Feature Manager and then the **Normal To** icon to get a top view of the tray. Next select the **Sketch** icon and draw a **Rectangle** feature across the inside of the tray. Constrain the rectangle to be **0.10** inches across and **3** inches from the outside of the Tray. See Figure 4-17. Select the four lines of the rectangle. Select the **Linear Sketch Step and Repeat** icon and supply the following criteria: **Number (3); Spacing (3); and Angle (180)**. If the preview of the array does not show the repeated pattern on the Tray, click on the icon next to the Angle input box (Figure 4-18) to change the direction of the array. If the preview is correct, select the **OK** button.

Figure 4-16.
Reference Plane
Menu.

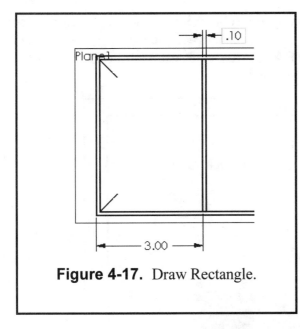

Figure 4-17. Draw Rectangle.

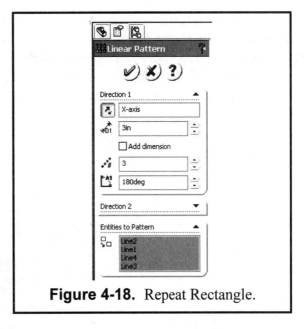

Figure 4-18. Repeat Rectangle.

You are now ready to extrude the patterns downward to the Tray Shell. Select **Insert, Boss, Extrude.** The extrusion arrow will be pointing upward. Click on the highlighted arrow and pull it downward. Then go to the **"Boss Extrude" menu** and select the **Up To Next** option (Figure 4-19) and click **OK**.

Your completed model should look like Figure 4-20.

Figure 4-19. Extrude Menu.

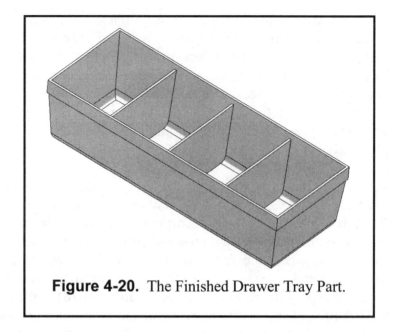

Figure 4-20. The Finished Drawer Tray Part.

Now save your model. Pull down the **File** menu and select **Save As**. On the "Save As" menu, select your appropriate file folder, type in the part name **DRAWER TRAY.SLDPRT**, then click **Save**.

To finish this exercise, you should print a hard copy for submission to your instructor. Open your **TitleBlock-Inches.drwdot**. Insert the image into the **Title Block** drawing sheet like in previous labs. Save your drawing as **DRAWER TRAY.slddrw**. **Print** a hard copy to submit to your lab instructor. The drawing should look like Figure 4-21.

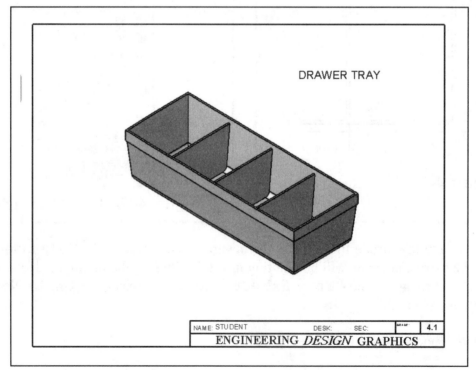

Figure 4-21. Drawer Tray Inserted onto the Title Block Sheet

Exercise 4.2: TAP-LIGHT DOME

Go to **File** and open **ANSI-INCHES.prtdot**. Pull down **File** again, select **Save As**, then name it **TAP-LIGHT DOME.sldprt** and save the file in your folder.

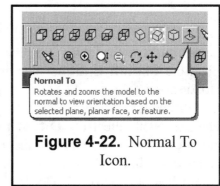

Figure 4-22. Normal To Icon.

Select the **Top Plane** in which to work, then click on the **Normal To** icon which looks like a square plate with an arrow pointing upwards out of the center of the plate. (Figure 4-22)

Select the **Sketch** icon and draw a **Circle** at the origin with a <u>**Radius**</u> of **2.35** inches.

Select the **Extrude** symbol (Figure 4-23) on the left side of the screen. Do a **Blind Extrude** of **0.375** inches. Click on the **OK** button, which will produce an image similar to Figure 4-24.

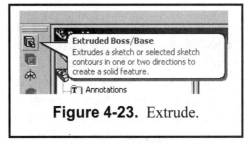

Figure 4-23. Extrude.

Click on the words "**Extrude**" in the Feature Manager twice (this is not a double click) and rename this feature as "**Dome Base**".

Select the **Top** plane of the **Dome Base**. Then go to **Insert, Features, Dome**. In the "**Dome**" features window give the **Dome Height** of **1.20 inches** (see Figure 4-25) and click **OK**. The dome operation should give you an object similar to Figure 4-26.

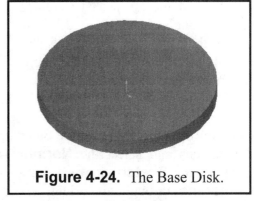

Figure 4-24. The Base Disk.

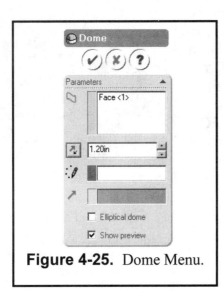

Figure 4-25. Dome Menu.

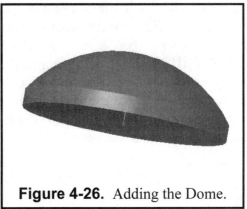

Figure 4-26. Adding the Dome.

Rotate the model so you can see the bottom face. Select the bottom face and pick the **Shell** icon (Figure 4-27) in the left tool bar. Give the shell thickness of **0.075** in the parameters box and **OK** the selection.

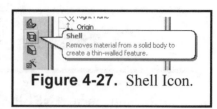

Figure 4-27. Shell Icon.

You might have to zoom in to select the bottom thin surface of the resulting shell. After you have selected the thin surface select the **Sketch Entities** icon and then select the **Convert Entities** icon (Figure 4-28). This converts the outer edges of that surface into a new sketch entity that can be used for a new feature. Next select the **Offset Entities** icon (Figure 4-29) and pick the black edge of the converted entity, enter the distance of **0.20** (Figure 4-30) outward so the new offset pattern lies outside of the Dome (Figure 4-31). **Extrude** this pattern upward by **0.075** inches.

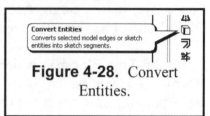

Figure 4-28. Convert Entities.

Figure 4-29. Offset Icon.

This should complete the basic shelled dome. The model should resemble Figure 4-32. What remains to be done is to cut the four holes in the lip of the dome where fastening screws pass to hold the body and the lens frame together. The holes in the lip of the dome are placed at rather unusual angles. This is done to insure that the dome can only be placed on the body of the light fixture in one position.

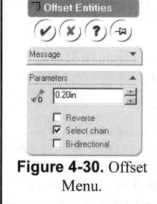

Figure 4-30. Offset Menu.

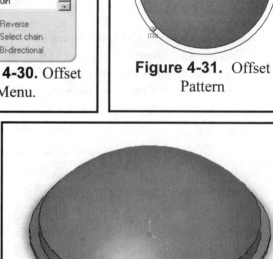

Figure 4-31. Offset Pattern

Click on the top surface of the outer lip of the domed lens and select the **Normal To** icon. Click on the **Sketch** icon and draw a vertical **Centerline** through the origin. Next **Draw** four radiating centerlines using the centerline option and a **Bolt circle with a diameter of 5.05** inches (be sure to check **FOR CONSTRUCTION** in the option box) as shown in Figure 4-33. The large bolt circle must be drawn since it is not the same diameter as the outer rim of the dome lip. Dimension the four radiating centerlines as shown in Figure 4-33.

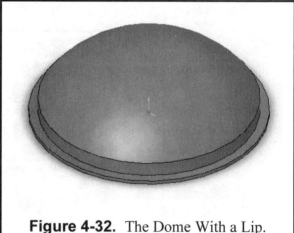

Figure 4-32. The Dome With a Lip.

Locate the four small holes and dimension them. Then draw the four circles for the through holes. Finally do the **Extrude Cut, Through All**.

Your final model should look similar to Figure 4-34.

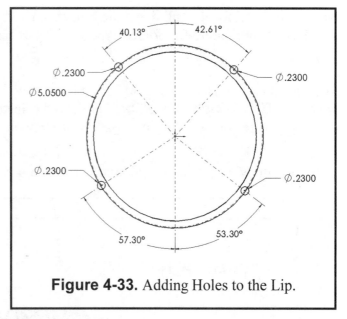

Figure 4-33. Adding Holes to the Lip.

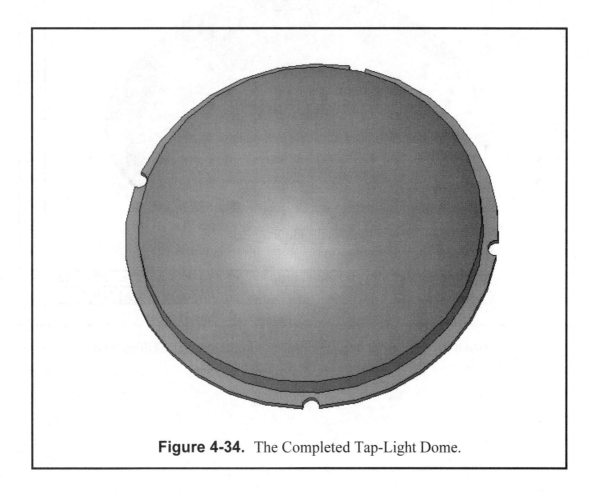

Figure 4-34. The Completed Tap-Light Dome.

Now save your model. Pull down the **File** menu and select **Save As**. On the "Save As" menu, select your appropriate file folder, type in the part name **LIGHT DOME.sldprt** and then click **Save**.

To finish this exercise, you should print a hard copy for submission to your instructor. First open your **TitleBlock-Inches.drwdot**. Follow the instructions given in Unit 1 for inserting the rendered image onto a Title Block Save your drawing as **LIGHT DOME.slddrw**.

Your final drawing should look similar to **Figure 4-35.**

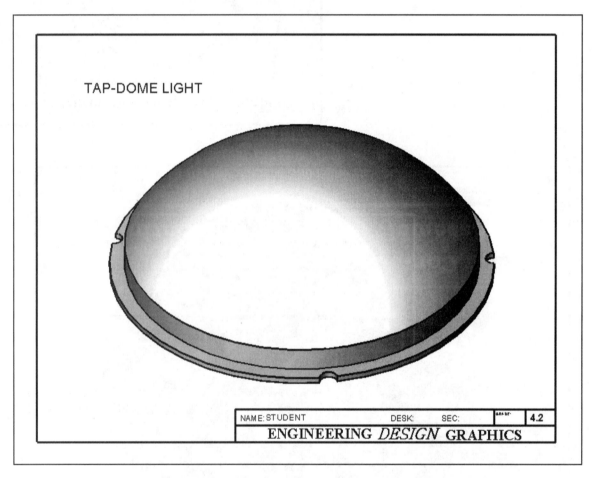

Figure 4-35. Tap-Dome Light Inserted onto the Title Block Sheet

Exercise 4.3:
ACME THREAD LEAD SCREW

Acme threads have been in use for more than 100 years in applications requiring smooth mechanical power transmission, repetitive conversion of rotary to linear motion, controlled traversing of cutting tool holders in lathes and milling machines, precision mechanical drives and instrument stages, and others. A typical example of a present day use is the jackscrew used to position the horizontal stabilizer in the tail assembly of multi-engine jet airliners. The Acme thread is a modified square profile and, like other thread designs, is normally cut on a single helical path, although multi-start thread designs are sometimes used for special purposes.

In this exercise you will create an Acme thread lead screw—a single standard acme thread cut onto a shaft, with other features that enable it to be connected with other drive components. To do this we will introduce the **Cut Sweep**, which creates the thread on a SolidWorks part by sweeping a given profile along a prescribed path with certain rules set by the designer. Other Boss and Cut entities, as well as Features, will be used to create the shaft and its details.

Notes On Manufacturing: This lead screw would be fabricated by machining the Acme thread profile into the surface of a beginning piece of metal stock, whose diameter is the major diameter of the thread profile. This is a material subtractive process, and if your modeling procedure is chosen to match the expected manufacturing process, you may choose to perform an extrude cut in a base revolve to create the thread profile.

Begin in the usual manner by going to your folder and open **ANSI-INCHES.prtdot**. Pull down **File** again, select **Save As**, then name it **LEAD SCREW.sldprt** and save the file in your folder.

Select the **Right Plane** to begin your drawing. **Sketch** a **Circle** at the origin that has a **diameter** of **3.00** inches and **Extrude** it **Mid Plane** to **10.5** inches **(See Figure 4-36)**. The result will look like **Figure 4-37**.

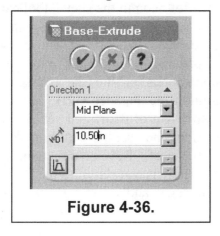

Figure 4-36.

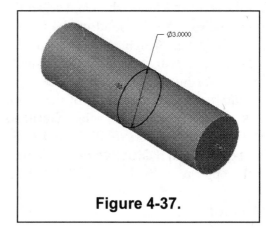

Figure 4-37.

Now select the surface of the **Right End** of the shaft and sketch a **Circle** centered on the shaft with a diameter of **2.230 inches** (Figure 4-38). **Insert – Cut – Extrude, Blind - Flipside to cut** to **1.5 inches** (See Figure 4.39).

Next select the left end of the shaft and repeat the previous process except do a **Flipside to cut** to **3.0 inches**. Your object should now look like Figure 4-40.

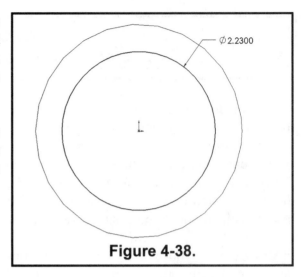

Figure 4-38.

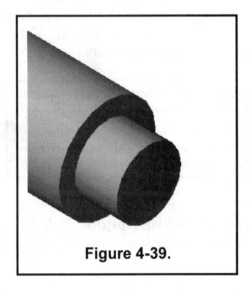

Figure 4-39.

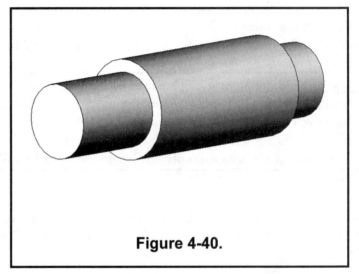

Figure 4-40.

THREAD CONSTRUCTION

Select the right end of the shaft and select the **Convert Entities** icon in the sketch tool bar. It is a good idea to have the solid model in the isometric view so you can see what is happening. While still in the Sketch mode, pull down **Insert, Curve, Helix/Spiral**. There are several options for specifying a helical path. Usually in a threaded pattern, the parameter of most interest is the pitch, or linear dimension between repeating points on a thread profile (the inverse of Pitch is the number of complete turns of the thread per unit length of the threaded part). In the **Helix Curve** menu, (Figure 4-41) select **Defined By: Pitch and Revolution** and set the pitch to **1.000-in**. and the total revolutions to **10** De-select Taper Helix, and set the **Starting Angle** to **270-degrees** and a **Clockwise** direction. You may have to select – Reverse direction, to make the helix appear on the shaft. Click **OK** to complete your selections and return to the Part. Your helix should resemble Figure 4-42. Go to the Feature Manager and rename Helix to **Acme Tooth Path**.

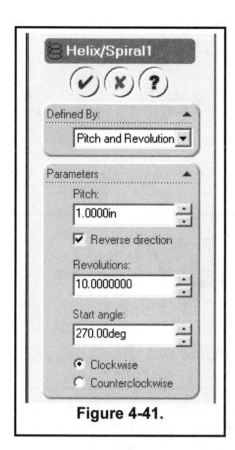

Figure 4-41.

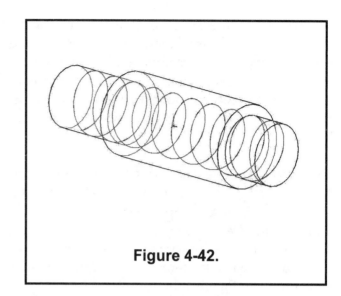

Figure 4-42.

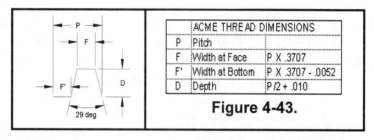

ACME THREAD DIMENSIONS		
P	Pitch	
F	Width at Face	P X .3707
F'	Width at Bottom	P X .3707 - .0052
D	Depth	P /2 + .010

Figure 4-43.

The general shape of an Acme thread profile is standardized as a function of Thread Pitch, as shown in Figure 4-43.

Tooth Profile: Now you are ready to create the tooth profile. In the manager tree **Select** the **Front Plane** since that plane passes through the end of the spiral helix. Enter the **Sketch** mode, and zoom into a region at the right end of the shaft. Select the **Center Line** icon and draw a vertical centerline along the edge view of the face of the shaft. Select the pull down menu **"Tools"**, Sketch Tools, **Dynamic Mirror**. As you **Sketch** a half profile of the tooth the **Dynamic Mirror** command will to produce the other half of the profile. Make sure that the profile of the tooth is **Colinear** with the edge of the cylinder. **Dimension** your sketch to correspond to those shown in Figure 4-44. Make sure the wide base of the tooth profile extends very slightly beyond the outer surface of the large cylinder.

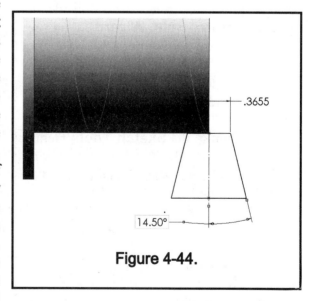

Figure 4-44.

Remember to close the tooth profile with straight lines (the exact dimensions of these are not critical, since this is a cut operation. When complete, exit the sketch mode by using the green √ button. Click **Rebuild**, and rename this sketch to **Acme Tooth Profile**. A dimetric view should show your profile and sweep path similar to Figure 4-45.

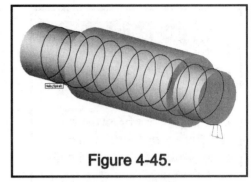

Figure 4-45.

Cut Sweep: Now you are ready to create the complete Acme thread. Pull down **Insert, Cut, Sweep** and observe the **Cut-Sweep** menu that appears. Under **Profile and Path**, using the mouse, select the Acme Tooth Profile and the Acme Tooth Path respectively. Your completed Acme thread should appear in diametric view similar to Figure 4-46.

Adding Shaft Features: Chamfer the shaft ends by selecting the edges of both ends, and pull down **Insert – Features - Chamfer...** and use the menu that appears to create **0.125-in**, **45-degree** chamfers

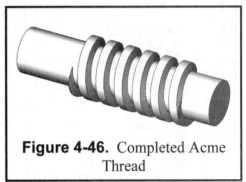

Figure 4-46. Completed Acme Thread

accordingly. Select the green √ to complete the chamfers. In addition, a precision part like the lead screw is normally held between special tools called <u>Live Centers</u> to support it for close tolerance turning or grinding. These centers require special angle drilled Center Holes accurately placed on the shaft centerline at each end of the part. Now create these center-drilled holes, which are similar in geometry to countersunk holes.

Select the end surface of the shaft where the hole is to be inserted, then pull down **Insert, Feature, Hole, Wizard...** and see the menu shown in Figure 4-47. Set the countersink hole parameters as shown, click **Next**, and under **Hole Placement**, instead of creating and setting dimensions to locate the hole on the sketch, use the **Add Relation** icon in the **Sketch Tools** menu. Now, select both the **center** of the hole being created by the Wizard, and the **origin** of the sketch, and select **Coincident** in the menu. This forces the hole to be concentric with the shaft, which is itself centered on the origin. Select out of the wizard to complete the drilled center hole, repeat the process on the opposite shaft end, rename these holes **Center Drill Hole A** and **B** in the Feature Manager, and compare your lead screw in Dimetric view to Figure 4-48.

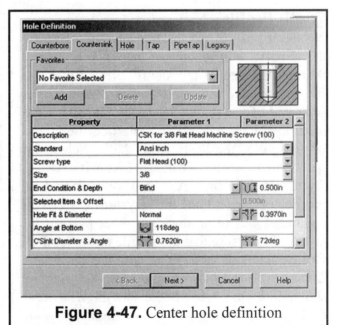

Figure 4-47. Center hole definition

Next, we will create a **Woodruff keyway** on the long shaft end. This keyway will locate a Woodruff key in a similar keyway on the inner diameter of a shaft coupling, commonly used to connect driven shafts to the output shaft of a motor or other prime mover. To create this feature, first select the **Front** plane, set a **Normal** view, and enter the **Sketch** mode. Create a profile using a **Circle** and closing it with trimmed **Lines**, and adjust the necessary dimensions as shown in Figure 4-49. Using this sketch, **Insert, Cut, Extrude, Mid-Plane** where the value is **0.25-in**. When this extrude cut is finished, rename it **Woodruff Keyway** in the Feature Manager.

Finally, we will install a pair of **Necks** on the short end of the lead screw shaft. Necks are narrow, shallow grooves cut or bored on the outer or inner diameter of a shaft, in which snap rings or other removable components seat, usually in order to hold parts on the shaft such as seals or bearing races to prevent their axial movement. Again, select the **Front** plane and **Normal** view, and create the profile shown in Figure 4-50. Use dimensions to control the geometry as shown, (make sure that you draw the axis center line) then pull down **Insert, Cut, Revolve** and set the parameters for a **One-direction, 360-deg** revolution. When complete, rename this feature **Necks** in the Feature Manager.

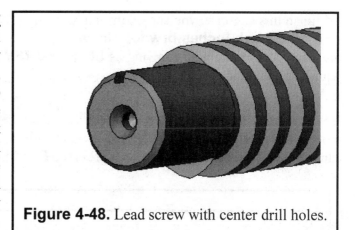

Figure 4-48. Lead screw with center drill holes.

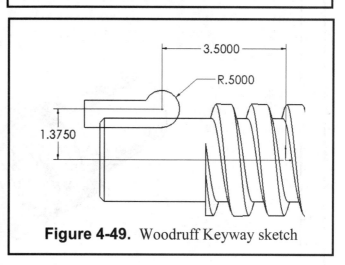

Figure 4-49. Woodruff Keyway sketch

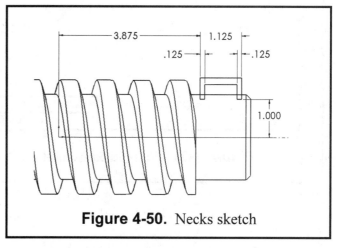

Figure 4-50. Necks sketch

Your **Lead Screw** model is now complete. When displayed in Dimetric view, it should resemble Figure 4-51. Choose a Shade color appropriate to your material selected. Now save your model. Pull down the **File** menu and select **Save As**. On the "Save As" menu, select your appropriate file folder, type in the part name **LEAD SCREW.sldprt**, and then click **Save**.

To finish this exercise, you should print a hard copy for submission to your instructor. First open your **TitleBlock-Inches.drwdot**. Insert the image into the **Title Block** drawing sheet like in previous labs. Save your drawing as **LEAD SCREW.slddrw**. **Print** a hard copy to submit to your lab instructor.

Before you print your copy, make sure you have set the **File**, **Page Setup** to **Landscape** mode. Now pull down the **File** and **Print Preview** commands from the top main menu. You can preview your print here, and then press the **Print** button to send it to the default printer.

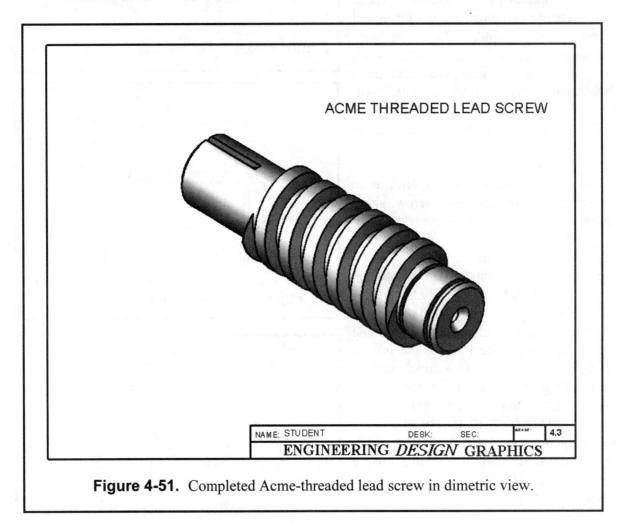

ACME THREADED LEAD SCREW

| NAME: STUDENT | | DESK: | SEC: | GRADE: | 4.3 |

ENGINEERING *DESIGN* GRAPHICS

Figure 4-51. Completed Acme-threaded lead screw in dimetric view.

Exercise 4.4: JACK STAND

Go to **File** and open **ANSI-INCHES.prtdot**. Pull down **File** again, select **Save As**, then name it **JACK STAND.sldprt** and save the file in your folder.

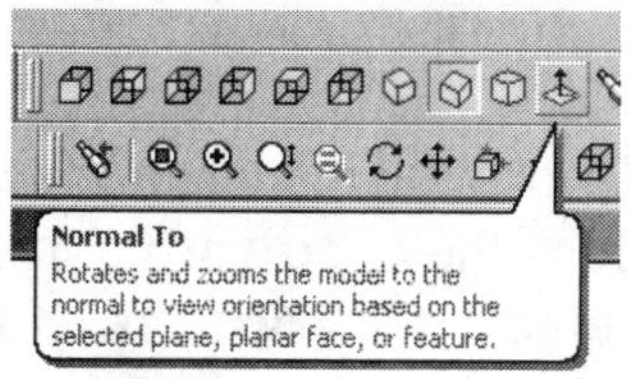

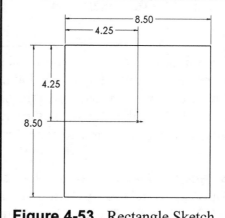

Figure 4-52. Normal to Icon.

Select the **Top Plane** in which to work, then click on the **Normal To** icon which looks like a square plate with an arrow pointing upwards out of the center of the plate (Figure 4-52).

Select the **Sketch** icon and draw a **Rectangle** centered on the origin. Constrain the rectangle as shown in Figure 4-53.

Before you can proceed with the next step you will have to establish a new work plane. To better see what is going to happen, go to the isometric view. Turn **Off** the **Sketch** icon. Select the **Top Plane** and then select **Insert, Reference Geometry, Plane.** Enter the distance of **6.5"**.

After you have created the reference plane, select it in the **Feature Manager Tree**. Select **Plane 1** and then the **Sketch** icon. Draw a **Circle** on the plane that is **3.5"** in diameter, centered on the origin.

Figure 4-53. Rectangle Sketch.

De-select the **Sketch** icon. **Select** the **Top Plane** again and then select **Insert, Reference Geometry, Plane** again. Enter the distance of **10"**. This plane will be labeled **Plane 2**. Select it and **Sketch** a **Circle** on it that is **2.5"** in diameter, centered on the origin. Go to an isometric view to see the configuration as shown in Figure 4-54.

After you De-select the **Sketch** icon, **Select** the **Loft** icon in the left-hand column. (See Figure 4-55).

The next operations are best seen in a pictorial **(Isometric)** view.

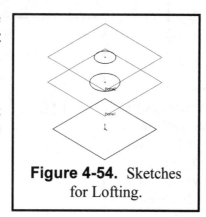

Figure 4-54. Sketches for Lofting.

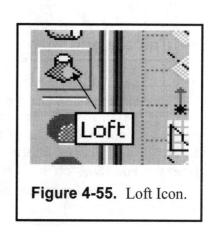

Figure 4-55. Loft Icon.

Select the three sketches in the order that they are to be lofted. The **bottom square first**, then the **circle in the middle** and last, the **top circle**. The order of the sketch selection will appear in the **Base – Loft Menu** (see Figure 4-56). As you select the sketches a preview of the loft will be shown on the screen. If it appears as the figure in Figure 4-57, select the (√) to finalize the process.

Rotate the model so you can see the **bottom face**. **Select** the **bottom face** and pick the **Shell** icon (Figure 4-58) in the left tool bar. Give the shell thickness of **0.1875"** in the parameters box and (√) **OK** the selection.

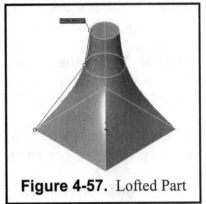

Figure 4-56. Loft Menu.

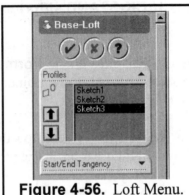

Figure 4-57. Lofted Part

Several other operations must be performed in order to make this a viable design. The top must be reinforced for a threaded adjustment screw and the sides are to be hollowed out to lighten the weight of the jack stand. (The thread formation has been omitted from this design).

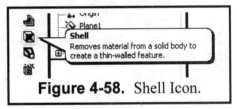

Figure 4-58. Shell Icon.

Select the **Top Surface** of the jack stand and **Select** the **Normal-To** icon. **Convert** the entity and do a **Boss Extrude** downward for **3"**. **Select** the **Top Surface** again and **Sketch** a **1.25** diameter **Circle**. Do a **Cut, Extrude, Through all** to create the hole as shown in Figure 4-59.

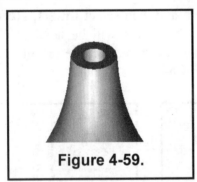

Figure 4-59.

The last two operations are the openings that need to be cut in the sides of the jack stand. **Select** the **Front Plane** and **Select Normal-To**. **Sketch** the **Triangle** and set the dimension constraints as shown in Figure 4-60. Also add a vertical relation between the top point of the triangle and the origin.

Execute a **Cut Extrude, Through All** in **Both Directions**.

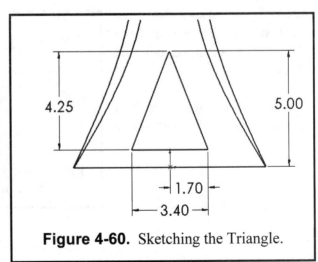

Figure 4-60. Sketching the Triangle.

Since you will be using the exact same sketch in the Right Plane, click on the **Previous Sketch,** go to the **Windows Edit** menu and select **Copy** (see Figure 4-61). Next go to the **Feature Manager Tree,** select the **Right Plane**, and **Go** to the **Windows Edit** menu and select **Paste**. Select the **Sketch** that resulted from this operation and repeat the **Cut Extrude, Through All** in **Both Directions** to complete the model. Your final model should look similar to Figure 4-62.

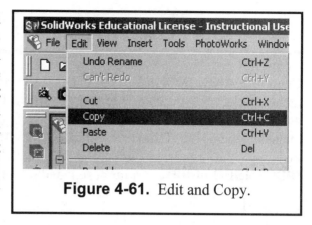

Figure 4-61. Edit and Copy.

Now save your model. Pull down the **File** menu and select **Save As**. On the "Save As" menu, select your appropriate file folder, type in the part name **JACK STAND.sldprt**, then click **Save**.

To finish this exercise, you should print a hard copy for submission to your instructor. First open your **TitleBlock-Inches.drwdot**. Follow the instructions given in Unit 1 for inserting the rendered image onto a Title Block. Save your drawing as **JACK STAND.slddrw** in your designated folder.

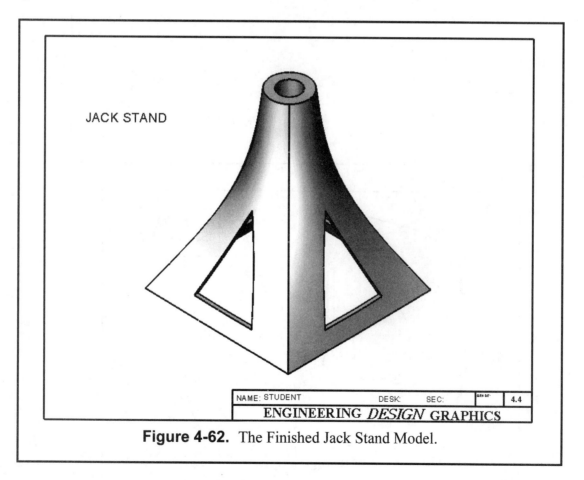

Figure 4-62. The Finished Jack Stand Model.

SUPPLEMENTARY EXERCISE 4-5 TAPE DISPENSER

Using the **ANSI-INCHES.prtdot**, Draw the profile of the Tape Dispenser and extrude it 0.75 inches. Select the front surface and fillet it to 0.05 inches. Select the back surface and the two interior surfaces as indicated in the second figure and SHELL the solid to a thickness of 0.10 inches. Open your **TitleBlock-Inches.drwdot**. Follow the instructions given in Unit 1 for inserting the rendered image onto a Title Block. Save your drawing as **TAPE DISPENSER.slddrw** in your designated folder.

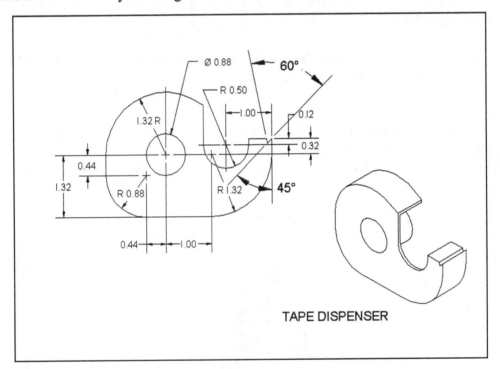

TAPE DISPENSER

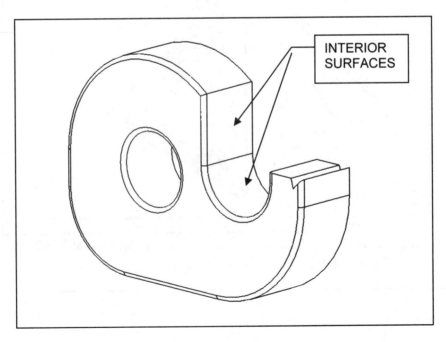

INTERIOR SURFACES

SUPPLEMENTARY EXERCISE 4-6 FUNNEL

Build a full size model of the Funnel below. Begin in the **Top Plane**. To get the desired model, each section must be lofted separately. Activate the right plane and sketch a guide curve connecting the left hand edges of the first two sketches. Repeat the process for the other two lofts. When the lofting process in completed, select the top and the bottom surfaces and shell the model to a wall thickness of 0.10 inches. Insert it onto a Title Block and title it **FUNNEL.slddrw.**

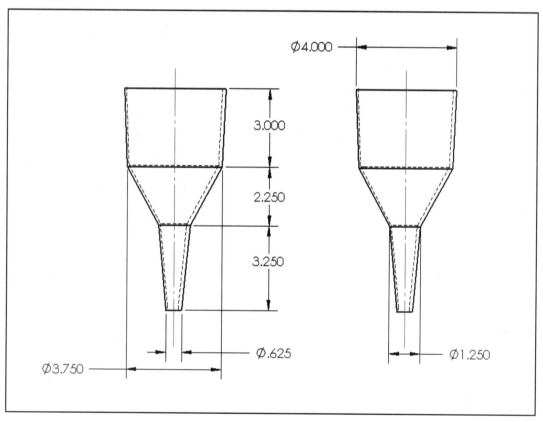

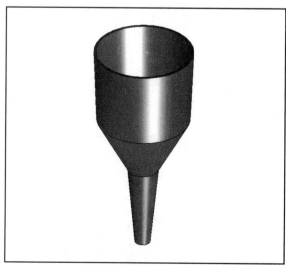

Notes:

Computer Graphics Lab 5:
Assembly Modeling and Mating

In this Computer Graphics Lab 5, you will build several parts of an assembly. You will then assemble the parts and fit them properly together using mating functions available in Solidworks. This introductory section will get you started and then two exercises, the Terminal Support Assembly and the Swivel Eye Block Assembly, are provided.

ASSEMBLY FILE

In the previous exercises, you started with a **File, New, Part** command sequence to start a new part file. SolidWorks offers two other choices when starting a new file, **Assembly** and **Drawing,** as shown in Figure 5-1. This is the normal way to start an Assembly.

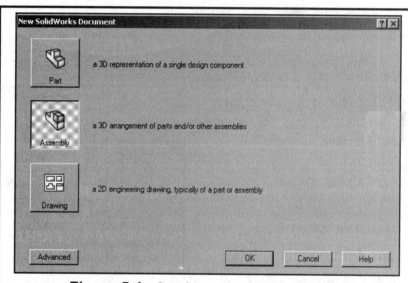

Figure 5-1. Starting a New Assembly File.

TILING THE WINDOWS

There are different ways to start the assembly. One easy way is to open all the parts to the assembly in SolidWorks, in addition to having the new assembly file open. You can then **Tile Vertically** the windows (see Figure 5-2) and then simply "Drag and Drop" the parts into the assembly file.

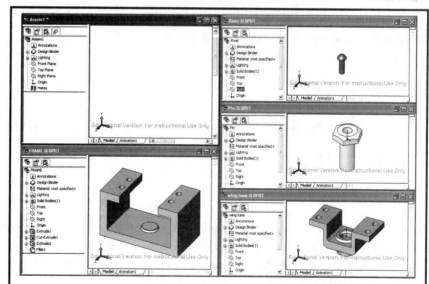

Figure 5-2. Tiling the Windows Vertically to Begin the Assembly

THE ASSEMBLY TOOLBAR

The Assembly toolbar is located on the left hand side of the screen when you are in the assembly mode. It contains the following commands:

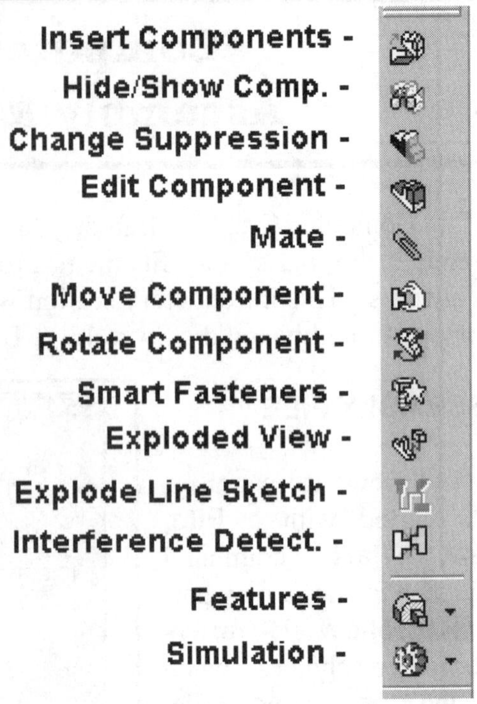

Insert Components – Allows you to insert an existing part into an assembly.

Hide/Show Component - You can toggle the display of assembly components. Turning off the display temporarily removes it from view, allowing you to work with underlying components.

Change Suppression - You can specify an appropriate suppression state for the components. The assembly rebuilds faster this way.

Edit Component - Editing a component while in an assembly allows you to modify a component without leaving the assembly.

Mate – Mates components in an assembly (see below for Mate Types).

Move Component – Moves an identified component in an assembly

Insert Components -
Hide/Show Comp. -
Change Suppression -
Edit Component -
Mate -
Move Component -
Rotate Component -
Smart Fasteners -
Exploded View -
Explode Line Sketch -
Interference Detect. -
Features -
Simulation -

Figure 5-3. The Assembly Toolbar

Rotate Component – Rotates an identified component in an assembly.

Smart Fasteners – This automatically adds fasteners (bolts and screws) to your assembly if there is a hole, hole series, or pattern of holes, that is sized to accept standard hardware.

Exploded View – This separates the components into an exploded view.

Explode Line Sketch – This can be used to add a 3-D line sketch to show the relationship between components in an exploded view.

Interference Detection – This can be used to detect any interference between components in an assembly.

Features – This brings up the features menu that you studied in the Chapter 3 introduction.

Simulation – This brings up the simulation tools menu to make a simulation of the assembly.

MATE TYPES

You can mate parts in an assembly by clicking the entities in the computer space and then select the **Mate** icon. The available list of mates is then displayed and listed below. _Note_: Only those mate types that are valid for the selected entities are available when this command is used. The valid mating relationships are:

Coincident - positions selected faces, edges, and planes (in combination with each other or combined with a single vertex) so they share the same infinite line. Positions two vertices so they touch.

Perpendicular - places the selected items at a 90-degree angle to each other.

Tangent - places the selected items in a tangent mate (at least one selection must be a cylindrical, conical, or spherical face).

Concentric - places the selections so that they share the same center point.

Parallel - places the selected items so they lie in the same direction and remain a constant distance apart from each other.

Distance - places the selected items with the specified distance between them.

Angle - places the selected items at the specified angle to each other.

Symmetry - places the selected items at an equal distance from a plane of symmetry.

VIEWING ASSEMBLIES

When you are building assemblies with many components, sometimes viewing of specific parts becomes difficult. One way to view a part in an assembly is to set the transparency of the other parts. Select the **Tools**, **Options**, **Display/Selection** tab. Then set the Assembly Transparency to **Force Assembly Transparency** with the slider at some value up to 100%. An example is shown in Figure 5-4.

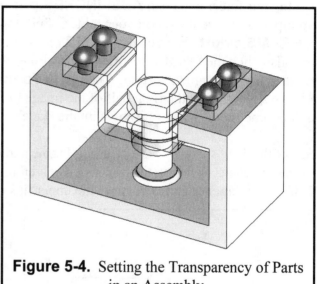

Figure 5-4. Setting the Transparency of Parts in an Assembly.

EXPLODING ASSEMBLIES

Assembly components can be exploded using the **Exploded View** icon on the assembly toolbar. This produces the **Assembly Exploder** menu on the screen, as shown in Figure 5-5. More on exploding assemblies will be covered in a later section.

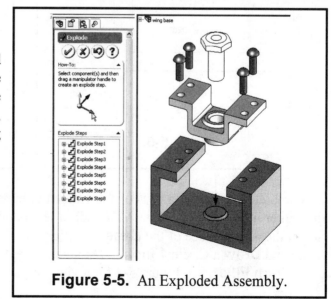

Figure 5-5. An Exploded Assembly.

Exercise 5.1: Terminal Support Assembly

The Terminal Support Assembly has three major components, the Frame, the Wing Base and the Pin. It also contains four standard rivet parts for attachment to the frame. You will start by designing the Frame part. After that you will model the Wing Base, the Pin and then finally create one version of the rivet. You will mate all of them in an assembly file, including bringing in the rivet version four times.

FRAME

Go to your folder and open **ANSI-INCHES.prtdot**. A good practice is to immediately name your part and save the file in your folder. Pull down **File** again, select **Save As**, and then name it **FRAME.sldprt**. Next click the **LMB** on the **Front** plane icon in the Feature Manager tree and also click the **Front** view orientation. Enter the **Sketch** mode and draw a vertical **Centerline** through the origin. Then go to **Tools, Sketch Tools**, and select **Dynamic Mirror**. Now, draw the right half of the image in **Figure 5-6**. You will see the left half drawn at the same time. When finished with the sketch, extrude it **3.00 inches – Mid Plane**.

Select the TOP surface of the resulting Frame and enter the Sketch Mode. Place the four holes in the sketch according to the dimensions given in Figure 5-7. Perform an **Extrude Cut – Blind** only far enough to penetrate the upper lips of the Frame.

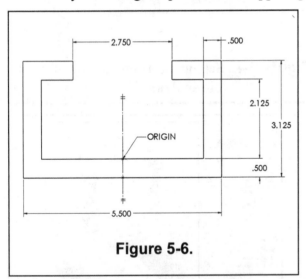

Figure 5-6.

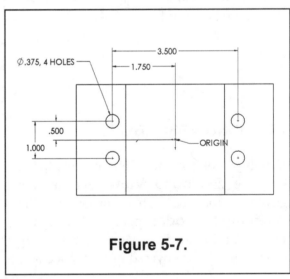

Figure 5-7.

To complete the Frame, a boss that is 1 inch in diameter and .125 inches high must be added to the center of the base and have a .10 inch fillet added where the boss intersects the Frame. Select the **Top** surface of the **Base** and click on the **Top** view orientation. Enter the **Sketch** mode and **Draw** a Circle **1 inch** in Diameter. Next **Extrude** this circle **.125 inches** and add the **.1 inch Fillet**. See Figure 5-8 for a view of the completed Frame.

You can now save the completed part. Pull down **File**, select **Save As**, and save the part as **FRAME.sldprt** in your folder. Now **Close** your Frame part. You are now ready to start the next part for the assembly.

WING BASE

Go to your folder and open **ANSI-INCHES.prtdot**. Immediately pull down **File** again, select **Save As**, and then name it **WING BASE.sldprt**. Next click the **LMB** on the **Front** plane icon in the Feature Manager tree and also click the **Front** view orientation. Set **Grid/Snap** major grids to **1** and minor girds per major to **8.** Be sure to check (√) "Display Grid" **On**.

Review the beginning sketch details shown on Figure 5-9. Enter the **Sketch** mode and use the **Line** tool to draw the outline. Add three sketch **Fillets** to the three corners with radii (**0.125** or **0.250**) as indicated. Draw a vertical **Centerline** through the origin. **Select** all geometry simultaneously (they all highlight *green*) and **Mirror** the half profile about the centerline.

Click the **Extrude Boss/Base** feature icon and use a **Mid Plane** end condition with **2.000** inches distance. Then click the green (√) button to execute the extrusion for the base part, as shown in Figure 5-10. Rename this "Base-Extrude" feature as **Base Part** in the Feature Manager.

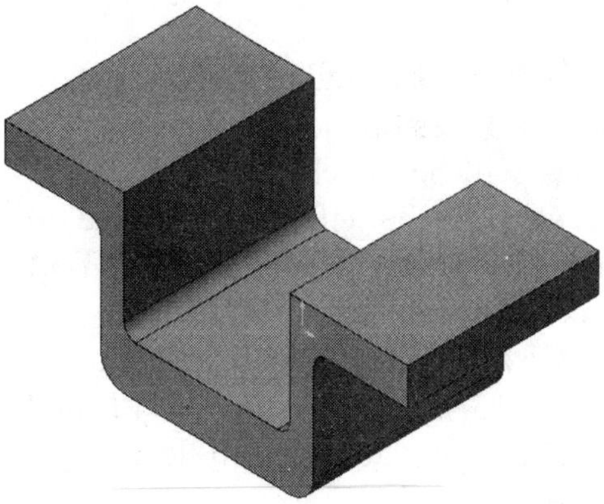

Click on the top surface of the bottom feature of this "Base Part" (not the top of the wings). It should turn *green*. Also choose a **Top** view orientation. **Sketch** a **Circle** on this surface, centered at the origin, with a <u>diameter</u> of **1.250**.
Click the **Extrude Boss/Base** feature icon. Set "Direction 1" (up) to **Blind** with a distance of **0.125** inch. Set "Direction 2" (down) to **Blind** with a distance of **1.00** inch. Then click the green (√) button. Rename this feature **Big**

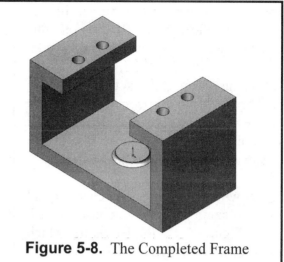

Figure 5-8. The Completed Frame

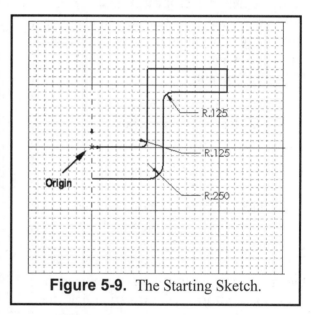

Figure 5-9. The Starting Sketch.

Figure 5-10. The Base Part.

Boss. Click on the top surface of this big boss, **Sketch** a **Circle** on this surface, centered at the origin, with a <u>diameter</u> of **0.75**. Click the **Extrude Cut** feature icon and cut the hole using the **Through All** end condition. Rename this new hole feature **Big Hole**. You now have a model that looks like Figure 5-11 in a **Rotated View** orientation.

You now need to add a 3-D chamfer and fillets to some of the edges just created. Study Figure 5-12 to determine which edges to chamfer and fillet. To better view these edges, change to a **Wireframe** view. Click the **Chamfer** icon on the features toolbar, pick the edge to chamfer with the cursor (it turns *green*), and set the following parameters on the "Chamfer" menu:

> Dot (•) "Angle Distance"
> Distance = **0.10** inches
> Angle = **45** degrees

Then click the green (√) button.

Next click the **Fillet** icon on the features toolbar, pick the two edges to fillet with the cursor (they turn *green*), and set the fillet radius to **0.125** inches. Then click the green (√) button. You can switch back to a **Shaded, Trimetric** view to better see the chamfer and fillets as shown in Figure 5-13.

The final features to add to the Wing Base are the four holes on the two wings where the rivets will be attached. Click on the top surface of the left wing feature to highlight it *green*. Also select a **Top** view orientation. Start a **Sketch** and draw a **Circle** on the surface as indicated by Figure 5-14. Use the **Grid** and **Dimension** tools to precisely locate this first hole.

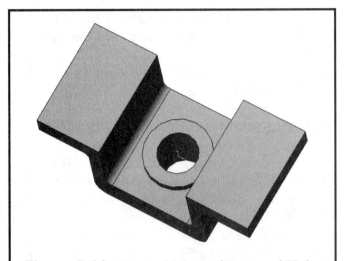

Figure 5-11. Rotated View of Boss and Hole.

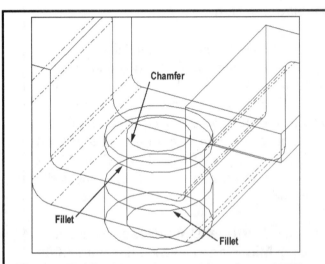

Figure 5-12. The Edges to Chamfer and Fillet.

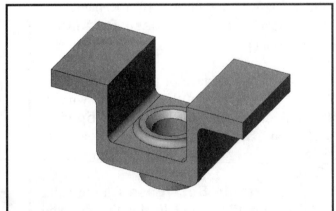

Figure 5-13. Adding the Chamfer and Fillets.

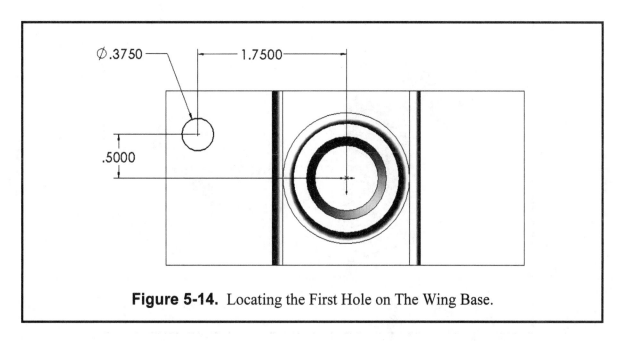

Figure 5-14. Locating the First Hole on The Wing Base.

Now select **Tools, Sketch Tools**, and **Linear Sketch Step and Repeat**. In the menu, supply the following parameters:

Direction 1
Number = **2**   Spacing = **3.500** inches   Angle = go to the **right**

Direction 2
Number = **2**   Spacing = **1.000** inches   Angle = go **down**

Click **Preview** (see Figure 5-15) to see if they are correct and then click **OK** to execute the command.

Click the **Extrude Cut** feature icon and cut the holes using the **Through All** end condition. Rename this new feature **Four Holes**. You now have a finished model of the Wing Base that looks like Figure 5-16 in a **Trimetric** view orientation.

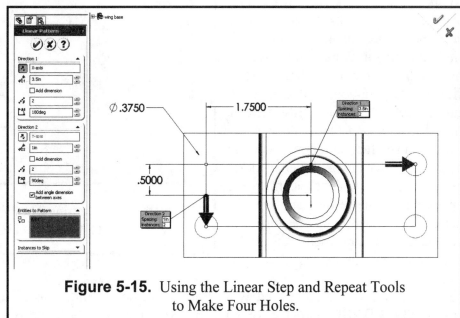

Figure 5-15. Using the Linear Step and Repeat Tools to Make Four Holes.

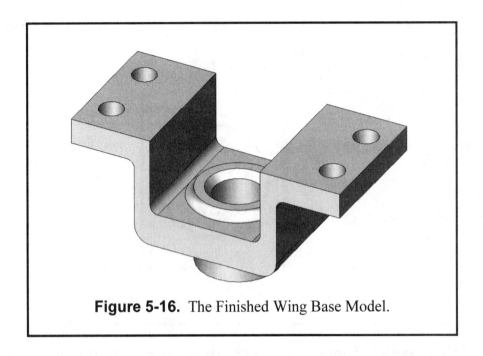

Figure 5-16. The Finished Wing Base Model.

The Wing Base has mild steel material properties that can be reflected by the color of the shaded image. Pull down **Tools**, select **Options**, and then select **Document Properties**. Click the **Color** tab on this menu and select **Shading** under "Model/Features Colors." Next Click the **Edit** button to get the Solidworks "Color" palette on the screen as shown in Figure 5-17. Click the **Steel Blue** color (second row, sixth choice from left). Then click the **OK** button, and then click another **OK**. The Wing Base will be shaded in the steel blue color. *Note:* You can also click on the part name in the Feature Manager and then click on the **Edit Color** (palette) icon on the top toolbar. The "Color and Optics" menu will appear in the feature tree area and you can make the color definition using this approach.

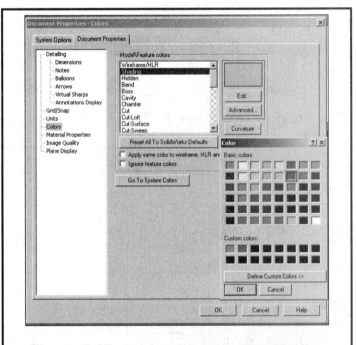

Figure 5-17. Setting The Wing Base Shading Color to Steel Blue.

You can now save the completed Wing Base. Pull down **File**, select **Save As**, and save the part as **WING BASE.sldprt** in your folder. Now **Close** your Wing Base part. You are now ready to start the next part for the assembly.

PIN

Go to your folder and open **ANSI-INCHES.prtdot**. Immediately pull down **File** again, select **Save As**, and then name it **PIN.sldprt**. Next click the **LMB** on the **Front** plane icon in the Feature Manager tree and also click the **Front** view orientation. Set **Grid/Snap** major grids to **1** and minor girds per major to **8.** Be sure to check (√) "Display Grid" **On**.

Review the beginning sketch details shown on Figure 5-18. Enter the **Sketch** mode and use the **Line** tool to draw the outline. Draw a vertical **Centerline** through the origin. Add the sketch **Fillet** to the corner with a radius of **0.125** as indicated. Click the **Revolve Boss/Base** feature icon and revolve the sketch profile **360** degrees. Rename this base part as **Pin Base** in the Feature Manager.

You now need to add the hex head feature to the top of the Pin. Click on the top flat surface of the Pin (it turns *green*) and also select a **Top** view orientation. Pull down **Tools**, **Sketch Entities**, and then select **Polygon**. Center the polygon at the origin and drag a corner point horizontally out to the right and click the corner on the perimeter edge of the Pin, as shown in Figure 5-19. Make sure the parameters in the "Polygon" menu are set correctly (see Figure 5-19), then click the green check (√) to close the menu.

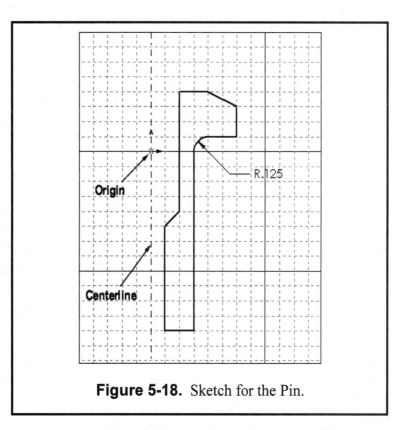

Figure 5-18. Sketch for the Pin.

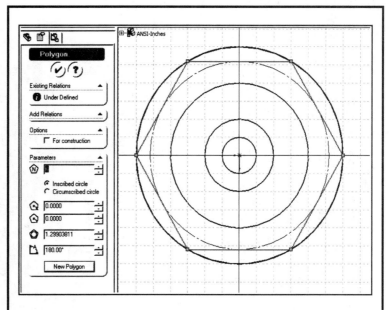

Figure 5-19. Adding a Hexagon to Cut the Hex Head.

Select an **Isometric** view orientation to better see the next operation. Click the **Extrude Cut** feature icon, and set the end condition to **Through all**. Also check (√) **on** the **Flip side to cut** so that the six slivers of the hex head will be cut away (see Figure 5-20). Click the green check (√) to close the "Cut-Extrude" menu and the hex head is cut along the rim of the Pin. Rename this feature to **Hex Cut** in the Feature Manager.

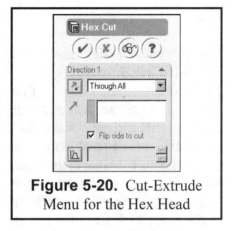

Figure 5-20. Cut-Extrude Menu for the Hex Head

The Pin is now finished as shown in Figure 5.21. However, you might want to change its color. The Pin has bronze material properties that can be reflected by the color of the shaded image. Pull down **Tools**, select **Options**, and then select **Document Properties**. Click the **Color** tab on this menu and select **Shading** under "Model/Features Colors." Next Click the **Edit** button to get the SolidWorks "Color" palette on the screen. Click the **Bronze Yellow** color (second row, second choice from left). Then click the **OK** button, and then click another **OK**. The Pin will be shaded in the bronze yellow color.

You can now save the final part. Pull down **File**, select **Save As**, and save the part as **PIN.sldprt** in your folder. Now close your session, pull down **File** and click **Close**. You are now ready to start the next part for the assembly.

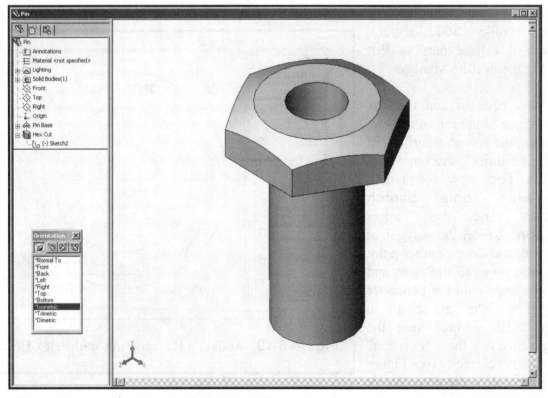

Figure 5-21. The Finished Pin Model.

RIVET

The Rivet is a simple part and you can create it in a number of ways. The method chosen here is to simply sketch a half-profile and then revolve it around a centerline. There are different types of rivets (flat head, pan head, etc.). For this case, you will design a "Button Head" rivet.

Study the geometry in Figure 5-22. Go to your folder and open **ANSI-INCHES.prtdot**. A good practice is to immediately name your part. Pull down **File** again, select **Save As**, and then name it **RIVET.sldprt**. Next click the **LMB** on the **Front** plane icon in the Feature Manager tree and also click the **Front** view orientation. Disregard the "Grid/Snap" settings, since you will just sketch an outline and then fix the geometry with the dimensioning tool.

Enter the **Sketch** mode and use the **Line** and **Centerpoint Arc** tools to draw the outline as indicated in Figure 5-22. Also draw a vertical **Centerline** through the origin. Then use the **Dimension** tool to set all the given dimensions. If they are placed correctly, all lines should turn *black* meaning the geometry is fixed. **_Note:_ The center of the arc is not at the origin.** If it happens to be at the origin in your case, then remove the "Coincident" relation between them by clicking the **Display/Delete Relations** icon (it looks like a pair of glasses).

Now click the **Revolve Boss/Base** feature icon and revolve the sketch profile **360** degrees. Rename this base part as **Rivet Base** in the Feature Manager. The finished rivet is shown in Figure 5-23 in an Isometric View.

Pull down **Tools**, select **Options**, and then select **Document Properties**. Click the **Color** tab on this menu and select **Shading** under "Model/Features Colors." Next Click the **Edit** button to get the SolidWorks "Color" palette on the screen. Click the **Red** color (second row, first choice from left). Then click the **OK** button, and then click another **OK**. The Rivet will be shaded in the red color.

You can now save the completed Rivet. Pull down **File**, select **Save As**, and save the part as **RIVET.sldprt** in your folder. Now close your session, pull down **File** and click **Close**. You are now ready to start the assembly.

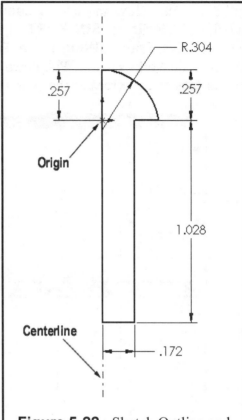

Figure 5-22. Sketch Outline and Geometry for the Rivet.

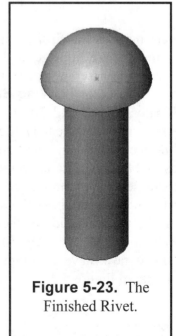

Figure 5-23. The Finished Rivet.

TERMINAL SUPPORT ASSEMBLY

Pull down **File**, **New** and select **Assembly**. Pull down **File** again, select **Save As**, and then save it as **TERMINAL SUPPORT**. Pull down **File** and **Open**, one-by-one, the four parts of the assembly: **Frame, Wing Base**, **Pin**, and **Rivet**. You now have five active files in your current SolidWorks session. Pull down **Window** and select **Tile Vertically**. You can now see all four files on the screen as shown in Figure 5-24.

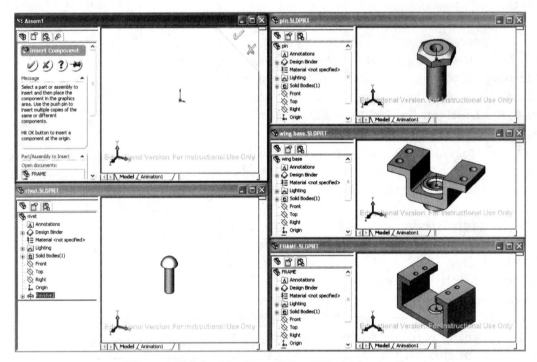

Figure 5-24. The Four Files Tiled Vertically.

Starting with the **Frame** file, **Select** its title in the Feature Manager and "Drag and Drop" it into the assembly file. Repeat this "Drag and Drop" with the **Wing Base** then the **PIN**. Finally, "Drag and Drop" the **RIVET** <u>four times</u> into the assembly file. You can try to line them up when you "Drop" them into the assembly, but more importantly you will mate them next. You no longer need the four part files so you can **Close** them by clicking the X on the top right side of their window. Then maximize the assembly file window. You should now have a computer screen layout similar to Figure 5-25.

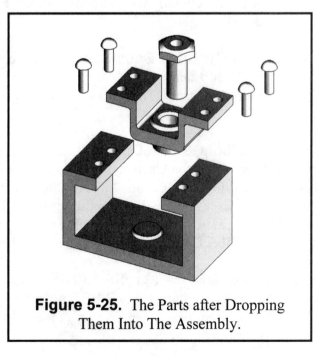

Figure 5-25. The Parts after Dropping Them Into The Assembly.

5-12

You will mate the Frame and the Wing Base first. Click the **Mate** icon on the left side Assembly toolbar (it looks like a paper clip), and the "Mate" menu comes up as indicated in Figure 5-26. Now pick the cylindrical hole on the Frame and the corresponding hole in the Wing base. Click on the **Concentric** mate setting. Repeat this process for two other corresponding holes. This will constrain the Wing Base with the Frame along the axes of the holes. The next operation will establish constraints in relation to the top surface of the Frame and the bottom surface of the upper wing of the Wing Base. Select the **Mate** icon and select the top surface of the Frame. Rotate the figure up so you can see the bottom surface of the Wing Base and select the corresponding surface. Click on the **Coincident** mate setting.

Now pick the outer cylindrical surface of the Pin (the surface that will go into the hole) and then pick inner cylindrical surface of the big hole on the Wing Base. They both should turn *green*. Now click the **Concentric** mate setting and then click the green check (√) to execute the mate. The Pin is now concentric with the hole and you should see it move over a little. You can look at it from a **Top** view if you wish to check it.

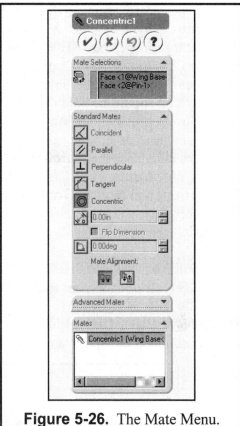

Figure 5-26. The Mate Menu.

Repeat this **Concentric** mate four times, one-by-one, between each Rivet and its respective small hole on the wing surfaces. Use an **Isometric** view and **Zoom** in as needed to complete these mates.

Now try something. Click the **Move Component** icon on the left side Assembly toolbar. Try to move the Pin or one of the Rivets around on the screen. You will see that its movement is constrained in a vertical direction that corresponds to the axis of its respective hole.

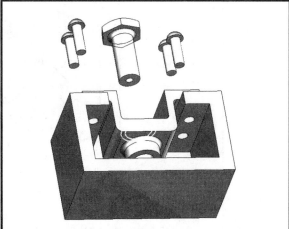

Figure 5-27. Using a Rotated View to See the Bottom Surface of the Hex Head.

You will now fix the parts to the Wing Base. Click the **Mate** icon again. Click the flat surface on the lip of the big hole. Next you need to click the bottom flat surface of the hex head, but it may be hard to select. So select the **Rotate View** icon and rotate the whole assembly around until you have a clear view of that surface. Now de-select the "Rotate View" icon (by clicking it off) to get back the pick cursor, and select the bottom of the hex head as shown in Figure 5-27.

Now on the "Mate" menu, click the **Coincident** mate setting and then click the green check (√) to execute this type of mate. You should see the Pin move into the correct position on the Wing Base and it is now fixed. Return to an **Isometric** view and use the **Move Component** icon to see if you can move the Pin up and down inside the big hole. It is fixed and you should not be able to move it out of the hole. Now click the **Rotate Component** icon on the Assembly toolbar. You should be able to rotate it around in the hole since that degree-of-freedom is not fixed. Now repeat this **Coincident** mating process for the four rivets, one-by-one. In each case, mate the flat bottom surface of the Rivet head with the top flat wing surface of its respective hole. Use the **Rotate View** feature as needed (or if you think you can get away with it, use a **Wireframe** view mode). After you have completed these four mates, try the **Move Component** and **Rotate Component** tools until you are satisfied that the assembly has been mated correctly. You are now finished with this mating process and your Terminal Support Assembly is complete.

Now pull down **File**, select **Save As**, and save the assembly as **TERMINAL SUPPORT.sldasm** in your folder. Insert the rendered Terminal Support Assembly image into your **Title Block** drawing sheet that was created in Chapter 1. Now save your drawing as **TERMINAL SUPPORT.slddrw** and **Print** it on this sheet (see Figure 5-28). Now close your session, pull down File and click Close. You are finished.

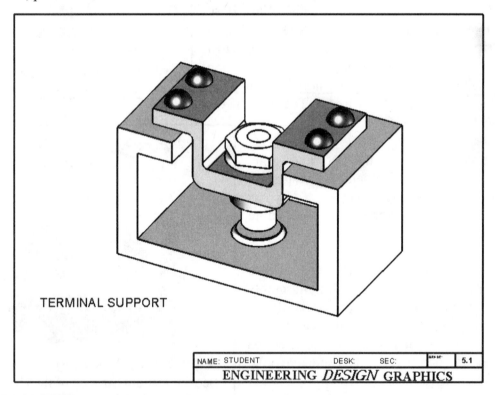

Figure 5-28. The Finished Terminal Support Assembly on the Title Block Sheet.

Be sure to save your assembly files for use in later lab exercises such as "Kinematics Simulation" where you will need to explode an assembly and make an animation file.

Exercise 5.2: Swivel Eye Block Assembly

The Swivel Eye Block Assembly is a common design used to hoist objects with a mechanical leverage advantage. It has four major part components: an Eye Hook, a Pulley Sheave, Spacer, and a Base Plate that is used twice. It is assembled using small rivets that are peened on one end to secure them and hold the components together. You will start the design by designing the Base Plate, which controls many of the dimensions of the other components.

BASE PLATE

Study the geometry of the Base Plate in Figure 5-29. Go to your folder and open **ANSI-INCHES.prtdot**. Immediately pull down **File** again, select **Save As**, and then name it **SBLOCK BASE PLATE.sldprt** Next click the **LMB** on the **Front** plane icon in the Feature Manager tree and also click the **Front** view orientation. Disregard the "Grid/Snap" settings, since you will just sketch an outline and then use the dimensioning tool.

Enter the **Sketch** mode and use the **Line** and **Circle** sketch tools to draw the outline as indicated in Figure 5-29. Start with a **Circle** at the <u>origin</u> and with a <u>radius</u> of **1.5625** inches. Then draw three **Lines**, approximating the tangent points. Click the **Add Relation** icon and make the **Tangent** relation with the bottom circle and left line, then make the **Tangent** relation with the bottom circle and right line. Use **Trim** to get rid of part of the circle not needed. Draw the two small **Circles** on the top of the profile, draw the center **Circle**, and make sure the top line is **Horizontal**. Finally use the **Dimension** tool to fix all the geometry in place. If done correctly, the lines should turn *black*. Select **Extrude Boss/Base**, use a **Blind** end condition and distance of **0.1250** inches (one-eighth inch). Using **Tools**, **Options**, and **Document Properties**, set the **Shading Color** to **Steel Blue** (second row, sixth choice from left). Then click the **OK** button twice. The Base Plate is finished as shown in Figure 5-30.

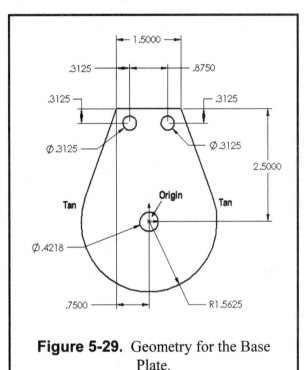

Figure 5-29. Geometry for the Base Plate.

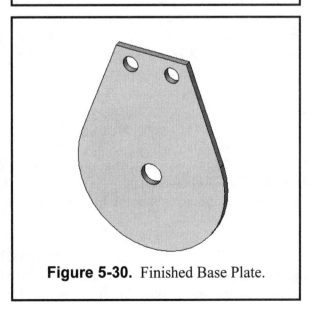

Figure 5-30. Finished Base Plate.

Be sure to **Save** your **SBLOCK BASE PLATE.sldprt** before you **Close** your file and then start a new part for the assembly.

PULLEY SHEAVE

Study the geometry of the Pulley in Figure 5-31. Go to your folder and open **ANSI-INCHES.prtdot**. Immediately pull down **File** again, select **Save As**, and then name it **SBLOCK PULLEY.sldprt**. Next click the **LMB** on the **Right** plane icon in the Feature Manager tree and also click the **Right** view orientation. Disregard the "Grid/Snap" settings for this part.

Enter the **Sketch** mode and use the **Line** and **Centerpoint Arc** sketch tools to draw the outline as indicated in Figure 5-31. Also draw a horizontal **Centerline** through the <u>origin</u>. Use the **Dimension** tool to fix all the geometry in place. If done correctly, the lines should turn *black*. Now select the **Revolve Boss/Base** feature icon and give the revolution a full **360** degrees parameter. You now have the pulley part of the assembly.

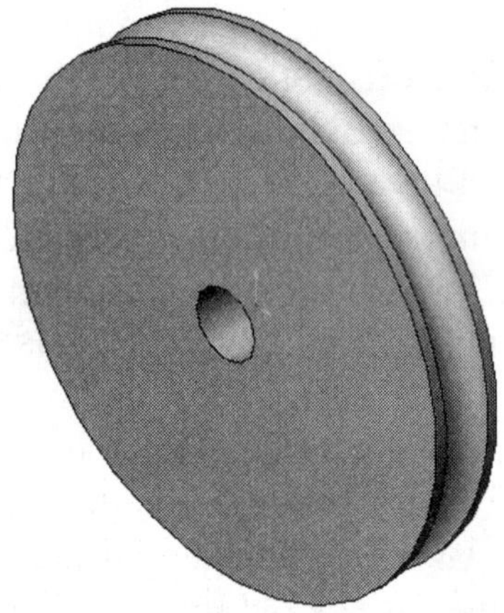

Using **Tools**, **Options**, and **Document Properties**, set the **Shading Color** to **Brass Yellow** (first row, second choice from left). Then click the **OK** button twice. The Pulley is finished as shown in Figure 5-32. Be sure to **Save** your **SBLOCK PULLEY.sldprt** before you **Close** your file.

SPACER

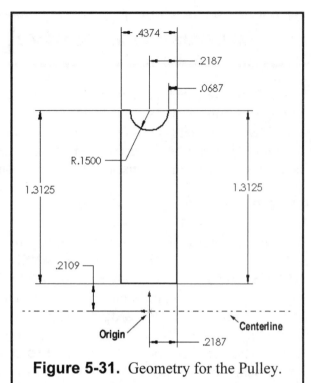

Figure 5-31. Geometry for the Pulley.

Figure 5-32. The Finished Pulley.

Study the geometry of the Spacer in Figure 5-33. Go to your folder and open **ANSI-INCHES.prtdot**. Immediately pull down **File** again, select **Save As**, and then name it **SBLOCK SPACER.sldprt**. Next click the **LMB** on the **Front** plane icon in the Feature Manager tree and also click the **Front** view orientation. Disregard the "Grid/Snap" settings for this part.

Enter the **Sketch** mode and use the **Line** and **Circle** sketch tools to draw the simple outline as indicated in Figure 5-33. Then use the **Dimension** tool to fix all the geometry in place. Be sure to dimension the position of the Spacer relative to the <u>origin</u>. If done correctly, the lines should turn *black*.

Select **Extrude Boss/Base,** use a **Mid Plane** end condition and distance of **0.5000** inches. _Note_: A Mid Plane end condition will extrude the sketch 0.2500 inches in both directions, using the sketch plane as the "mid plane."

Now click on the top surface of the Spacer and **Sketch** a **Circle** centered at the origin and with a diameter of **0.3500** inches, as shown in Figure 5-34. Select **Extrude Cut** and cut the hole **Through All** the Spacer.

Using **Tools**, **Options**, and **Document Properties,** set the **Shading Color** to **Metallic Green** (first row, fourth choice from left). Then click the **OK** button twice. The Spacer is finished. Be sure to **Save** your **SBLOCK SPACER.sldprt** before you **Close** your file.

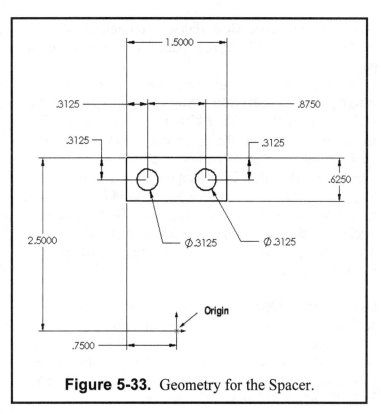

Figure 5-33. Geometry for the Spacer.

EYE HOOK

The Eye Hook part can be made by simply revolving a circle and then extruding a circle in their respective planes. Go to your folder and open **ANSI-INCHES.prtdot**. Immediately name your part by pulling down **File** again, select **Save As**, and then name it **SBLOCK EYE HOOK.sldprt**. Next click the **LMB** on the **Right** plane icon in the Feature Manager tree and also click the **Right** view orientation. Set the **Units** to **Inches** and **4** decimal places. Disregard the "Grid/Snap" settings for this eye hook part.

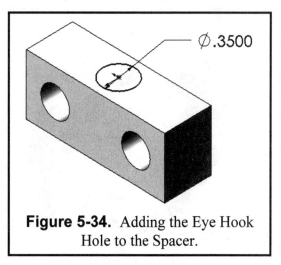

Figure 5-34. Adding the Eye Hook Hole to the Spacer.

Sketch a **Circle** in the position indicated in Figure 5-35. Also draw a horizontal **Centerline** above this circle. Click the **Add Relations** icon, and make the "Circle" and "Origin" have a **Vertical** relation. Add a **Horizontal** relation to the "Centerline" just to be safe. Now use the **Dimension** tool to add the three dimensions that will fix all the geometry.

Select the **Revolve Boss/Base** icon and revolve the circle through a **360** degrees path. This creates the top part of the Eye Hook.

Select the **Top** plane in the Feature Manager. Pull down **Insert**, select **Reference Geometry**, and then **Plane**. Define the plane to be **2.875** inches above the Top plane, and then click the green check (√) mark. Now click on this new plane (called **Plane 1** in the Feature Manager). **Sketch** a **Circle** on it centered at the plane's local origin and with a diameter of **0.3475** inches, as shown in Figure 5-36. Next **Extrude Boss/Base** the circle to a **Blind** distance of **1.2500** inches downward. This completes the geometric construction of the Eye Hook as shown in Figure 5-37.

Using **Tools**, **Options**, and **Document Properties**, set the **Shading Color** to **Metallic Orange** (fourth row, second choice from left). Then click the **OK** button twice. The Eye Hook now is finished and has a very nice color. Be sure to **Save** your **SBLOCK EYE HOOK.sldprt** before you **Close** your file.

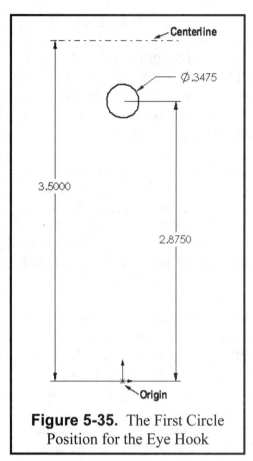

Figure 5-35. The First Circle Position for the Eye Hook

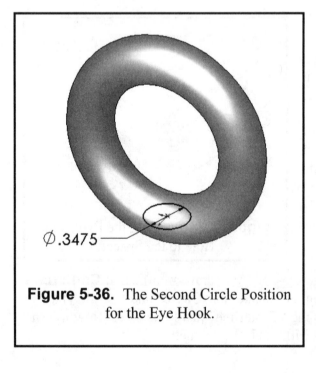

Figure 5-36. The Second Circle Position for the Eye Hook.

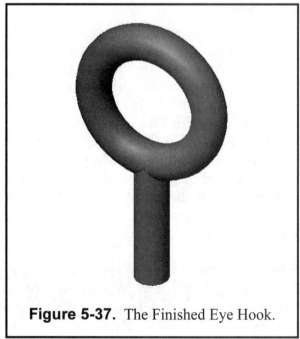

Figure 5-37. The Finished Eye Hook.

RIVETS

The final parts to create are the Big and Small Rivets. These are standard parts with dimensions that can be obtained from a handbook. In <u>each case</u>, go to your folder and open **ANSI-INCHES.prtdot**. and **Sketch** the given outline in a **Front** plane. Use the **Dimension** values given in Figure 5-38 and 5-39 for the Big Rivet and Small Rivet, respectively. Center your data according to the given origin. *Note:* **Do not draw the arcs for the rivets at the origin.** When you **Dimension** the **Centerpoint Arc** entity, the center of that arc moves down slightly below the origin. Be sure to draw a vertical **Centerline** through the origin. **Revolve Boss/Base** the Rivet outline **360** degrees. Give it the **Shading Color** of **Red** (second row, first choice from left on the SolidWorks color palette). **Save** the Big Rivet as **SBLOCK BIG RIVET.sldprt** before you **Close** your file. **Save** the Small Rivet as **SBLOCK SMALL RIVET.sldprt** before you **Close** your file.

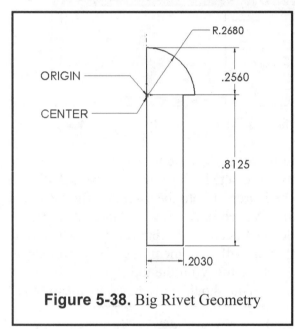

Figure 5-38. Big Rivet Geometry

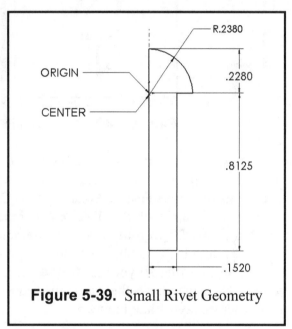

Figure 5-39. Small Rivet Geometry

SWIVEL EYE BLOCK ASSEMBLY

Pull down **File, New** and select **Assembly**. Pull down **Tools, Options, Document Properties** and select **ANSI** and then Select **Units**. Make sure you indicate **IPS** (Inch, Pound, Second) and **OK** the selections. Pull down **File** again, select **Save As**, and then save it as **SWIVEL EYE BLOCK.sldasm**. Pull down **File** and **Open,** one-by-one, the four main parts of the assembly:

> **SBLOCK BASE PLATE.sldprt**
> **SBLOCK PULLEY.sldprt**
> **SBLOCK SPACER.sldprt**
> **SBLOCK EYE HOOK.sldprt**

You will add the Rivets later. You now have five active files in your current SolidWorks session (the Assembly file and the four Part files). Pull down **Window** and select **Tile Vertically**. You can now see all five files on the screen as shown in Figure 5-40.

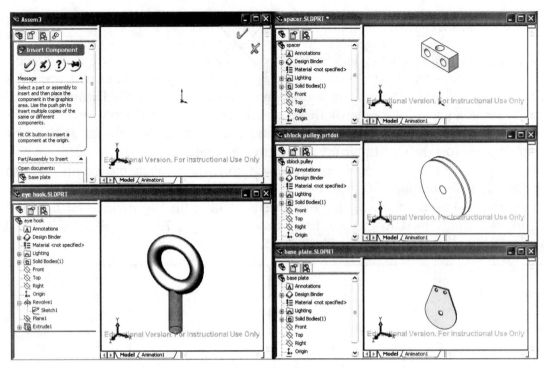

Figure 5-40. The Five File Windows Tiled Vertically.

The first part dropped into the assembly is fixed and becomes the base to which all other parts are mated. It cannot be moved unless its constraints are deleted. Starting with the **SPACER** file, select its title in its Feature Manager and "Drag and Drop" it into the assembly file. Repeat this "Drag and Drop" with the **PULLEY** and then the **EYE HOOK**. Finally, "Drag and Drop" the **BASE PLATE** <u>two times</u> into the assembly file. You can try to line them up when you "Drop" them into the assembly, but more importantly you will mate them next. You no longer need the four part files so you can **Close** them by clicking the X on the top right side of their window. Then maximize the assembly file window. You should now have an **Isometric** computer screen layout like Figure 5-41.

You will first mate the Front Base Plate with the Spacer. Click the **Mate** icon on the left side Assembly toolbar (it looks like a paper clip), and the "**Mate**" menu comes up as indicated in Figure 5-42. Now pick the upper left small cylindrical hole surface of the front Base Plate and then pick the inner left cylindrical hole surface of the Spacer. They both should turn *green*. Now click the **Concentric** mate setting and then click the green check (√) to execute the mate. Repeat this **Concentric** mate process by picking the upper right small cylindrical hole surface of the Base Plate and then pick the inner right cylindrical hole surface of the Spacer. Use an **Isometric** view and **Zoom** in as needed to perform these mates.

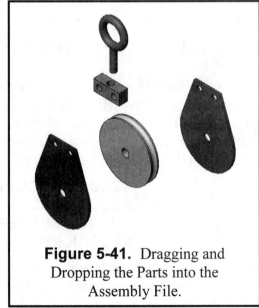

Figure 5-41. Dragging and Dropping the Parts into the Assembly File.

Now their holes are concentric but the front Base Plate and Spacer may not touch. Click the **Mate** icon and then pick the front surface of the Spacer and the back surface of the front Base Plate. (*Note:* You probably can not find a view orientation that allows you to see and pick both of these surfaces simultaneously, so use the **Rotate View** icon or the **Wireframe** view mode to assist you in clicking these two surfaces.) Once you have selected the two flat surfaces, they should turn *green*. Now in the "Mate" menu, select the **Coincident** mating condition, and click the green (√) **OK** button. You should now see the front Base Plate move towards the front surface of the Spacer, and they are now mated properly.

Repeat this process with the back side of the Spacer and the back Base Plate. This includes three **Mates**:

- o **Concentric** holes on left side
- o **Concentric** holes on right side
- o **Coincident** surfaces that touch

The two Base Plates are now mated to the Spacer as shown in an **Isometric** view in Figure 5-43. You can look at it from a **Front** view orientation if you wish to check it and see the holes going all the way through as shown in Figure 5-44.

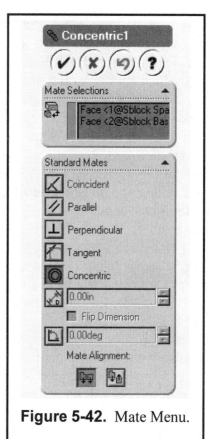

Figure 5-42. Mate Menu.

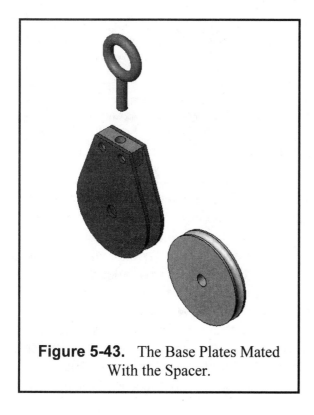

Figure 5-43. The Base Plates Mated With the Spacer.

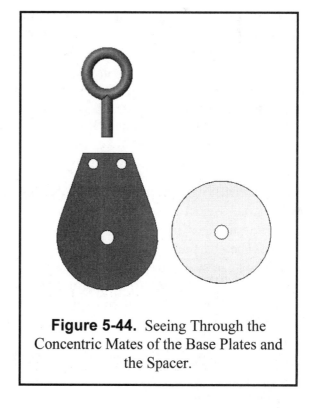

Figure 5-44. Seeing Through the Concentric Mates of the Base Plates and the Spacer.

Now you will mate the Pulley into the Base Plates that will sandwich it. Click the **Mate** icon. Now pick the large center hole surface of the front Base Plate (*or* you could *instead* pick the large center hole surface of the back Base Plate). Next pick the center hole surface of the Pulley. Give it a **Concentric** mate and then click the green (√) button. Notice the Pulley aligns concentrically with the center Base Plate holes, but in all likelihood is not sandwiched exactly between them. Switch to a **Right** view orientation to better see this. You could just move it into position by clicking the **Move Component** icon and then moving the Pulley into position by "eyeball." However that is not the right way to do it. You need a second mating condition.

The Spacer is 0.5000 inches thick and the pulley is 0.4374 inches thick. So you need to position the Pulley (0.5000-0.4374)/2 = 0.0313 inches away from the Base Plates. Click the **Mate** icon. Select the front round face of the Pulley and then select the back face of the front Base Plate. You may need to use the **Zoom** and **Rotate View** icons to get these faces highlighted simultaneously. Once they are highlighted (turned *green*), select the **Distance** mate setting, key in the value of **0.0313**, and then click the green (√) button. The Pulley moves into position and is now fully mated. Use a **Right** view orientation to see this latest mate, as shown in Figure 5-45. Make sure there is a small gap.

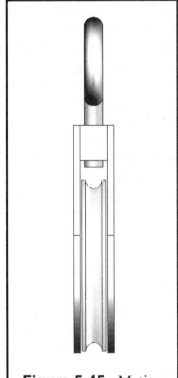

Figure 5-45. Mating the Pulley Between the Two Base Plates.

While you are at it, notice the "Mates" branch in your Feature Manager tree structure. It lists all the mates made to date for the Swivel Eye Block Assembly, as shown in Figure 5-46. You can "right click" on the mate of interest and **Edit Feature** of the mate.

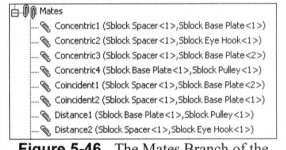

Figure 5-46. The Mates Branch of the Feature Menu.

Now you will mate the Eye Hook to the assembly. Return to an **Isometric** view. Click the **Mate** icon. Select the circular shaft of the Eye Hook and the top circular hole on the Spacer. The two surfaces turn *green*. Now give them a **Concentric** mate and click the green (√) button. The shaft now mates with the hole, but it probably does not go far enough down the hole. You can switch to a **Right** view and **Zoom** into the area where the shaft goes through the Spacer hole. Use the **Move Component** assembly feature and move the shaft through the hole until it sticks out of the bottom of the Spacer. Use the **Rotate View** display icon and rotate your view until you can see both the flat bottom of the shaft and the bottom surface of the Spacer. Click **Mate** and then click both the flat bottom of the shaft and the bottom of the Spacer surfaces. Give them a **Distance** mate of **0.1250** inches. **Preview** the selection (see Figure 5-47) and if it is correct, then click the green (√) button. If it does not look correct, you can try **Flip Dimension**.

The major parts of the assembly are now mated completely, and you will next add the Rivets. First though, take note of the degrees-of-freedom that still remain with these parts. The two Base Plates and the Spacer are fixed in space because of the two concentric and one coincident mate conditions. However the Pulley and Eye Hook can still rotate in one degree-of-freedom. Select the **Rotate Component** icon on the assembly toolbar. Now with the cursor, move the Pulley around its concentric mate and see it turn effortlessly. Now move the Eye Hook as it swivels around in its hole, but you can not move it out of the hole because of the distance mate. Try to leave the Eye Hook in a position such that the Eye feature is parallel to the Base Plate, as shown in the final Figure 5-47.

Pull down **File** and **Open** both the **SBLOCK BIG RIVET** and **SBLOCK SMALL RIVET** files. Pull down **Windows** and select **Tile Vertically**. Drag and drop the "Big Rivet" into the assembly window, and then drag and drop the "Small Rivet" <u>twice</u> into the assembly window (see Figure 5-48). Each rivet will fit into its respective hole and will have the same two identical **Mate** characteristics. The first characteristic will be a **Concentric** mate between the rivet shaft and the inner surface of its respective hole. The second mate is a **Coincident** mate between the back flat part of the rivet head and the front face of the front Base Plate. So now execute these mates for the Big Rivet going through the center holes

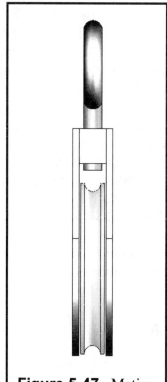

Figure 5-47. Mating the Eye Hook with the Spacer.

and then for the two Small Rivets going through their respective holes on the top of the assembly. You may have to use the **Move Component**, **Zoom** and **Rotate View** icons to get these faces highlighted simultaneously when you are mating. Once you are finished, you should have a final Swivel Eye Block Assembly as shown in Figure 5-49 in a **Trimetric** view.

Manufacturing Note: If you **Rotate View** and look at the back of your assembly, you can see the Rivets sticking out about 0.0625 inches (one sixteenth of an inch). The normal process used to secure the Rivet to the Base Plate is a peen operation. *Peening* the end of the Rivet with a hammer, for example, causes the surface to expand in a spherical direction, and thus prevents the Rivet from coming out of the hole. We will leave this peening operation for a later day, and your assembly modeling and mating exercise is over.

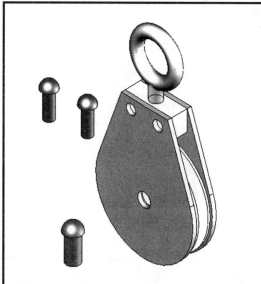

Figure 5-48. Dragging and Dropping the Rivets into the Assembly.

Pull down **File**, select **Save As**, and save the assembly as **SWIVEL EYE BLOCK.sldasm** in your folder. Now close your session, pull down **File** and click **Close**. You are finished with this exercise.

Before you close this file you should save it and also get a hard copy printout. Insert the rendered Swivel Eye Block Assembly image into your **Title Block** drawing sheet that was created in Chapter 1. Now save your drawing as **SWIVAL EYE BLOCK ASSEMBLY.slddrw** and **Print** it on this sheet (see Figure 5-50). If you have access to a *Color Printer*, use it to show the nice colors of your assembly.

Figure 5-49. The Finished Swivel Eye Block Assembly in a Trimetric View.

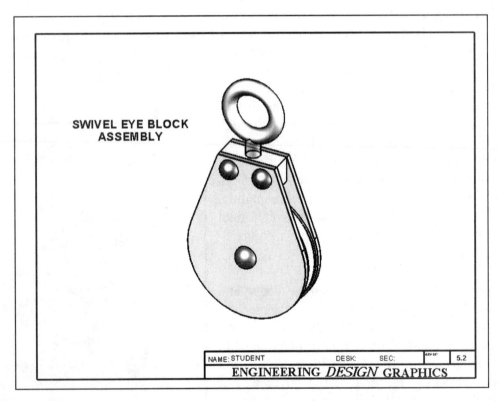

SWIVEL EYE BLOCK
ASSEMBLY

NAME: STUDENT		DESK:	SEC:	DRAWN BY:	5.2
ENGINEERING *DESIGN* GRAPHICS					

Figure 5-50. The Swivel Eye Block Assembly Image Inserted Onto the Title Block Sheet.

Be sure to save your assembly files for use in later lab exercises such as "Kinematics Simulation" where you will need to explode an assembly and make an animation file.

Computer Graphics Lab 6: Analysis and Design Modification I

In this Computer Graphics Lab 6, you will be introduced to some of the advanced analysis and design modification capabilities of SolidWorks. Solid modeling is a new tool for engineering design that offers many new advantages over conventional practice. One of these advantages is the ability to analyze the design directly from the digital database without the need to build a physical part. In this laboratory, you will analyze various design properties of the solid model using the **Measure** and **Mass Properties** commands. You will also be exposed to **Design Tables,** which can be used to build a family of similar parts.

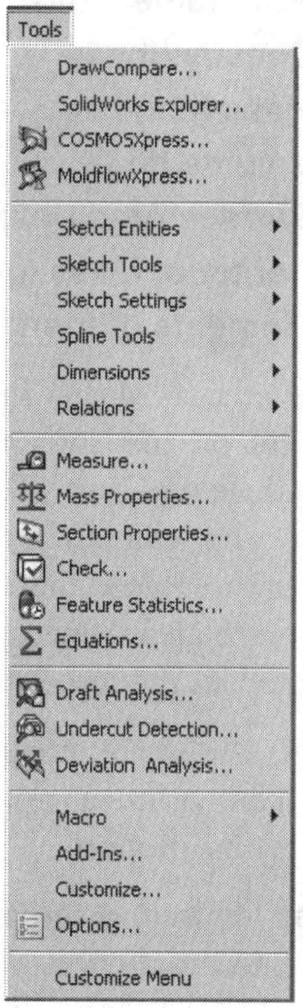

THE MEASURE FUNCTION

The **Measure** function can be found in the **Tools** pull-down menu (see Figure 6-1). When you use this function, a ruler appears on the cursor and you can pick the entity of interest in the computer screen area. This function includes the following capabilities as examples. They can be applied either to a 2-D sketch or to a 3-D solid model.

Line returns the length of the line.

Arc returns the length of the arc and the diameter. If the arc is a full circle, the length ends up being the circumference (see Figure 6-2).

Flat Surface returns the square area of the surface and the length of the perimeter around the flat surface.

Circular Surface returns the square area of the surface, the diameter, and the perimeter. If it is a through hole, then the perimeter will be the circumference of one end plus the circumference of the other end.

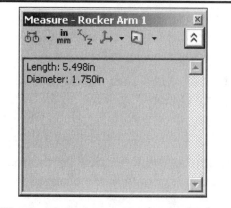

Figure 6-1. The Measure Function.

Figure 6-2. Measure Screen Menu.

THE MASS PROPERTIES FUNCTION

Selecting the **Mass Properties** command in the **Tools** pull-down menu (see also Figure 6-1) will open an on-screen window that reports the mass properties of the current solid model. Before you can calculate the mass properties accurately, you need to set the density of the material for the solid model part. The density is set in the **Options** command of the **Tools** pull down menu under the **Document Properties** then select **Material Properties** tab. Here you can set the "Density" of the material as shown in Figure 6-3. See also Table 6-1 for some common density values.

Once the density of the part material is set, you can then select the **Mass Properties** command. The result will be reported in the "Mass Properties" Report in the on-screen window, as shown in Figure 6-4. The mass property values and units reported include the following (see the Appendix, page 6-11, for definitions):

Part Name

Density (lbs/in$^{3)}$

Mass (lbs)

Volume (in3)

Surface Area (in2)

Center of Mass (in)

Moments of Inertia (lbs/in^2)

Once the "Mass Properties" Report appears on the screen, you can review the values reported. To see all of them at once, you can stretch the lower right corner to enlarge the on-screen window. There are also some options buttons you can click at the top of the menu.

Print will open the print menu where you can print a copy of the "Mass Properties" Report.

Copy will copy the entire report to the computer clipboard. Then you can open a word processing routine like MS-Word or WordPad and paste it directly into the document. This allows you to edit the report in order to get a customized hardcopy of it.

Close will simply close the on-screen "Mass Properties" window.

Options will open another "Mass Property Options" window on the screen as shown in Figure 6-5. Here you can custom set the units and density values.

Recalculate will recalculate the mass properties after options are changed.

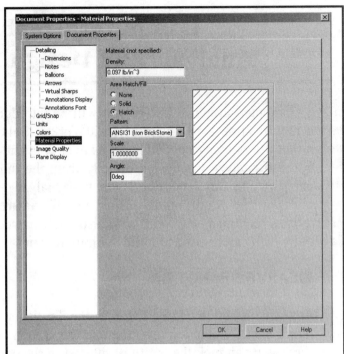

Figure 6-3. Setting the Materials Properties.

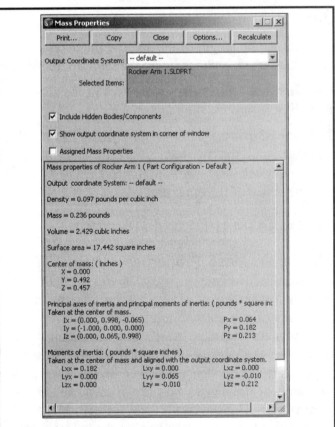

Figure 6-4. Mass Properties On-Screen Report.

ABOUT THE MASS PROPERTIES UNITS

Some mass properties are based on the geometric distribution of the object and are independent of the material's density (assumed to be uniform). Examples of these kinds of properties are volume and center of mass (centroid). Other properties, such as mass and moments of inertia, are dependent on the material's density. Table 6-1 lists the densities of some common engineering materials. You can use these density values to set the material properties of your part. Weight and Mass are often confused. Below is an example of the correct way to calculate them for a unit one-inch cube. _Note_: The "Density" value used by SolidWorks (see Figure 6-3) is actually the value of the "Unit Weight" listed below in Table 6-1. This lack of uniformity in terminology contributes to the general confusion on this matter.

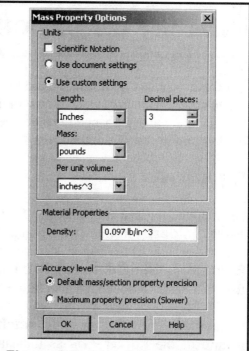

Figure 6-5. Mass Property Options.

Example Calculation: Material is Mild Steel (density is 0.728×10^{-3} lbs-sec^2/in^4)

Weight $= $ (unit weight)x(volume) $= (0.281$ lbs/in$^3)$ x $(1.00$ in$^3) = 0.281$ lbs.

Mass $\quad = $ (density)x(volume) $= (0.728 \times 10^{-3}$ lbs-sec^2/in^4)x$(1.00$ in$^3) = 0.728 \times 10^{-3}$ lbs-sec^2/in.

$\qquad = $ (weight) / (gravity) $= (0.281$ lbs) / $(386$ in/sec$^2) = 0.728 \times 10^{-3}$ lbs-sec^2/in.

Table 6-1. Some Unit Weights and Densities of Common Materials.

Material	Unit Weight (lbs/in^3)	Density (lbs-sec^2/in^4)
Aluminum	0.097	0.251×10^{-3}
Brass	0.307	0.794×10^{-3}
Chromium	0.259	0.671×10^{-3}
Copper	0.323	0.837×10^{-3}
Magnesium	0.063	0.163×10^{-3}
Plastic	0.036	0.093×10^{-3}
Rubber	0.041	0.106×10^{-3}
Steel	0.281	0.728×10^{-3}
Titanium	0.163	0.422×10^{-3}

Exercise 6.1: ROCKER ARM MASS PROPERTIES

For this Exercise 6.1, you will build the basic geometry of the rocker arm, which is designed to rotate about a principal axis. You will then copy the first rocker arm data into a second rocker arm file and make a change in its geometry. Mass Properties analysis will be performed on both models and the results will be compared to each other.

ROCKER ARM 1

Open **ANSI-INCHES.prtdot** and **Save** it as **ROCKER ARM 1.sldprt**. In the **Front** plane, **Sketch** a **Circle** with a <u>diameter</u> of **1.75** inches and centered at the origin. **Extrude** it a **Blind** distance of **1.00** inches out from the front plane. You now have the bottom base boss.

Return to the **Front** plane and **Sketch** the back upright feature of the Rocker Arm as indicated in Figure 6-6. Draw the three **Lines** such that the bottom of the profile slightly extends into the extruded base. Draw the outer top arc using the **Tangent Arc** tool. Draw the **Circle** below this arc. Now **Add Relations** to the profile as follows:

- o The small circle and origin are **Vertical**.
- o The small circle and top arc are **Concentric**.
- o The left-side line and top arc are **Tangent**.
- o The right-side line and top arc are **Tangent**.

Finally use the **Dimension** tool to apply the three dimensions given in Figure 6-6. Now **Extrude** this upright sketch **0.75** inches out from the front plane. You will get the beginning model of the Rocker Arm as shown in Figure 6-7.

Now you will draw the final sketch to cut the hole and keyway through the bottom boss. Click on its front surface (it turns *green*) and enter the **Sketch** mode. Set **Units** to inches and **3** decimal places. Use a **Front** view orientation to draw the big **Circle** with a <u>radius</u> of **0.50** inches and centered at the origin. Draw three short **Lines** to make the keyway at the top of the circle and then use the **Trim** tool to cut away the pieces that are not needed. Refer to Figure 6-8 to see how it should look at this point. Use the **Dimension** tool to dimension the features in accordance with Figure 6-8.

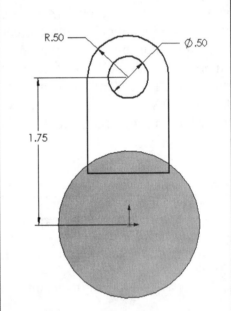

Figure 6-6. Dimensions for the Upright Part of the Rocker Arm.

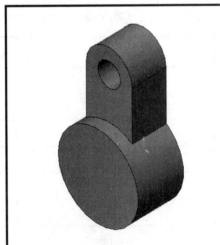

Figure 6-7. The Beginning Rocker Arm.

6-4

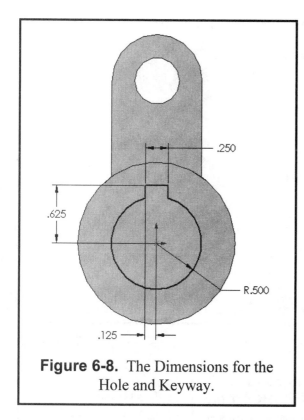

Figure 6-8. The Dimensions for the Hole and Keyway.

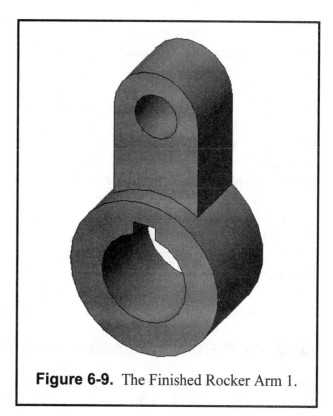

Figure 6-9. The Finished Rocker Arm 1.

Now **Extrude Cut** the sketch profile using a **Through All** end condition. The Rocker Arm 1 is finished as shown in Figure 6-9 in a **Trimetric** view. Use the **Rotate View** icon to see the through hole and keyway features. **Save** your model as **ROCKER ARM 1**. Do <u>not</u> close your file.

ROCKER ARM 2

You will design Rocker Arm 2 by using the general database of Rocker Arm 1. So now **Save** your screen model as **ROCKER ARM 2.sldprt**. The two differences for the new Rocker Arm 2 are the width of the upright feature (now 1.25 inches) and the depth of this upright feature (now only 0.50 inches). These changes can be accomplished easily using the feature editing capabilities of SolidWorks.

In the Feature Manager tree, click over the **Sketch2** label with a right mouse click ("Sketch2 is under the second "Extrude" feature). Select the **Edit Sketch** option and the old "Sketch2" definition appears on the screen. Change the value of the large arc from R0.500 to **R0.625** as shown in Figure 6-10. Then click the **Rebuild** icon to execute this change in the upright features width.

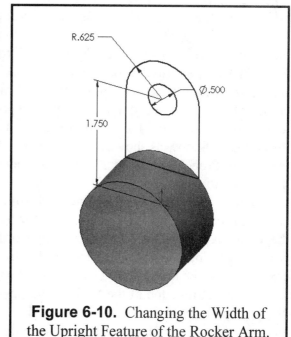

Figure 6-10. Changing the Width of the Upright Feature of the Rocker Arm.

Now change the extrusion depth of the upright feature. Right mouse click the second "Extrude" label in the Feature Manger tree. Select the **Edit Feature** option. The "Boss-Extrude" menu will now appear. In this menu, leave the end condition as **Blind**, but change "Distance" to **0.500** inches. Then click the green **OK** button. The solid model will now be rebuilt with the new extrusion depth. The Rocker Arm 2 is now finished as shown in Figure 6-11 in a **Trimetric** view. Use the **Rotate View** icon to see the through hole and keyway features. **Save** your model as **ROCKER ARM 2**. Then **Close** your SolidWorks file to start the next phase of this analysis exercise.

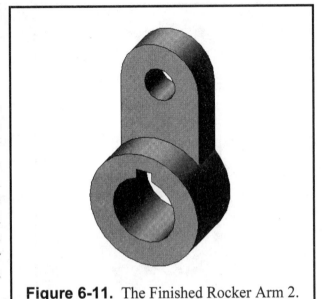

Figure 6-11. The Finished Rocker Arm 2.

MASS PROPERTIES ANALYSIS OF ROCKER ARM 1

You will start your mass properties analysis with Rocker Arm 1. Pull down **File**, select **Open**, and open the **ROCKER ARM 1** file from your folder. Now you need to set the material for the Rocker Arm 1. Right click on the **Material** icon (Figure 6-12) in the Feature Manager and select **Edit Material**. Under **SolidWorks Materials** in the "Materials Editor" menu (Figure 6-13), expand the **Steel** library of materials and select **CAST CARBON STEEL.** If you do not want the part color to change with material assignment, then click **off** the "**Use Material Color**" box.

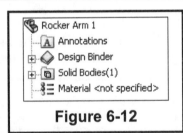

Figure 6-12

Pull down **Tools**, and select the **Mass Properties** command. The "Mass Properties" report window will now appear on the screen showing all the mass properties for Rocker Arm 1 for cast carbon steel. If you cannot see all of the report, pull down on the lower right corner of the window border to stretch the "Mass Properties" window as shown in Figure 6-14. Recall the options of the "Mass Properties" buttons, which includes the ability to print this report to a local printer. However, you may prefer to place your name and other data on the hard copy report. So, in the "Mass Properties" window, click the **Copy** button. This will copy the entire report to the computer's clipboard. Now open some word processing software like MS Word. Use the **Edit** and **Paste** commands in the software to paste the clipboard data directly onto a new page. At the top of the Mass Properties report, type in: Your **Name,** Your **Seat** Number, and Your **Section** Number. Also add an opening sentence of the Mass Properties report: "Mass Properties of Rocker Arm 1 with Cast Carbon Steel Material" in order to identify the part name and assigned material.

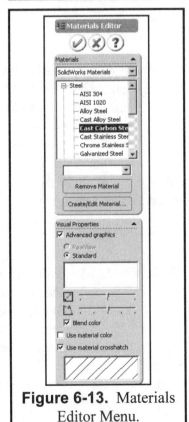

Figure 6-13. Materials Editor Menu.

Next **Print** a hard copy on your local printer. You may want to then select **File** and **Save** in the word processing software to save the word file as **ROCKER ARM 1 - STEEL**. Then close your word processing software and return to SolidWorks.

When you return to SolidWorks, the "Mass Properties" window is still open, so click the **Close** button. You will now repeat this mass properties analysis for Rocker Arm 1 using aluminum as the material.

Right click on the **Material** (currently Cast Carbon Steel) icon (Figure 6-12) in the Feature Manager. Under **SolidWorks Materials**, expand the **Aluminum** library of materials and select **1060 ALLOY**. This sets all the properties for this item. If you do not want the part color to change, click the "**Use Material Color**" box **off.**

Pull down **Tools**, and select the **Mass Properties** command. The "Mass Properties" report window will now appear on the screen showing all the mass properties for Rocker Arm 1 with aluminum material, as shown in Figure 6-15. Now repeat the **Copy** to clipboard and **Paste** in a word processing software procedure used previously to get a hard copy of the Mass Properties for Rocker Arm 1 for aluminum. Be sure to include your pertinent data and material on the print out. **Save** your **ROCKER ARM 1 - ALUMINUM** file and then you can close the word processing software.

When you return to SolidWorks, **Close** your "Mass Properties" window. You can then **File**, **Close** your **ROCKER ARM 1** part file to start analysis on Rocker Arm 2.

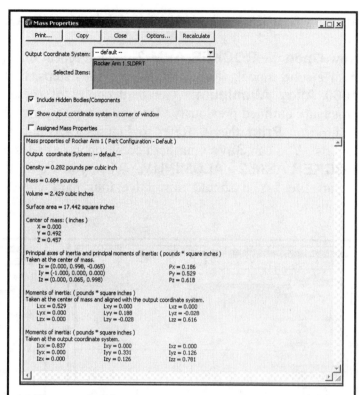

Figure 6-14. Mass Properties for Steel Rocker Arm 1.

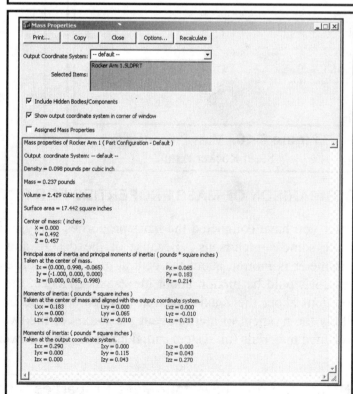

Figure 6-15. Mass Properties for Aluminum Rocker Arm 1.

MASS PROPERTIES ANALYSIS OF ROCKER ARM 2

Now **Open** the **ROCKER ARM 2** file and repeat this mass properties analysis with the Rocker Arm 2 solid model. Repeat all the previous steps, first for **Cast Carbon Steel** and then for **1060 Alloy Aluminum**. Get hard copies of these two reports using the copy and paste procedure outlined previously. Be sure to type your name, class data and material on the reports before you **Print** them. Refer to Figures 6-16 and 6-17 as needed for these mass property reports. You can **Save** your hard copy reports as files named **ROCKER ARM 2 - STEEL** and **ROCKER ARM 2 - ALUMINUM**. When you are finished, **Close** down your **ROCKER ARM 2** part file. You should now have four hard copies of various mass property reports for submission.

Figure 6-16. Mass Properties for Steel Rocker Arm 2.

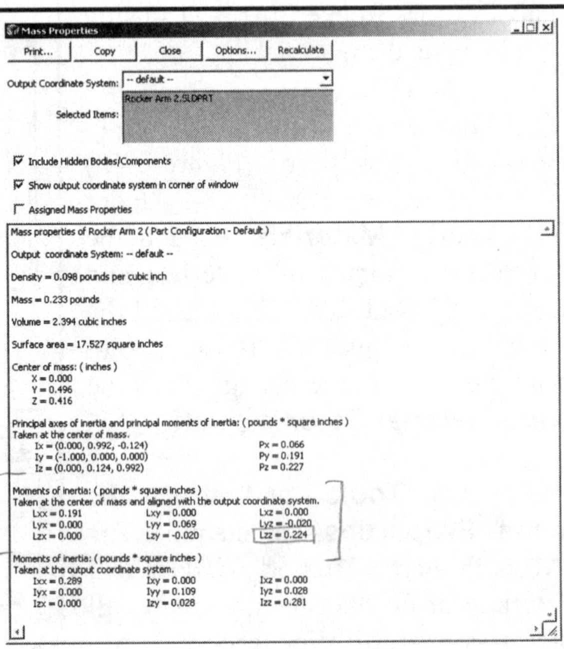

Figure 6-17. Mass Properties for Aluminum Rocker Arm 2.

COMPARISON OF MASS PROPERTIES FOR ROCKER ARMS 1 and 2

After you have completed the mass properties analysis for both Rocker Arms 1 and 2, you can make some comparisons. Because of the design and functionality of the rocker arm, a key parameter is motion about the central axis of the large cylindrical hole on the bottom. In this case, it would be motion about the Z-axis. Hence, the moment of inertia (resistance to steady rotation) about the Z-axis taken at this center would be considered a critical physical property. Study the moment of inertia about the Z-axis of the two rocker arm designs for each of the two assigned materials (mild steel and aluminum), and answer the question below.

> **Note:** You now have four Mass Properties reports. Identify on the correct one, which combination of geometry and material yields a Rocker Arm design that is easiest to rotate (requires the least torque) about the central Z-axis?

CREATING A SHADED IMAGE OF THE TWO ROCKER ARMS

You will now create shaded images of the two Rocker Arms, side-by-side, and obtain a plot for submission to your instructor. You will do this using an assembly model. Pull down **File**, select **Open**, and then select the **ROCKER ARM 2** part file. Repeat this **File, Open** sequence for **ROCKER ARM 1** also. Now pull down **File** and select **New**. This time open a new **Assembly**. This will create a blank assembly file. Pull down **File**, select **Save As**, and then give your new assembly file the name **Rocker Arm Assembly**. At first, all of this computer screen images (viewports) land on top of each other. To see all three screens, pull down **Window** and select **Tile Vertically**. This will result in a screen image as shown in Figure 6-18.

To assemble your two Rocker Arms, just pick, drag, and drop your parts into the assembly window. Click on the **ROCKER ARM 1** icon in its Feature Manager window. Drag it into the assembly window and drop it into an area around the origin. In like manner, go to the **ROCKER ARM 2** icon in its Feature Manager window and drag and drop it into an area just to the right of Rocker Arm 1. Both parts are now in the assembly. You no longer need the two Rocker Arm files, so you can close both of those windows by clicking in the box ☒ symbol at the upper right corner of their window borders. Also, you can now stretch or maximize your Rocker Assembly window by clicking the maximize box in the upper right corner of its window border.

The Rocker Arms may have been dropped into somewhat arbitrary positions. So first try a **Trimetric** View Orientation. Now arrange Rocker Arm 2 to be on the right side of Rocker Arm 1. Select the **Move Component** icon (refer back to Figure 5-3) from the Assembly Toolbar. With the move cursor, pick Rocker Arm 2 and move it to an acceptable position (see Figure 6-19 as a guide). You can also use **Zoom** and **Pan** to arrange your image. You may now save your assembly, so pull down **File** and select **Save As**. save your **ROCKER ARM ASSEMBLY** file.

Open the **TitleBlock-Inches.drwdot** from your folder and insert an isometric view of the Assembly in the same manner that you have been doing with single solid parts. Before you print a hardcopy of your image, you need to label the Rocker Arms. Pull down the **Insert** menu, select **Annotations**, and then select **Note**. The on-screen "Note" menu appears. Type in the label "**ROCKER ARM 1**" in the note window. You may want to dictate the font size also, so click **off** the check mark in the "Use Documents Font" window. Click the **Font** button and the "Choose Font" on-screen menu appears. Here you can set the font type and height. Use the **Arial** font type with a **Bold** setting and set the height to **0.18** inches. Then click **OK** twice to close the on-screen menus, and the note appears on the screen. In all likelihood, the note is not positioned correctly, so drag it with the LMB to an appropriate position above **ROCKER ARM 1**. Repeat this annotation process for **ROCKER ARM 2**. Refer to Figure 6-19 for an example of an acceptable screen layout.

Now preview your print file by pulling down **File** and select **Print Preview**. See your image as it will appear when printed as shown in Figure 6-19, and then click the **Close** button. Then pull down **File** and select **Print**. Make sure the proper printer is selected, and then click **OK**. This finishes the Lab Exercise 6.1 and you can pull down **File** and click **Close** to exit.

Note: Attach your Rocker Arm Assembly printout to your four Mass Properties reports and submit them to your instructor before you leave the lab.

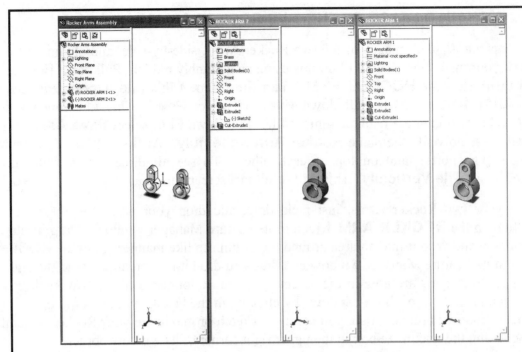

Figure 6-18. The Rocker Arm Assembly, Rocker Arm 1, and Rocker Arm 2 Windows Tiled Vertically.

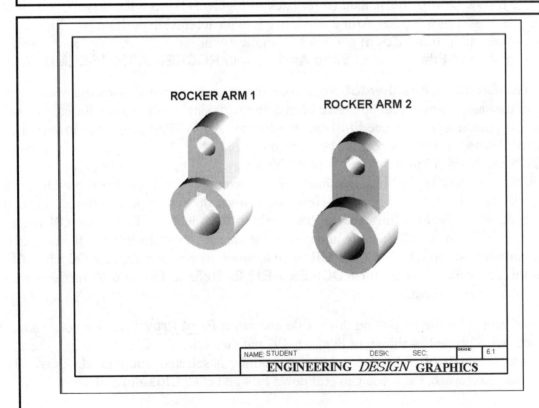

Figure 6-19. A "Print Preview" of the Finished Image Just Before Obtaining a Hard Copy.

Appendix

SOLID MODEL MASS PROPERTIES IN SOLIDWORKS

1. **DENSITY** is the weight per unit volume of the material the part is made from.

2. **MASS**: The mass of a body is the measure of its property to resist change in its steady motion. The mass depends on the volume of the body and the density of the material of which the body is made. In this case with SolidWorks, mass is equivalent to weight.

3. **VOLUME**: The volume of a body is the total volume of space enclosed by its boundary surfaces.

4. **SURFACE AREA**: The surface area is the total area of the boundary surfaces defining the solid model.

5. **CENTER OF MASS**: Center of Mass (or Centroid) of a volume is the origin of coordinate axes for which first moments of the volume are zero. It is considered the center of a volume. For a homogeneous body in a parallel gravity field, mass center and center of gravity coincide with the centroid.

6. **PRINCIPAL AXES OF INERTIA AND PRINCIPAL MOMENTS OF INERTIA**: Principal moments of inertia are extreme (maximal, minimal) moments of inertia for a body. They are associated with principal axes of inertia which have its origin at the centroid, and the direction of each usually given by the three unit-vector components. For these axes, the products of inertia are zero.

7. **MOMENTS OF INERTIA**: A moment of inertia is the second moment of mass of a body relative to an axis, usually X, Y, or Z. It is a measure of the body's property to resist change in its steady rotation about that axis. It depends on the body's mass and its distribution around the axis of interest.

Exercise 6.2: SOCKET PLUG DESIGN TABLE

In Exercise 6.2, you will make a family of parts of the Socket Plug using a Design Table. A Design Table allows you to build multiple configurations of parts or assemblies by specifying parameters in an embedded Microsoft Excel worksheet. The parameters can be the dimensions of key features of the design object that will vary from one part configuration to the next. Once the design table is built, you can go to the "Configuration Manager" to sequence through the different parts. You can then load all your configured parts into an assembly image to display them.

Open **ANSI-INCHES.prtdot** and **Save** it as **SOCKET PLUG.sldprt**. Start a **Sketch** in the **Front** plane. Use the **Line** and **Centerline** tools to create the sketch profile shown in Figure 6-20. Make sure the vertical centerline goes through the origin, and that the lower left corner of the profile is at the origin also. Now carefully **Dimension** the sketch profile **in this order**.

First, the bottom **1.00** overall width.
Second, the **2.00** inch overall height
Third, the **0.50** inch gap on the top
Fourth, the **0.25** inch thickness on the top
Fifth, the **0.50** inch outer plateau height
Sixth, the **0.50** inch inner plateau height

While you have been applying and fixing these dimension values, SolidWorks has also been keeping track of them with a more general approach. It names each dimension with a standard variable name "D#@Sketch#" where the first # is the order the dimension was applied to the sketch and the second # is the Sketch number. For example, the first 1.00 inch dimension should be labeled "D1@Sketch1." This information is critical in the creation of a Design Table in SolidWorks, since you can assign different values to this general dimension variable.

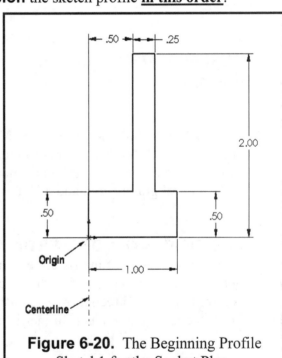

Figure 6-20. The Beginning Profile Sketch1 for the Socket Plug.

Now explore this dimension numbering scheme and revise your sketch accordingly. In the **Select** mode, position your mouse over the first 1.00 dimension and right click it (**RMB**). Now select the **Properties** option on the pop-up menu that appears. The "Dimension Properties" menu now appears as shown in Figure 6-21. Notice the window on the menu that has the "Full Name" of **D1@Sketch1**. Now on the bottom of the menu click **Modify Text**. The "Modify Text of Dimension" menu now appears. In the "Dimension Text" box, after <DIM>, type in **(D1)** as shown in Figure 6-22. **Make sure this number corresponds to the dimension name in the Dimension Property window.** Observe the "Preview" below it and then click **OK** twice to add this label to the **1.00 (D1)** dimension on your sketch. This is just a reference label to help you later identify it in your Design Table.

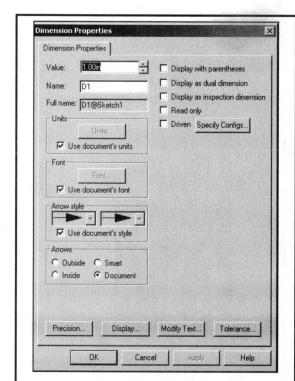

Figure 6-21. The Dimension Properties Menu.

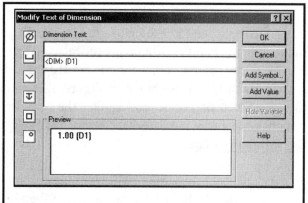

Figure 6-22. Adding the D1 Label to the First 1.00 Dimension.

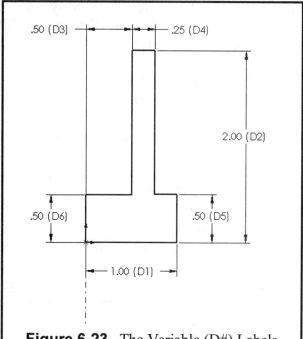

Figure 6-23. The Variable (D#) Labels Now Added to the Sketch1 Dimensions.

Now using this same procedure, add the corresponding (D#) labels to the remaining five dimensions in the same order you applied them earlier. In each case, use the following same steps:

> **RMB** on top of the dimension
> Select **Properties** option
> The "Dimension Properties" Menu appears
> Observe its "Full Name"
> Click **Modify Text**
> Type in the proper **(D#)** in the "Text Box"
> Observe the "Preview"
> Click **OK** twice.

When you are finished, your sketch and corresponding dimensions should appear as shown in Figure 6-23. Study these to make sure they correspond to the order in which they were applied (for instance, the top 0.50 inch gap dimension should be labeled D3). Now click the **Base Revolve** icon and revolve the sketch **360** degrees to create the base part for the Socket Plug, as shown in Figure 6-24.

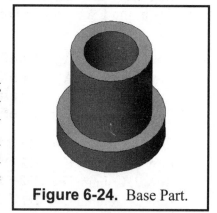

Figure 6-24. Base Part.

Now you will add a slot feature to the Socket Plug design using a second sketch. Click on the **Right** plane on the Feature Manager and also select a **Right** view orientation. In the **Sketch** mode, draw a **Rectangle** as shown in Figure 6-25. Use the **Dimension** tool to apply the nominal dimension values indicated in Figure 6-25. **Use the following order.**

First, the bottom **1.50** height from the origin
Second, the **0.30** inch overall width of the slot
Third, the **0.15** inch distance from the origin
Fourth, the **2.00** inch overall height of the slot.

Then use the previous steps to **Modify Text** of each dimension so that its label **(D#)** appears with its value, as shown in Figure 6-25.

Now click the **Extrude Cut** icon, and extrude it **Through All** in "Direction 1" and **Through All** also in "Direction 2." Then click the green (√) mark to execute the command. The slot feature is now added and the default model is complete as shown in Figure 6-26. You should **Save** it as **SOCKET PLUG.sldprt**.

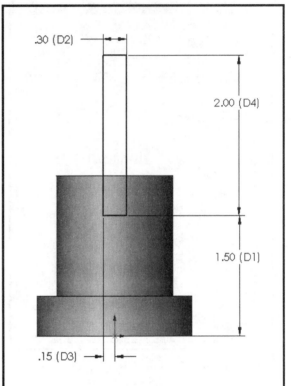

Figure 6-25. The Sketch2 for the Slot.

You are ready to make a Design Table. Pull down **Insert**, select **Design Table**, and then select **Blank** on the Design Table menu. A blank Excel spreadsheet will appear on your screen as suggested in Figure 6-27. There is some preliminary default data on the spreadsheet. Row 1 will have a label stating "Design Table for: Socket Plug" and row 3, column A will have "Instance 1." Key in the following new configuration titles and dimension variables in the Excel editing box (in the top toolbar area):

Row 3, Column A = **Config 1**
Row 4, Column A = **Config 2**
Row 5, Column A = **Config 3**
Row 6, Column A = **Config 4**

Row 2, Column B = **D1@Sketch1**
Row 2, Column C = **D2@Sketch1**
Row 2, Column D = **D3@Sketch1**
Row 2, Column E = **D1@Sketch2**

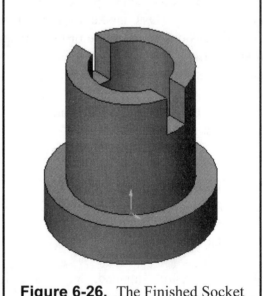

Figure 6-26. The Finished Socket Plug Default Model.

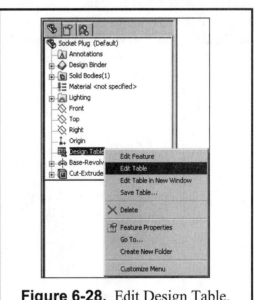

Figure 6-27. The Design Table for the Four Configurations of the Socket Plug.

	A	B	C	D	E	F	G
1	Design Table for: Socket Plug						
2		D1@Sketch1	D2@Sketch1	D3@Sketch1	D1@Sketch2		
3	Config 1	1	2	0.5	1.5		
4	Config 2	1.25	2.5	0.65	1.75		
5	Config 3	1.5	3	0.8	2		
6	Config 4	1.75	3.5	0.95	2.25		
7							
8							
9							
10							

Now study the data in the Design Table in Figure 6-27. Carefully key in the dimension values for D1@Sketch1 for Configurations 1 through 4 in its proper place under column B. Repeat this data entry for D2@Sketch1 under column C, D3@Sketch1 under column D, and D1@Sketch2 under column E. *Note:* Be careful to keep your cursor <u>inside</u> the spreadsheet's confines, because when you click outside of it, the Design Table is executed and the spreadsheet disappears. So when you are finished entering the data, just click on the computer screen to launch the Design Table.

If you have done this correctly, a Design Table icon is added to the Feature Manager tree, as shown in Figure 6-28. From here you can right mouse click (**RMB**) and **Edit Table** of the Design Table to get it back on the screen. *Note:* Sometimes when you are completing a Design Table, you may make a mistake or inadvertently close it before you are finished. Right click on the Design Table icon in the Feature Manger and Edit Table to get it back on the screen. Even if you believe you entered the data correctly, it might be a good idea to <u>check it again</u> before going forward.

You are now ready to see the four different design configurations created by the Design Table. First click the **Rebuild** icon (green light symbol) to rebuild all your design data. You might also want to **Save** your part file now to be safe.

Notice the small configuration icon at the top of the Feature manger column, as indicated in Figure 6-29. Click this **Configuration Manager** icon to turn the Feature Manger area into a "Configuration Manager" tree, as shown in Figure 6-30.

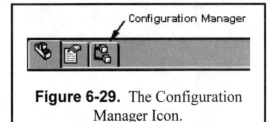

Figure 6-28. Edit Design Table.

Figure 6-29. The Configuration Manager Icon.

Now in an **Isometric** view, one-by-one, double click on the **Config 1**, **Config 2**, **Config 3**, and **Config 4** labels in this tree to see the four different configurations of the Socket Plug. You may have to **Rebuild** your data during this process. Also click on the **Default** configuration, which also happens to be the same as "Config 1," because the values entered in row 3 just happen to be exactly the same as your original sketch data. *Note*: Config 1 does not have to be the same as the "Default" configuration. **Save** your file again.

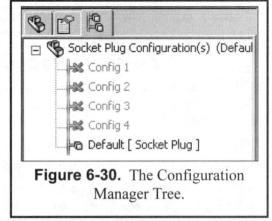

Figure 6-30. The Configuration Manager Tree.

Since this is a family of parts, it would be nice to view them all together to see their variations in size and shape. One way to do this is to "drag and drop" them all into an assembly. So pull down **File**, **New** and select **Assembly**. Pull down **Window** and **Tile Vertically**. Now "drag and drop" the configurations one-by-one, into the assembly window. Start by selecting the "Config 1" label in the Configuration Manger tree, then "Config 2," then Config 3," and finally "Config 4." You can now maximize the assembly window to see the operation better. Arrange them in the assembly window using the **Move Component** icon tool to get a layout as suggested in Figure 6-31 without the labels. Once aligned, save as an assembly. Open **TITLEBLOCK-INCHES** and insert your assembly drawing in the same way you have been inserting your solid models. Add **Insert, Annotation** titles and **Print** the image to hand in to your instructor before you leave the lab. **Save** your file as **SOCKET PLUG ASSEMBLY.slddrw** and then logoff.

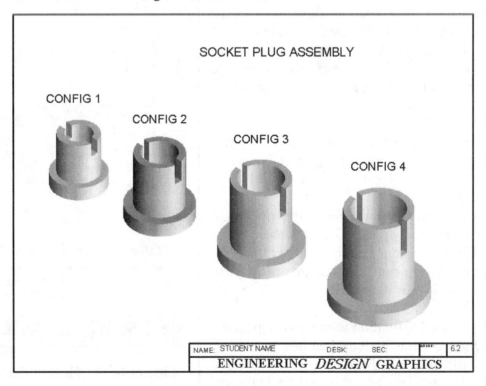

Figure 6-31. A "Print Preview" of the Finished Image Just Before Obtaining a Hard Copy.

Computer Graphics Lab 7:
Analysis and Design Modification II

INTRODUCTION

SolidWorks parametric modeling software allows the designer to build and modify 3-D solid models easily by editing the dimensions and constraints imposed on the 2-D sketch, and then rebuilding the model. In this lab exercise, you will build a 3-D model of a pillow block model using an initial design concept. The initial 3-D model database will then be analyzed using the COSMOSWorks add-in. You will perform a finite element analysis (FEA) on the pillow block to test the stress in the part during its primary function, which is to support a rotating shaft. The FEA results will then suggest modifications to the initial design of the pillow block in order to improve its strength and performance. You will then redesign the pillow block using the parametric features of SolidWorks. Once the second design concept is completed, you will make a second study of the pillow block to see if the design changes improved the performance of the pillow block.

Procedure for Finite Element Analysis using COSMOSWorks

The purpose of this exercise is to learn the stage in the design process subsequent to modeling the object. This is the Finite Element Analysis of the solid model. The results of this analysis are used to evaluate the design of the component. Finite Element Analysis allows the user to simulate a variety of load conditions that the part would be subjected to in the environment that it is designed for and evaluate the performance of the part under them before physically building the part. It is also extremely useful when destructive testing of the part in question is prohibitively expensive. COSMOSWorks in conjunction with SolidWorks offers a powerful tool for FEA. The part can be built as a solid model and COSMOSWorks can be used to analyze the performance of the part.

The object of this exercise is to build a simple part (a Pillow Block) in SolidWorks and analyze it using COSMOSWorks. Before beginning the exercise COSMOSWorks should be installed as an "Add In" to SolidWorks. The steps for accomplishing this are outlined below:

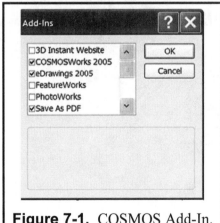

Figure 7-1. COSMOS Add-In.

1. Open SolidWorks
2. Open the **Tools** Menu and click on **Add-Ins**
3. The Add-Ins Dialog box opens (see Figure 7-1). Click on **COSMOSWorks 2006** and see that the small box beside it is checked
4. Click on **OK**.

This adds the COSMOSWorks menu to the Menu Bar and a set of COSMOSWorks command buttons appear as a Tool Bar. The menu and the tools are displayed when a new file is created or an existing file is opened. The Cosmos Load Tool Bar will have the following Icons. The name of each of the icons is given in Figure 7-2 and a verbal description of each of the commands is given in the Table 7-1

Table 7-1 Definitions	
Restraints	Applies restraints to the selected entities for the active structural study (static, frequency, or buckling).
Pressure	Applies pressure to the selected faces for the active structural study (static, frequency, or buckling).
Force	Applies force, torque, or moment to the selected entities for the active structural study (static, frequency, or buckling). The specified value is applied to each selected entity.
Gravity	Defines gravity loading for the active structural study (static, frequency, or buckling).
Centrifugal Force	Applies centrifugal forces for the active structural study (static, frequency, or buckling).
Remote Load	Applies remote loads for structural studies
Rigid Connection	Applies rigid connection between selected faces in structural studies
Bearing Load	Applies bearing loads on selected faces of different components
Temperature	Applies temperatures on the selected entities for the active thermal or structural (static, frequency, or buckling) studies.

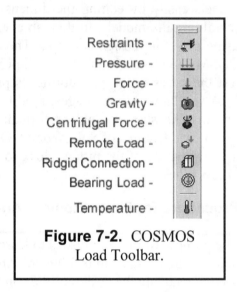

Figure 7-2. COSMOS Load Toolbar.

Exercise 7.1: Finite Element Analysis of a Pillow Block

DESIGNING THE FIRST VERSION OF THE PILLOW BLOCK

You will start by building the preliminary Pillow Block. Study the needed geometry for this version in Figure 7-3. To start, Open **ANSI-INCHES.prtdot** from your folder. Pull down **File** again, select **Save As**, key in the name **PILLOW-1.sldprt**, make sure the directory is set to your folder, and then click the **Save** button. Notice that the part name is now "Pillow1" in the Feature Manager tree structure on the screen.

Select the **Front** plane in the Feature Manager. Enter the sketch mode by clicking the **Sketch Mode** icon on the Sketch Toolbars and reproduce the front profile with the center of the large hole at the origin and then extrude the profile about **Mid-Plane** to the depth of **1.40** inches (See Figure 7-4). In the **Feature Manager,** select the **Top Plane**. **Extrude-Cut** the through holes in the base according to the dimensions given in Figure 7-5.

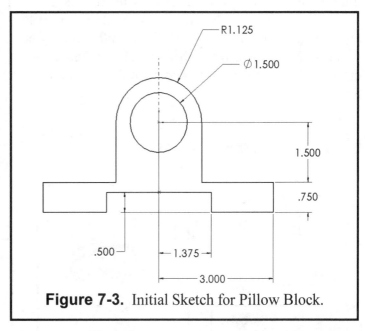

Figure 7-3. Initial Sketch for Pillow Block.

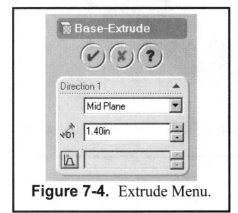

Figure 7-4. Extrude Menu.

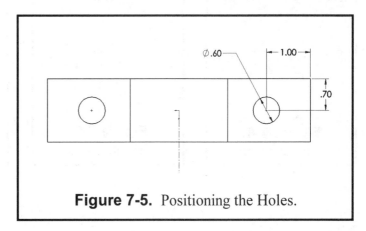

Figure 7-5. Positioning the Holes.

When finished, your solid model should look like the Pillow Block in Figure 7-6. **Save PILLOW1.sldprt** to your folder.

Now you will build a shaft that fits into the large hole of the Pillow Block. To start, open **ANSI-INCHES.prtdot**. Pull down **File** again, select **Save As**, key in the name **SHAFT.sldprt**, make sure the directory is set to your folder, and then click the **Save** button. Notice that the part name is now Shaft in the Feature Manager tree structure on the screen.

Select the **Front** plane in the Feature Manager. Click the **Sketch Mode** icon on the Sketch Toolbars and draw a **Circle** with a diameter of **1.50** inches at the origin (See Figure 7-7) and then extrude the profile about the **Mid-Plane** to the depth of **7.00** inches (See Figure 7-8). Add a **Chamfer** of **0.125** (Figure 7-9) on both ends of the shaft to complete this solid model. See Figure 7-10.

Save SHAFT.sldprt to your folder.

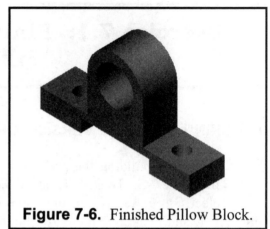

Figure 7-6. Finished Pillow Block.

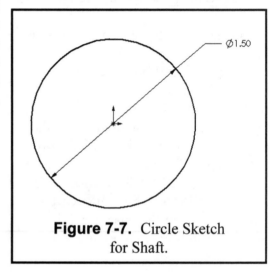

Figure 7-7. Circle Sketch for Shaft.

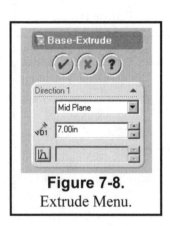

Figure 7-8. Extrude Menu.

Figure 7-9. Chamfer Menu.

Figure 7-10. The Finished Shaft.

ASSEMBLY OF PARTS

At this time you are to make an assembly of the two parts. Make sure that you have Pillow1 and Shaft open. Go to **File**, **New** and select **Assembly**, set the **Units** to **MMGS.** Go to the pull-down **Tools** menu and select **Add-Ins.** Check **COSMOSWorks** from the available list. **Save As "PILLOW ASSEMBLY-1".** First, **Select** the Pillow Block and drag it to the **Origin (When you see a double set of arrows)** of the Assembly drawing. Next **Select** the **Shaft** and drag it to the **Origin (When you see a double set of arrows)** of the Assembly Drawing. This will center the shaft inside of the hole of the pillow block. Maximize the Assembly file Window and view the assembly in isometric (See Figure 7-11).

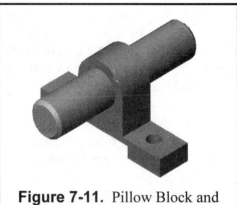

Figure 7-11. Pillow Block and Shaft Assembly.

FINITE ELEMENT ANALYSIS USING COSMOSWORKS

The actual analysis of the pillow block could be a complex procedure even with COSMOSWorks, since analysis of the pillow block would have to include the effects of the rotating shaft and thermal stress on the shaft and the pillow bock. In this case only a simple static analysis of the pillow block will be carried out.

Figure 7-12. COSMOSWorks Icon.

To begin analyzing the part, a Study needs to be defined. The steps required for defining a study are:

1. Click on the **COSMOSWorks Manager Icon** at the top of the Feature Manager Tree (Figure 7-12).
2. Press the **RMB** on the part name in the **COSMOSWorks** Manager Tree and click **Study** (Figure 7-13).
3. Click in the box below Study name, and name the study (e.g. **Study-1- with your last name**) as

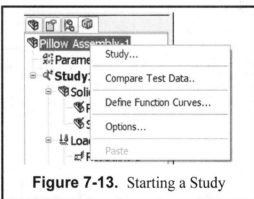

Figure 7-13. Starting a Study

shown in Figure 7-14. Next click in the box below "Analysis type." A pull down menu appears. Select the type of study as **STATIC**. Next, click in the box below "Mesh type" and select **SOLID MESH,** then click **OK.**
4. Right click on the Study name in the Feature Manager Tree and select **Properties.** A window labeled **Static** indicating the type of study that will be conducted appears. Under the **OPTIONS** tab select **FFE** and Click **OK.**

Assigning Material to the Parts

COSMOS has a large material library, which contains the properties of a wide variety of materials. It also allows the user to create a new material with properties defined by the user. The procedure to apply a material is outlined below:

1. Go to the Feature Manager and right-click on the Part Name **Pillow1** (Figure 7-15), and select the **Apply/Edit Material** option.
2. In the Material window (Figure 7-16) select **From Library File – SolidWorks materials.** Assign **Cast Alloy Steel** to the **Pillow Block.** Verify that the "**Type**" is set at **Linear Elastic Isotropic** and that the "**Units**" are set to **SI** and Click on **OK**. This assigns the material to the **Pillow Block**.
3. Repeat this process to the **Shaft** using **Alloy Steel** as the material.
4. A *red check mark* appears on icon next to the name of the model under the Solids folder in the COSMOSWorks Feature Manager indicating that a material has been defined

Applying Restraints:

A restraint is placed on the bottom surfaces of the pillow block to fix the object for a simple static analysis. The sequence of steps for this is follows:

1. Holding down the **CTRL** button, select the two bottom surfaces of the **Pillow Block** (See Figure 7-17).

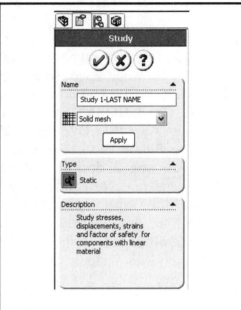

Figure 7-14. Defining a Study.

Figure 7-15. Apply/Edit Material.

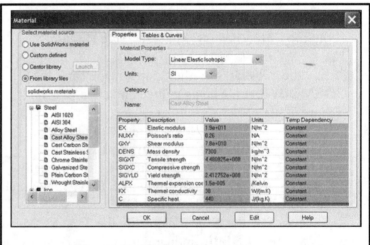

Figure 7-16. Material Assignment

2. Click on the **Restraint** icon in the COSMOS toolbar. See Figure 7-18. Select **Fixed** as restraint type. Click on **OK** and green arrows will appear on these two surfaces as shown in Figure 7-19.

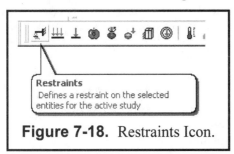

Figure 7-18. Restraints Icon.

Figure 7-17. Applying Restraints on the Bottom Surfaces.

Applying the Force on the Shaft

In the static analysis the Pillow Block will react to the force the shaft exerts. The sequence of steps to apply this force is described below:

1. Click on the cylindrical surface of the shaft.
2. Click on the **Force** icon in the Cosmos toolbar (See Figure 7-20).
3. Select – Type – **Apply Force/Moment**
4. Under **Force (Per Entity)** Activate the second force and enter the value of the force **(-200000 N)** and ensure that the units are set to **SI** system, and click **OK** (Figure 7-21). Forces appear as lavender arrows.

   Note: Make sure that the value in the second box is a negative 200,000 N.

Figure 7-19. Applied Restraints.

This completes the application of restraints, and forces (Figure 7-22) to the Pillow Block and the Shaft. The next step is to create the Mesh required for analysis.

Figure 7-21.

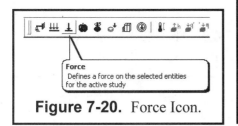

Figure 7-20. Force Icon.

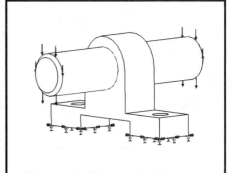

Figure 7-22. Applied Forces.

Creating the Mesh:

The mesh is the division of the solid into a number of small geometric divisions. The effect of the stress on these divisions is computed and then integrated to provide a stress analysis of the entire part. This is an extremely simplistic way of looking at the mesh generation process, which in reality is extremely complicated and takes a relatively long time to execute even on today's fastest computers. The procedure to create the mesh for this analysis is detailed below:

In the COSMOSWorks Manager tree, click the **RMB** on **Mesh** and click on **Create** (Figure 7-23).

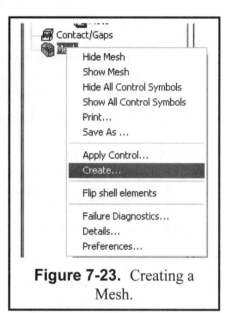

1. This opens up the mesh dialog box, which allows the user to define the mesh size for the analysis. A smaller mesh yields better results, but takes longer to mesh as well as analyze. Hence it is a tradeoff between mesh size and computation time. Change the units to **mm**. Set the **Global Size** to **5** for a slightly finer mesh and **Tolerance** to **0.25** (Figure 7-24).
2. Click on **OK** to accept the values and the Meshing process begins.
3. At the end of the meshing process, a check mark is placed against Mesh in the COSMOSWorks Feature Manager Tree. This causes the mesh to be displayed on the solid as shown in Figure 7-25.

Figure 7-23. Creating a Mesh.

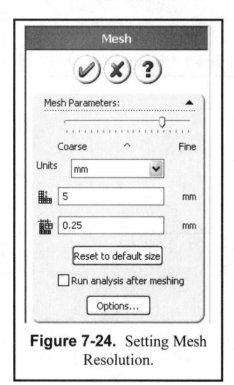

Figure 7-24. Setting Mesh Resolution.

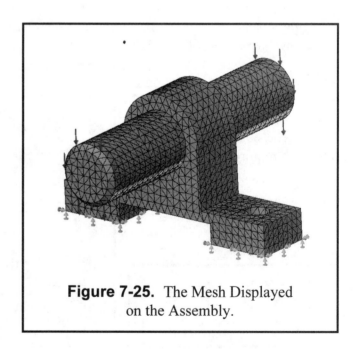

Figure 7-25. The Mesh Displayed on the Assembly.

To Run Static Analysis

The mesh generation is now complete and all parameters required for running the analysis have been defined. To run the Static Analysis, click the **RMB** on the name of the study and click on **Run**. The analysis begins. This process also takes a long time to complete and the execution time depends on the mesh size. The program displays a message once the static analysis is completed. Click on **OK**.

Post-processing

In this section the analysis has been completed and the results are visualized and interpreted. Five new items now appear in the **COSMOSWorks** feature manager (Figure 7-26). They are **Stress, Displacement, Strain, Deformation** and **Design Check**. You can click on the **+** sign in front of these menu items and expand the menu item. Under each item you will find a **Plot1**. Each of these plots depicts what is happening in that part of the study. **Right Mouse Click** on each **Plot1** to get a pull-down menu. Select **Show** to view the results of each portion of the study.

In this section you will be dealing primarily with Von Mises Stress. The sequence of steps to generate the von Mises stress distribution on the Pillow Block is listed next.

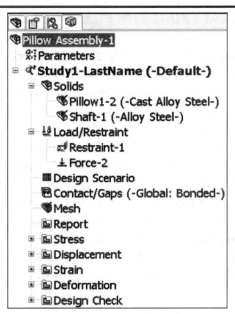

Figure 7-26. New Items on the COSMOSWorks Feature Manager.

1. Click on the **+** sign next to the **Stress** folder. The **Plot 1** icon appears.
2. Right click on **Plot 1** and **Edit Definition** to get the Design Check Wizard dialog box.
3. Select **Pillow1** as the solid part and in the **Criterion** box choose **Maximum von Mises** stress.
4. Click on **Next** to go to **Step 2**.
5. In the **Set Stress Limit** box, choose **To Ultimate Strength** and click on **Next**.
6. In **Step 3**, select **Non-dimensional Stress Distribution**.
7. Click on **Finish**. The stress distribution is displayed on the model as shown in Figure 7-27. You may want to rotate the model to see the model underneath.
8. Repeat these steps to get a design check plot of the **Shaft**. To hide the Restraint and Force vectors, right click on them in the Feature Manager and select **Hide**.

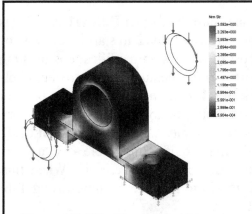

Figure 7-27. Von Mises Stresses.

Go to the **STRESS** report, right click on **Plot 1** and choose **Print**. Go to **Properties** and change the print format to **Landscape**. Then Click on **OK** and the plot will be printed out.

Insert the **Pillow-1 Assembly** rendered image onto a **Title Block** drawing sheet that was created in Chapter 1 and **Print** it on this sheet. This sheet along with the print of the **Stress - Von Mises Stresses Plot - 1** are to be turned in to your instructor.

ANALYZING THE PILLOW BLOCK FOR STRESSES

One of the powerful applications of solid modeling using SolidWorks is the ability to easily interface the database with analysis software. In this case, the pillow block was analyzed for stress distributions when forces were applied to it during its normal function, which is to support a rotating shaft.

The FEA study determines how the stresses and strains were distributed throughout the solid material of the pillow block when the given forces were applied. The results are readily displayed as color contour maps that show the stress distribution. Areas where stresses concentrate can be detected and the FEA results can lead to an improved design of the part. Figure 7-27 shows the results of this FEA study. It can be seen that the stresses tend to concentrate in the thin cylindrical wall surrounding the shaft hole, and also at the right angle where the upright feature emerges from the pillow block base. These two design features are likely candidates for further consideration and re-design when you create the next version of the pillow block. With the results of all this analysis, you are now ready to start the design modification stage.

DESIGN MODIFICATION OF THE PILLOW BLOCK

After studying the results of the FEA, several modifications are suggested for the pillow block to create a second version.

EDITING THE PILLOW BLOCK

Make sure the former **Pillow1** part file is **OPEN** on your computer screen, and then **SAVE AS** the part as **Pillow2** to start a new version of the part. You will now see how easy it is to make most of the design modifications by simply editing the sketch that was used to extrude the base part. In the Feature Manager tree, click the **+** sign on the **Base/Extrude** step to expose the **Sketch1** icon on the tree. Move the mouse cursor over that **Sketch1** icon and click it with the right mouse button **(RMB)**. This invokes a pop-up menu that allows you to edit that sketch. On the pop-up menu, select the **Edit Sketch** option and click it with the **LMB**. Using either Table 2 "Design Modification Table – A" and/or Figure 7-28, make the changes to modify the sketch to conform to the new criteria. When this is completed repeat the above process on the **Cut-Extrude** to relocate the holes using Table 2 "Design Modification Table – A" and/or Figure 7-29.

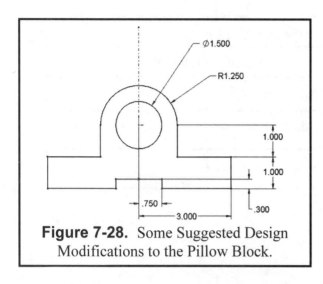

Figure 7-28. Some Suggested Design Modifications to the Pillow Block.

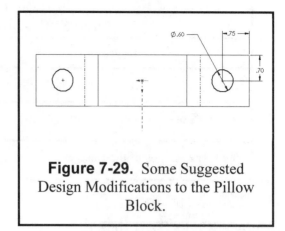

Figure 7-29. Some Suggested Design Modifications to the Pillow Block.

Table 2. Design Modification Table - A	
Feature	**Change Order Request**
Outer Radius Around Shaft Hole	Change Radius from 1.125 to 1.25 inches
Change the thickness of the Base	Change Height from 0.75 inches to 1.00 inch
Center of the Shaft Hole Distance from Base	Change Height from 1.50 to 1.00 inch
Vertical Bolt Holes	Change Position from 1.00 to 0.75 inches from the ends.

Basically, the thickness of the material around the shaft hole was too thin and the outer radius of the pillow block needs to be increased in order to thicken the material surrounding the hole. Sharp 90 degree angles are generally not a good idea for mechanical design, and fillets can be added to bolster the strength at these junctures. Also the slot, which is used primarily to save on material waste and part weight, is poorly designed. The width should be reduced and fillets added to compensate for the downward pressure. Finally the vertical bolt holes (Figure 7-29) need to be centered on the new foot-pad bases.

Once all the current changes have been made, select **Rebuild**. The new Pillow2 will appear in its current state (Figure 7-30).

After the design has been up-dated to look like Figure 7-30, **add fillets** to the Pillow block according to Table 3 –"Design Modification Table - B." When this is completed, your object should look like the Pillow Block in Figure 7-31.

Figure 7-30. Some Modifications to the Pillow Block.

Table 3. Design Modification Table - B	
Feature	**Change Order Request**
Right Angle Surface Intersections (2 Places)	Add Fillets with 0.375 inch Radius
Bottom Slot – Upper Two Corners	Add .25 inch Fillets.
The Upper Edges of the Base	Add .25 inch Fillets

Study – 2 – LAST NAME

After you have finished the design modifications, go to **File**, select **New**. Click on **Assembly** and **Save As "Pillow Assembly-2"**. Repeat the assembly process you used to create the first assembly. The two parts that make up the new assembly are **Pillow-2** and the **Shaft**.

You will now **Repeat** the **COSMOSWorks** process, using the same criteria and procedure performed on the original design. **Save** the **Assembly** and the **Cosmos/Study2 – Your last name** to your folder. Insert the **Pillow-2 Assembly** rendered image onto a **Title Block** drawing sheet that was created in Chapter 1 and **Print** it on this sheet. This sheet along with the prints of the **Stress - Von Mises Stresses Plot - 1** for the second study are to be turned in to your instructor.

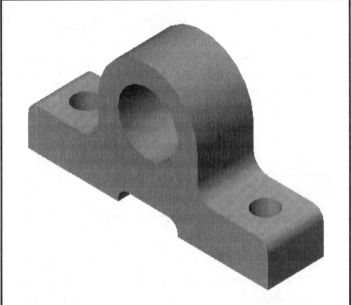

Figure 7-31. The Finished Pillow Block after all Design Modifications.

Exercise 7.2: Finite Element Analysis of a Piston

An internal combustion engine piston is a simple component, yet very complex variables affect its performance in service. Engine designers must consider friction, wear, temperature transients, fatigue, shock, corrosion, vibration, noise, and chemical and material properties among the many factors that affect engine performance. Small wonder that the automobile engine has undergone constant modification and improvement for more than 100 years, and that much work remains to be done.

In this exercise you will construct a 3-D solid model of an automobile engine piston. Then the material properties, loads, reactions, and constraints typical for such a part will be discussed. Finite element analysis will be used to visualize the resulting distributed stress and strain on the piston, and appropriate design changes will be ordered to improve part performance. The part will be analyzed again to determine the effect of the design changes.

Constructing the Model

We begin with a sketch for the base revolve. Open **ANSI-INCHES.prtdot** from your folder. Go to the pull-down **Tools** menu and select **Add-Ins**. Check **COSMOSWorks** from the available list. Then do a **Save As - Piston-1.sldprt**. Select **Front** as the sketch plane, go to **Sketch** mode, and create the profile as shown in Figure 7-32. When finished, use this sketch as the basis for your **Base Revolve**, which should appear as in Figure 7-33.

Next we will create the wristpin bearing journals, but first we must create a reference plane for the necessary sketch. Select the **Front** plane in the Feature Manager. Go to **Insert**, choose **Reference Geometry** and **Plane**. Use **Offset Distance** and enter **0.75-in.** (the direction of the offset is not important; we

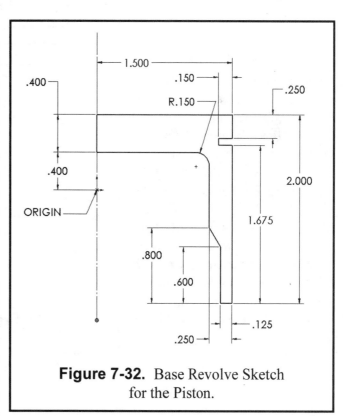

Figure 7-32. Base Revolve Sketch for the Piston.

will mirror this feature later). Use the green √ to complete the dialog and you will see that **Plane 1** has been created in the Feature Manager. Select **Plane 1** and create the **Sketch** shown in Figure 7-34. The **Tangent Arc** tool will assist you with this sketch. While still in the

Sketch mode, go to **Insert Boss Extrude** and choose the **Up To Next** option, then √ out of the dialog box. Rename this feature as **Journal** in the Feature Manager.

Next we will create the opposite Journal, which will be mirrored from the original. Highlight both the **Front plane** and the **Journal** icons in the Feature Manager (use Ctrl for a multiple selection) and then select the **Mirror** icon 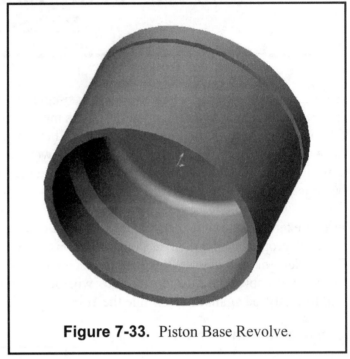 from the tool bar at left of the Feature Manager. You will then see the Journal previewed as a mirrored feature on the other side of the piston. Use √ to accept this and leave the dialogue. A new feature called **Mirror** will now appear under Journal in the Feature Manager, and your model should appear as in Figure 7-35.

Figure 7-33. Piston Base Revolve.

The final feature in the solid model will be the hole for the wrist pin (which we are not modeling). Select one of the two interior Journal faces, and go the **Sketch** mode. Draw a **Circle** in this sketch that is concentric with the **Tangent Arc** of the Journal and is 0.500-in. diameter (one way to create this circle is by using the **Offset** tool). When complete, perform a **Both Direction, Through All Cut Extrude** based on this sketch, and your completed model will appear in Figure 7-36.

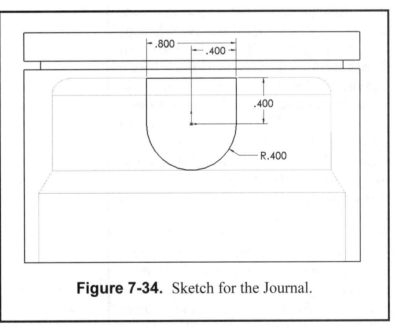

Figure 7-34. Sketch for the Journal.

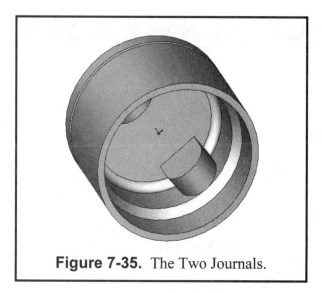

Figure 7-35. The Two Journals.

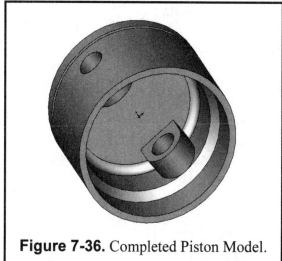

Figure 7-36. Completed Piston Model.

Finite Element Analysis of the Piston

Accurate modeling of the distributed stresses and strain in a real engine piston would require a high fidelity, time-dependent model that includes such factors as temperature distribution in addition to applied loads, counteracting forces, and friction. We can get a good idea of bounding levels of stress and strain if we assume steady state conditions at peak applied load on the piston; that is the basis for the discussion that follows. In addition, we will assume no temperature transients or gradients (constant temperature throughout the part).

Starting the Study

Set up a **Study** as you did in Exercise 7.1. Right click on the part name and select **Study**. Name it **Piston Study – your last name**, make it **Static** with **Solid Mesh** type (Figure 7-37).

Figure 7-37. Defining a Study.

Right mouse click on the part name under the Solids, (Figure 7-38). Select **FFE** in the solver dialog. From the COSMOSWorks menu choose **Apply/Edit Material**.

In the pop up window (Figure 7-39) select **From Library File – SolidWorks materials**, Assign **Aluminum Alloy -6061** to the **Piston**. Verify that the **"Type"** is set at **Linear Elastic Isotropic** and that the **"Units"** are set to **SI** and Click on **OK**.

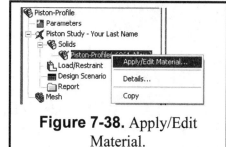

Figure 7-38. Apply/Edit Material.

Right click on the Study name in the Feature Manager Tree and select **Properties.** A window labeled **Static** indicating the type of study that will be conducted appears. Under the **OPTIONS** tab select **FFE** and Click **OK**.

Adding Restraints

The piston is constrained to move in only certain directions and modes. First select the outer cylindrical faces of the piston. Select the **Restraints** icon. Select **On Cylindrical Surface**. Under **Displacement** select all three choices, **Radial, Circumferential, and Axial**, (Figure 7-40). The value of each is **0.0**. Select out of this dialog.

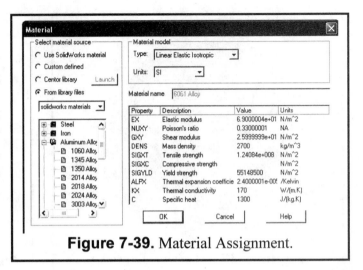

Figure 7-39. Material Assignment.

Figure 7-40.
Restraints.

Next the wrist pin journal holes will be constrained to remain straight and co-cylindrical (Note: this is NOT an accurate assumption but for the purpose of this simplified analysis the error will be small). Select both journal holes, and Select the **Restraints** icon as before. Select **On Cylindrical Surface**. Under the **Displacement** select all three choices, **Radial, Circumferential, and Axial,** (Figure 7-40). The value of each is **0.0**. Select out of the dialog.

Adding Loads

Now we apply external loads to the piston. We will model the distributed pressure of the combustion byproducts on the piston top face, and the reaction forces of the crankshaft transmitted to the piston journals via the wrist pin. Select the **top** face of the piston, Select the **Pressure** icon, and select **Normal to Selected Face**. Under the **Pressure Value,** set the value to **3,900,000 Pascals (Pa = N/m^2),** (Figure 7-41). Select out of the dialog.

Next select the cylindrical surfaces of the two journal holes. Select the **Force** icon. Under Force (per entity) choose the second box and enter the value of **35571 N,** (Figure 7-42). This total force will balance the integrated force of the distributed pressure on the piston top face.

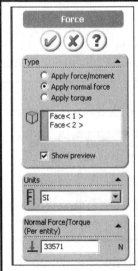

Figure 7-42.
Force.

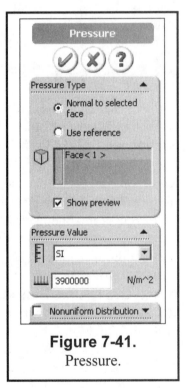

Figure 7-41.
Pressure.

Creating the Mesh

The Mesh is the method of dividing the solid model into an ordered set of finite elements; analysis of the equations of equilibrium/motion at each element, with boundary conditions due to the contribution of neighboring elements, is used to solve for distributed stress and strain and other continuous properties (the same method can be used to solve for electrodynamic and electrostatic behavior of a part or system).

In the COSMOSWorks feature manager, right click on **Mesh** and select **Create**. Set the mesh size to **3mm** (you may experiment with settings to create a different resolution, but the smaller the mesh the slower it will be to compute mesh). When you select out the mesh will appear on your piston as shown in Figure 7-43.

Running the Analysis

Run the static analysis by right clicking on the name of the **Study** in the COSMOSWorks Feature Manager and select **Run**. A dialog box will announce when the Run is complete.

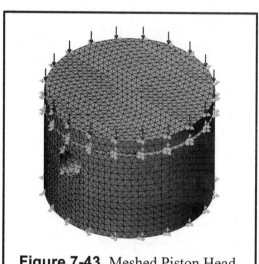

Figure 7-43. Meshed Piston Head.

Post Processing

Expand the Design Check folder in the Feature Manager. **Right click** on **Plot 1**, and select **Edit Definition**. Under **Criterion**, **Select Maximum von Mises** and under **Set Stress Limit** select **To Ultimate Strength**. In the Plot Results box, select **Non-Dimensional Stress Distribution**, then **Finish**. The resultant surface stresses are indicated on the piston by the color monograph. **Right click** on **Plot 1** of the **Design Check** and select **Print to get** a hard copy of this stress plot.

Explore the stresses on the piston. Where is the stress the highest? Where does it change most suddenly? It might be apparent that some local areas are stressed near to the ultimate strength of the material, while large regions of material may be very lightly stressed. This indicates a non-optimum design—the piston is not only operating near failure in some areas, but also it is too heavy overall.

Redesigning the Piston

Modify the piston design with two objectives—first, reduce the peak stress by adding a fillet or chamfer to the sharp corner where it occurs. Then, reduce the mass of the piston by removing material (using cuts or drafts) in selected non-critical areas of the piston, and calculate the reduction in mass due to the redesign. Verify that your new design doesn't move the region of peak stress to a new location within the piston.

Be creative! Look at a real automotive engine piston and see if you can tell where design engineers have tried to smooth and reduce peak stress, and cut to reduce total mass. Is there an optimum shape for a piston that will deliver highest specific power at lowest possible mass, with acceptable margin of safety?

Print a hard copy of your final design with the usual annotations and hand in to your instructor.

Computer Graphics Lab 8: Kinematics Animation and Rapid Prototyping

In Computer Graphics Lab 8, you will explode a previously built assembly file using SolidWorks "Assembly Exploder." You will set the direction and distance of the exploded parts of the assembly. You will then create a simple animation of this exploding assembly using SolidWorks "Animation Wizard." You will save the animation as an .AVI file that can be played on an external viewer, like Windows Media Players. You will also be briefly introduced to SolidWorks Physical Simulation capabilities. A second objective of this Computer Graphics Lab 8 is to produce an .STL (stereolithography) file of a SolidWorks part. The .STL file is then transferred to a rapid prototyping machine to make a physical prototype of the part.

ASSEMBLY TOOLBAR

In the earlier Computer Lab 5, you were introduced to the **Assembly Toolbar** as shown in Figure 8-1. When you open a completed assembly file, you can use these tools to manipulate the assembly components. When you click on the **Exploded View** icon, the **Explode** menu appears on the screen, as shown in Figure 8-2. This menu can be used to explode the assembly by manually editing the explode process.

For example, in Figure 8-3 the Pin of the Terminal Support assembly has been

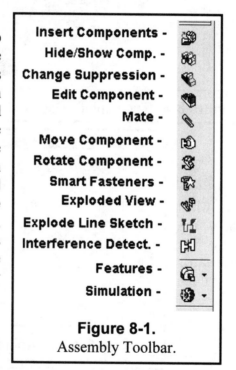

Figure 8-1.
Assembly Toolbar.

exploded upward as shown. The user first would highlight the **Part** window on the **Settings** tab (it turns pink) and then pick the Pin part on the assembly. The Pin part identification (like *pin-1@ wing base*) now appears in the window. Next, highlight the **Direction** window (it turns pink) and pick the direction arrow (like *Y@ wing base*). Then key in the **Distance** to be 6.00 inches. Then toggle the **Direction** button so the Pin goes upward. To preview, click the **Apply** button. To finish, click the **Done** button and *Chain 1* is done.

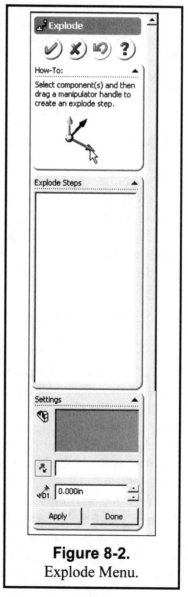

Figure 8-2.
Explode Menu.

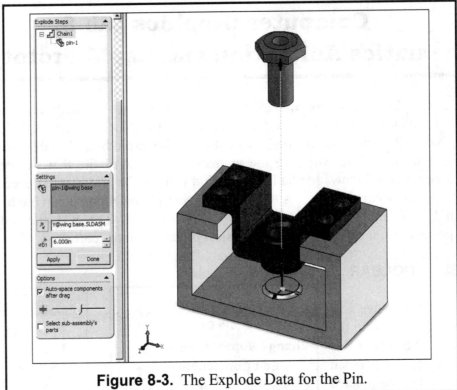

Figure 8-3. The Explode Data for the Pin.

ANIMATION WIZARD

The "Animation Wizard" is an easy tool to create simple animations when you have a part or assembly file loaded. It can be activated by first loading the SolidWorks **Animator** "Add-In" program. It has three features (see Figure 8-4):

       Rotate Model
       Explode Model
       Collapse Model

If you select **Rotate Model** it asks for an axis to rotate around and the number of rotations. You then get to the next menu (see Figure 8-5), which asks about the duration (in seconds) for the animation. In order to select the other two choices in the "Animation Wizard" you must first **Insert** an **Exploded View** of an assembly. You can then create an **Explode** animation or a **Collapse** (reverse of explode) animation.

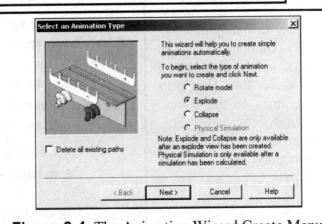

Figure 8-4. The Animation Wizard Create Menu.

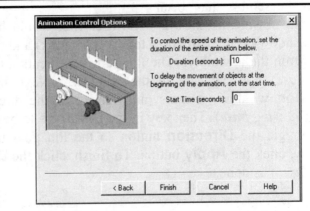

Figure 8-5. The Animation Control Options Menu.

ANIMATOR PULL-DOWN MENU

When you load the **Animator** "Add-in" module, the Animator pull-down menu will appear in the main menu on the top of the screen. There are several options you can select as shown in Figure 8-6.

New will launch the "Animation Controller and Script" area on the bottom of the screen (as shown later in Figure 8-7).

Options will display the "Animator Options" color palette.

Screen Capture will turn on the screen capture capability when you play an animation on the screen.

Customize Menu allows you to decide which options will appear on this pull-down menu.

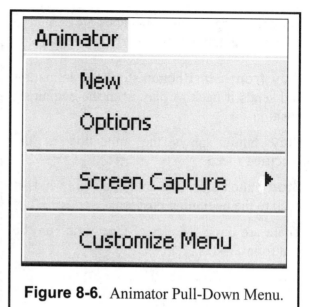

Figure 8-6. Animator Pull-Down Menu.

ANIMATION CONTROLLER AND SCRIPT

The "Animation Controller and Script" appears on the bottom of the screen when you select a **New** animation from the **Animator** pull-down menu, as shown in Figure 8-7.

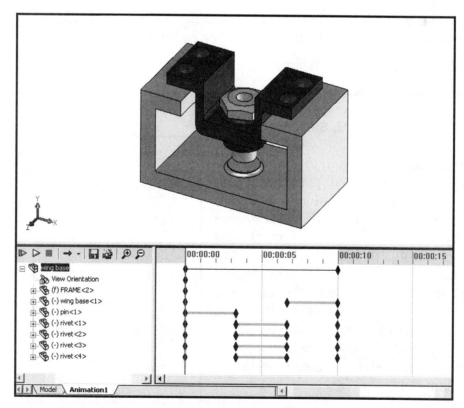

Figure 8-7. The Animation Controller and Script Area.

The following button commands are available on the "Animation Controller" (Figure 8-8).

Play from Start button stops the animation and sends it back to play from the beginning position.

Play button plays the animation at the specified speed.

Stop button stops the animation and sends it back to the beginning position.

There are three "Modes of Operation" on the controller.

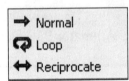

Figure 8-8. The Animation Controller.

Normal Mode button sets the animation to run once from start to end at the specified speed.

Loop Mode button sets the animation to run over and over again in a continuous loop.

Reciprocate Mode button sets the animation to first run forward, and then run backwards, and repeat this reciprocation in a continuous fashion.

Save as AVI File button will open the "Save Animation to File" menu and allows you to save the animation as an .AVI file. It can then be played on an external media player.

Animation Wizard launches the "Animation Wizard" tool (see Figures 8-4 and 8-5).

Zoom In and **Zoom Out** buttons allow you to zoom the script in or out on the screen.

INTRODUCTION TO PHYSICAL SIMULATION

Physical Simulation allows you to simulate the effects of motors, springs, and gravity on your assemblies. Physical Simulation combines simulation elements with SolidWorks tools such as mates and Physical Dynamics to move components around your assembly. If you pull down **View, Toolbars,** and click **Simulation,** the **Simulation Toolbar** will appear on the screen. You can move it to the left side under the Assembly Toolbar. The icons on the Simulation Toolbar are shown in Figure 8-9. These options include the ability to add a Linear Motor, Rotary Motor, a Linear Spring, or Gravity to your model.

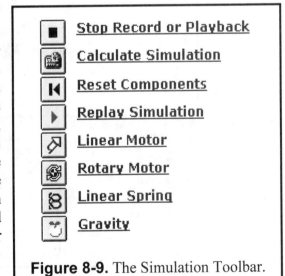

Figure 8-9. The Simulation Toolbar.

Exercise 8.1: Exploded Animation of the TERMINAL SUPPORT ASSEMBLY

Recall in Computer Graphics Lab 5, you created some assembly models in SolidWorks. If you created and saved the Terminal Support Assembly, you can now work this Exercise 8.1. If you created and saved the Swivel Eye Block Assembly, you should go to Exercise 8.2. If you did not save either assembly file, then you need to return to Computer Graphics Lab 5 and re-build one of the assemblies first and then return to this Lab 8.

LOADING THE ANIMATOR PLUG-IN

Before beginning this exercise, SolidWorks' Animator should be installed as an "Add-In" software package. Pull down the **Tools** Menu and click on **Add-Ins.** The "Add-Ins" Dialog box opens. Click on **SolidWorks Animator** and make sure its small box is checked (√). Then click on **OK.** This adds the Animator menu to the top menu (see earlier Figure 8-6)

EXPLODING THE ASSEMBLY

Pull down **File** and **Open** the previous **Terminal Support.sldasm** assembly file in your designated folder. You will create the animation by first exploding the assembly. To do this, choose the **Insert** menu and click on **Exploded View** (or click the Exploded View icon on the Assembly Toolbar). The "Explode" menu now appears in the Feature Manager area as shown in the earlier Figure 8-2.

Now the first part to explode is the Pin. Click in the **Part** area of **Settings** window (it turns pink). Next click on the Pin part of the model and the part gets selected using some SolidWorks code like *Pin-1@wing base*. Go to the model and pick the **upward direction arrow** to get the correct direction, named by a SolidWorks code like *Y@ wing base*. Then key in the **Distance** to be **6.00** inches. Then toggle the **Direction** button so the Pin goes upward. To preview, click the **Apply** button. To finish, click the **Done** button and *Explode Step 1* is done. These correct explode settings for the Pin part are shown in Figure 8-10.

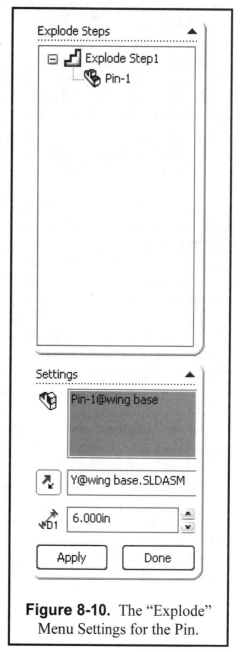

Figure 8-10. The "Explode" Menu Settings for the Pin.

New explode the four Rivets together. Click in the **Part** area of **Settings** window (it turns pink). Pick the four Rivets. They appear in the Part window using some SolidWorks code like *Rivet-1@wing base*, etc. Go to the model and pick the **upward direction arrow** to get the correct direction, named by a SolidWorks code like *Y@ wing base*. Then key in the **Distance** to be **5.00** inches. Then toggle the **Direction** button so the Rivets go upward. To preview, click the **Apply** button. To finish, click the **Done** button and *Explode Step 2* is done. These correct explode settings for the Rivet parts are shown in Figure 8-11.

Finally, explode the Wing Base part. . Click in the **Part** area of **Settings** window (it turns pink), and then pick the Wing Base on the assembly model. It appears in the Part window using some SolidWorks code like *Wing Base-1@wing base*. Go to the model and pick the **upward direction arrow** to get the correct direction, named by a SolidWorks code like *Y@ wing base*. Then key in the **Distance** to be **3.00** inches. Then toggle the **Direction** button so the Wing Base goes upward. To preview, click the **Apply** button. To finish, click the **Done** button and *Explode Step 3* is done. These correct explode settings for the Wing Base part are shown in Figure 8-12. The Terminal Support is now exploded, as shown in Figure 8-13.

Figure 8-11. "Explode" Settings for the Rivets.

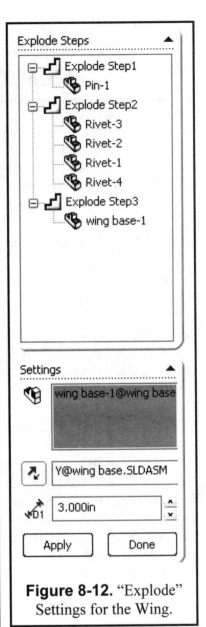

Figure 8-12. "Explode" Settings for the Wing.

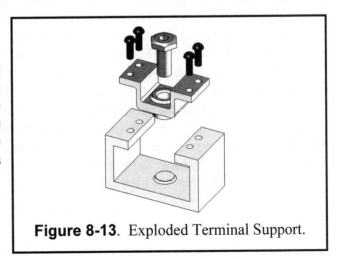

Figure 8-13. Exploded Terminal Support.

CREATING THE ANIMATION

Now you will create the animation using the automatic Animator Wizard. Click on **Animator** in the top menu bar and choose **New**. The "Animator Controller and Script" area appears on the bottom of the screen as shown in earlier Figure 8-7. Select the **Animation Wizard** button on the Controller (see the choices on Figure 8-8). Next click **on** the **Explode** radial dial on the "Select an Animation Type" menu. Then click the **Next** button. In the next dialog menu (see Figure 8-5) enter the animation "Duration" of **10** seconds and "Start Time" as **0**. Finally click the **Finish** button.

PLAYING THE ANIMATION

Study the various buttons on the "Animation Controller" as shown in earlier Figure 8-8. Press the **Play** button and see the animation on your screen. Try some of the other animation buttons. **Play** the animation in the **Normal Mode**. **Play** the animation in the **Loop Mode** and see the assembly move in a repeated fashion until you click **Stop**. **Play** the animation in the **Reciprocate Mode** and see the assembly move in a reciprocating mode until you click **Stop**. Try several combinations of options for this exploded animation (see Figure 8-14). When you have selected a desired animation mode, <u>show it to your instructor or lab teaching assistant</u>.

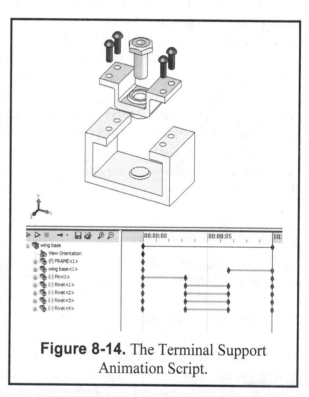

Figure 8-14. The Terminal Support Animation Script.

SAVING THE ANIMATION

Return to the "Animation Controller" buttons and select the **Save** button. The "Save Animation to File" menu now appears on the screen as shown in Figure 8-15. Name the file **Terminal Support** and use an **.AVI file** type. Use the **SolidWorks screen** as the Renderer and set the frames per second rate to **15**. Then click the **Save** button. Click on **OK** in the "Video Compression" dialog box that next appears, in order to accept the default settings. This causes the exploded model animation to be recorded to your file as well as played on screen. It may move slowly at this point because it is saving data to a file. <u>Note:</u> You may have to adjust your model viewport to fit the whole animation on your screen as it is being captured.

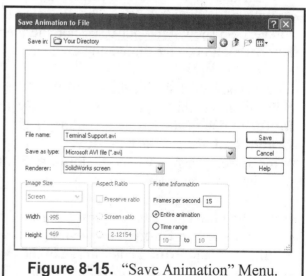

Figure 8-15. "Save Animation" Menu.

At this point you are finished with the animation, so you may want to **Save** your exploded assembly file as **EXPLODED TERMINAL SUPPORT**.

PHYSICAL SIMULATION EXAMPLE

Return to the original Terminal Support file. Pull down **File** and **Open** the previous **Terminal Support.sldasm** assembly file in your designated folder. Make sure it is collapsed and in the original mating position. If it is not collapsed, select the **Move Component** icon on the Assembly Toolbar, and move the Pin down to its mated position. Now you need to remove one of the mating constraints. Click the **Mates** tab ⊞ in the Feature Manager Tree, and see all the mated features for the Terminal Support Assembly. Right click (RMB) on the **Coincident(X) Wing Base<1>,Pin** mate, and then select **Delete** as shown in Figure 8-16. Then answer **Yes** to the "Confirm Delete" menu. This allows you to move the Pin upward.

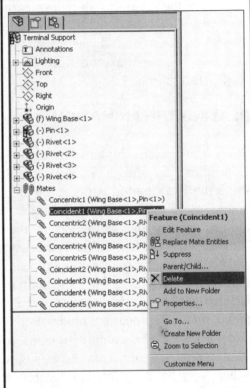

Figure 8-16. Deleting the Coincident Mate between the Pin and the Wing Base Will Allow You to Move the Pin.

Select the **Move Component** icon on the Assembly Toolbar, and move the Pin up from its mated position to be above the rest of the mated assembly. Next select the **Rotary Motor** icon from the Simulation Toolbar (see Figure 8-9). Click on the cylindrical shaft of the Pin. Next set the **Velocity** slider to the middle speed as shown in Figure 8-17. Then click the green (√) check. Now select the **Calculate Simulation** icon button on the Simulation Toolbar. The computer will now calculate the physical simulation and play it on the screen as shown in Figure 8-18. The Pin simulation will rotate forever. So show it to your instructor and then press the **Stop Record** button on the Simulation Toolbar.

You can now click the **Replay Simulation** icon button on the Simulation Toolbar if you want. Now try to add a **Linear Motor** to one of the Rivets. You may have to first **Delete** a **Coincident** mate to get the Rivet to move away from the Wing Base. Then click the **Calculate Simulation** icon to start the new simulation.

Before you leave the lab, your instructor may need a hard copy of your work. So **Open** your previously saved assembly file, **Explode** it, and **Print** a color image of the exploded assembly on a Title Block" drawing sheet, as shown in Figure 8-19.

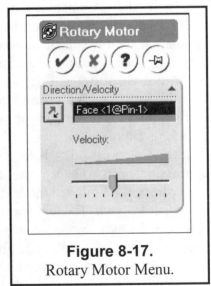

Figure 8-17. Rotary Motor Menu.

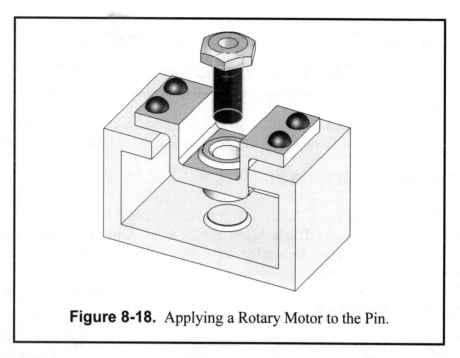

Figure 8-18. Applying a Rotary Motor to the Pin.

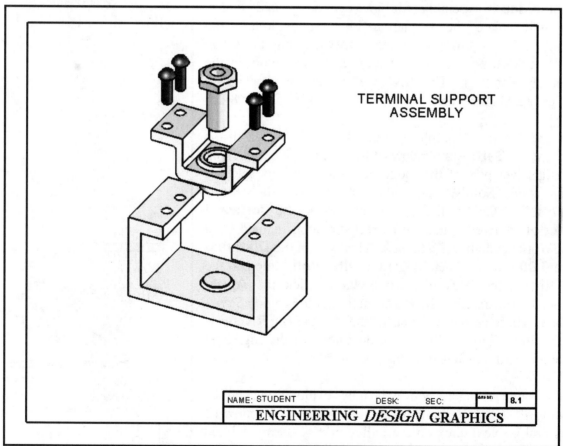

TERMINAL SUPPORT
ASSEMBLY

NAME: STUDENT		DESK:	SEC:	GRd DE:	8.1

ENGINEERING *DESIGN* GRAPHICS

Figure 8-19. The Exploded Terminal Support Assembly Image on a Title Block Sheet.

Exercise 8.2: Exploded Animation of the SWIVEL EYE BLOCK ASSEMBLY

Recall in Computer Graphics Lab 5, you created some assembly models in SolidWorks. If you created and saved the Swivel Eye Block Assembly, then you should work this Exercise 8.2.

LOADING THE ANIMATOR PLUG-IN

Before beginning this exercise, SolidWorks' Animator should be installed as an "Add-In" software package. Pull down the **Tools** Menu and click on **Add-Ins.** The "Add-Ins" Dialog box opens. Click on **SolidWorks Animator** and make sure its small box is checked (√). Then click on **OK.** This adds the Animator menu to the top menu.

EXPLODING THE ASSEMBLY

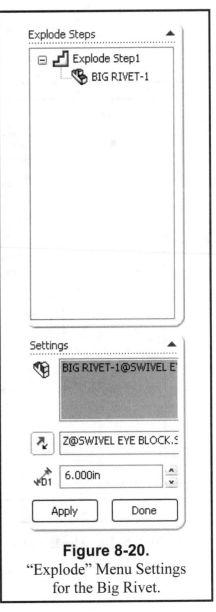

Pull down **File** and **Open** the previous **Swivel Eye Block.sldasm** assembly file in your designated folder. You will create the animation by first exploding the assembly. To do this, choose the **Insert** menu and click on **Exploded View** (or click the Exploded View icon on the Assembly Toolbar). The "Explode" menu now appears in the Feature Manager area as shown in the earlier Figure 8-2.

Now the first part to explode is the Big Rivet. Click in the **Part** area of **Settings** window (it turns pink). Next click on the Big Rivet part of the model and the part gets selected using some SolidWorks code like *Sblock Big Rivet-1@Sblock*. Go to the model and pick the **leftward direction arrow** to get the correct direction, named by a SolidWorks code like *Z@Sblock*. Then key in the **Distance** to be **6.00** inches. Then toggle the **Direction** button so the Big Rivet goes leftward. To preview, click the **Apply** button. To finish, click the **Done** button and *Explode Step 1* is done. These correct explode settings for the Big Rivet part are shown in Figure 8-20. You should now see the Big Rivet move leftward 6 inches from the assembly.

In the same manner, you will now explode the pulley downward. Click in the **Part** area of **Settings** window (it turns pink). Next click on the Pulley part of the model and the part gets selected using some SolidWorks code like *Sblock Pulley-1@Sblock*. Go to the model and pick the **upward direction arrow** to get the correct direction, named by a SolidWorks code like *Y@Sblock*. Then key in

Figure 8-20.
"Explode" Menu Settings for the Big Rivet.

the **Distance** to be **4.00** inches. Then toggle the **Direction** button so the Pulley goes downward. To preview, click the **Apply** button. To finish, click the **Done** button and *Explode Step 2* is done. These correct explode settings for the Pulley part are shown in Figure 8-21. You should now see the Pulley move downward 4 inches from the assembly.

You can complete the exploding of the remaining parts by repeating the above steps, one-by-one, for each part. These steps are as follows.

- Click in the **Part** area of **Settings** window (it turns pink).
- Click on the desired **Part** in the assembly model.
- Click on the correct direction arrow.
- Key in the correct **Distance** value.
- Toggle the **Direction** button to get the correct explode direction.
- Click the **Apply** button to preview the explode.
- Click the **Done** button to complete the Chain.

Use the following data table for completing this Swivel Eye Block assembly explosion process. Note that the Spacer will stay in place and will not move in this explosion process.

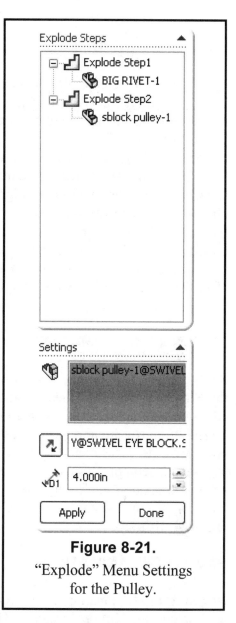

Figure 8-21.
"Explode" Menu Settings for the Pulley.

Step	Component	Direction	Distance Value
Explode Step 3	Small Rivet 1	Leftward	6.00 inches
Explode Step 4	Small Rivet 2	Leftward	6.00 inches
Explode Step 5	Front Base Plate	Leftward	3.00 inches
Explode Step 6	Back base Plate	Rightward	3.00 inches
Explode Step 7	Eye Hook	Upward	3.50 inches

Once this table is completed, click the **OK** button to close the "Explode" menu. You should now have an exploded Swivel Eye Hook assembly as shown in Figure 8-22.

CREATING THE ANIMATION

Now you will create the animation using the automatic Animator Wizard. Click on **Animator** in the top menu bar and choose **New**. The "Animator Controller and Script" area appears on the bottom of the screen as shown in earlier Figure 8-7. Select the **Animation Wizard** button on the Controller (see the choices on Figure 8-8). Next click **on the Explode** radial dial on the "Select an Animation Type" menu. Then click the **Next** button. In the next dialog menu (see Figure 8-5) enter the animation "Duration" of **10** seconds and "Start Time" as **0**. Finally click the **Finish** button.

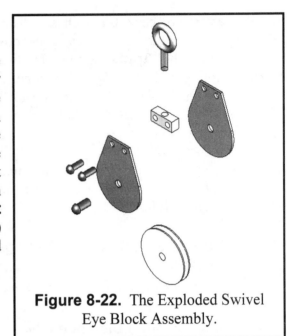

Figure 8-22. The Exploded Swivel Eye Block Assembly.

PLAYING THE ANIMATION

Study the various buttons on the "Animation Controller" as shown in earlier Figure 8-8. Press the **Play** button and see the animation on your screen. Try some of the other animation buttons. **Play** the animation in the **Normal Mode**. **Play** the animation in the **Loop Mode** and see the assembly move in a repeated fashion until you click **Stop**. **Play** the animation in the **Reciprocate Mode** and see the assembly move in a reciprocating mode until you click **Stop**. Try several combinations of options for this exploded animation. When you have selected a desired animation mode, show it to your instructor or lab teaching assistant. At this point, you may want to **Save** your exploded assembly file as **EXPLODED SWIVEL EYE BLOCK.sldasm**.

SAVING THE ANIMATION

Return to the "Animation Controller" buttons and select the **Save** button. The "Save Animation to File" menu now appears on the screen as shown in Figure 8-23. Name the file **Swivel Eye Block** and use an **.AVI file** type. Use the **Solidworks screen** as the Renderer and set the frames per second rate to **15**. Then click the **Save** button. Click on **OK** in the "Video Compression" dialog box that next appears, in order to accept the default settings. This causes the exploded model animation to be recorded to your file as well as played on screen. It may move slowly at this point because it is saving data to a file. Note: You may have to adjust your model viewport to fit the whole animation on your screen as it is being captured.

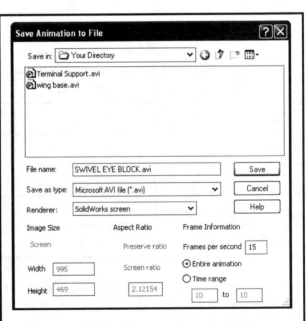

Figure 8-23. "Save Animation" Menu.

PHYSICAL SIMULATION EXAMPLE

Return to the original Swivel Eye Block. Pull down **File** and **Open** the previous **Swivel Eye Block** assembly file in your designated folder. Make sure it is collapsed and in the original mating position (see Figure 5-46). If it is not collapsed, select the **Move Component** icon on the Assembly Toolbar, and move the parts into their mated positions. Now you need to remove some of the mating constraints. Click the **Mates** tab ⊞ in the Feature Manager Tree, and see all the mated features for the Terminal Support Assembly. Right click (RMB) on the **Coincident(X) Spacer<1>, Base Plate<1>** mate, and then select **Delete** as shown in Figure 8-24. Then answer **Yes** to the "Confirm Delete" menu. Continue this process and **Delete** <u>all</u> the mates associated with the Front Base Plate, <u>all</u> the mates associated with the three Rivets, and the Distance mate between the Spacer and the Eye Hook.

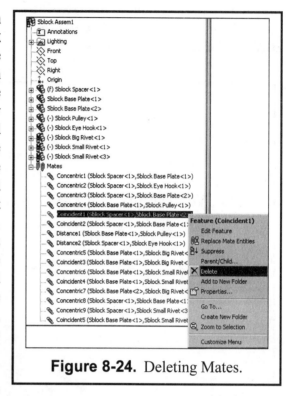

Figure 8-24. Deleting Mates.

Select the **Move Component** icon on the Assembly Toolbar, and move all three Rivets away from the assembly. Then move the front Base Plate away from the assembly. Finally move the Eye Hook up from the assembly. See Figure 8-25 as a preview of the current screen arrangement. Next select the **Rotary Motor** icon from the Simulation Toolbar (see Figure 8-9). Click on the flat circular front face of the Pulley. Next set the **Velocity** slider to the middle speed (see previous Figure 8-17). Then click the green (√) check. Now select the **Calculate Simulation** icon button on the Simulation Toolbar. The computer will now calculate the physical simulation and play it on the screen as shown in Figure 8-25. The Pulley simulation will rotate forever. So <u>show it to your instructor</u> and then press the **Stop Record or Playback** button on the Simulation Toolbar. You can now click the **Replay Simulation** icon button on the Simulation Toolbar if you want.

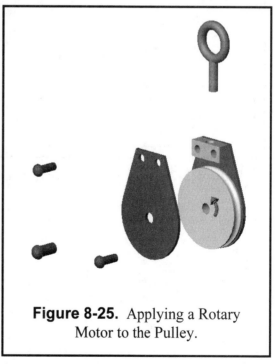

Figure 8-25. Applying a Rotary Motor to the Pulley.

Now try to add a **Linear Motor** to one of the Rivets or the Eye Hook. You may have to first **Delete** a **Coincident** mate to get the Part to move away from the assembly model. Then click the **Calculate Simulation** icon to start the new simulation.

Before you leave the lab, your instructor may need a hard copy of your work. So **Open** your previously saved assembly file, **Explode** it, and **Print** a color image of the exploded assembly on the Title Block drawing sheet, as shown in Figure 8-26. Save your drawing as **SWIVEL EYE BLOCK ASSEMBLY.slddrw**.

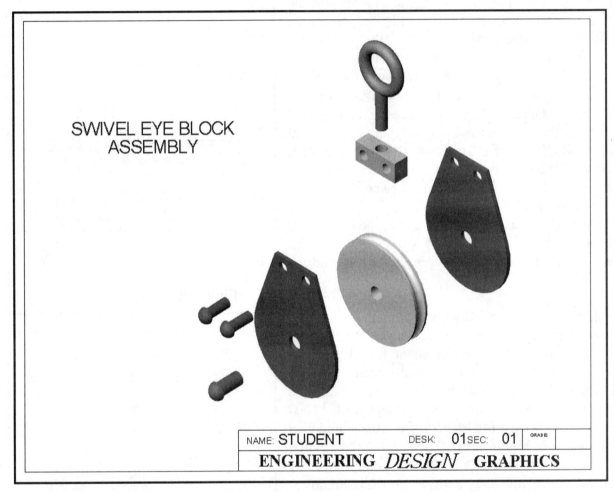

SWIVEL EYE BLOCK ASSEMBLY

NAME: STUDENT   DESK: 01 SEC: 01   GRADE

ENGINEERING *DESIGN* GRAPHICS

Figure 8-26. The Exploded Swivel Eye Block Assembly Image on a Title Block Sheet.

Exercise 8.3: Rapid Prototyping of a Solid Model Part

In this Exercise 8.3, you will build a solid model (or presumably already have one built), as assigned by your instructor. You will then save it in a file format that is the standard in the rapid prototyping industry. This file format is called stereolithography and is abbreviated .STL. You will then send your .STL file to an available rapid prototyping machine to make a rapid physical model of your part.

SAVING THE SOLID MODEL AS A STEREOLITHOGRAPHY (.STL) FILE

You can now build your **New** solid model in SolidWorks, or **Open** a model that has already been built. When you have completed the solid model, do a **Save As**, select "Save as Type" and select **.STL** Files (see Figure 8-27). Some example rapid physical prototypes of solid models are shown in Figure 8-28.

Note: If you need some ideas for solid models for this exercise, examine the accompanying Assignments 8.3.1 to 8.3.4.

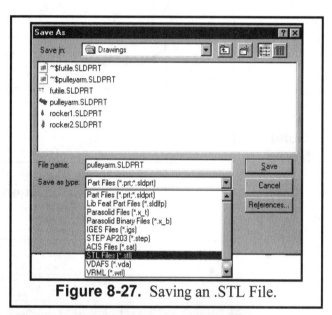

Figure 8-27. Saving an .STL File.

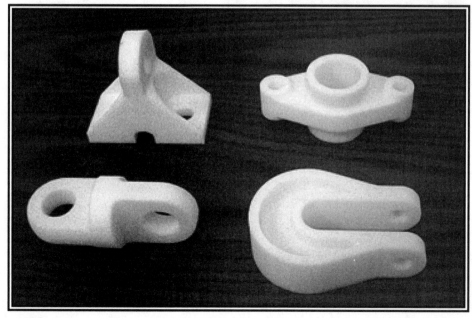

Figure 8-28. Some Rapid Prototype Models of Parts Shown in Assignments 8.3.1 to 8.3.4.

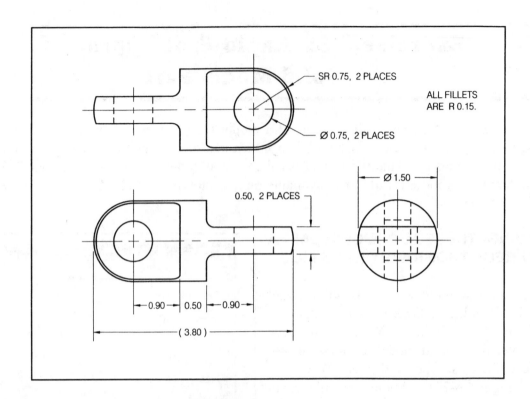

Solid Model

SR 0.75, 2 PLACES

ALL FILLETS
ARE R 0.15.

Ø 0.75, 2 PLACES

0.50, 2 PLACES

Ø 1.50

0.90   0.50   0.90

(3.80)

Assignment 8.3.1

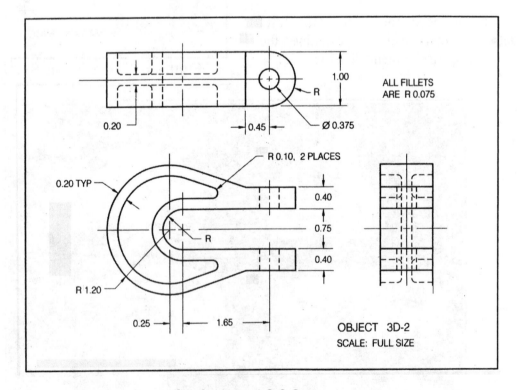

Solid Model

1.00

ALL FILLETS
ARE R 0.075

R

0.20

0.45

Ø 0.375

R 0.10, 2 PLACES

0.20 TYP

0.40

0.75

R

0.40

R 1.20

0.25   1.65

OBJECT 3D-2
SCALE: FULL SIZE

Assignment 8.3.2

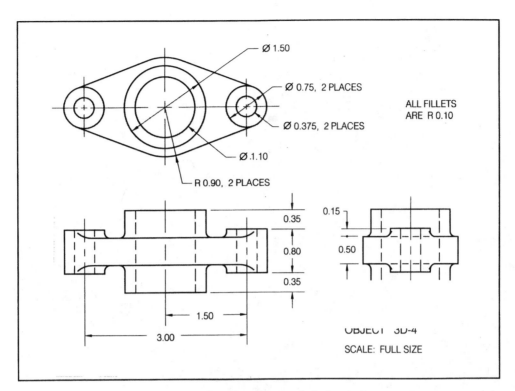

Solid
Model

Assignment 8.3.3

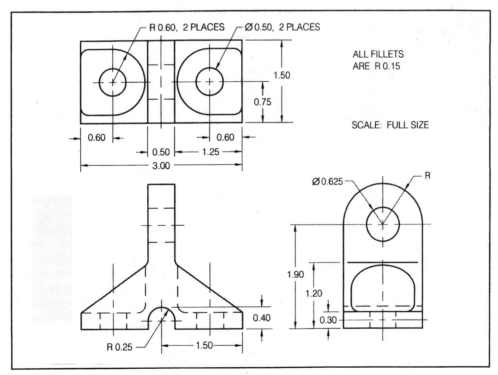

**Solid
Model**

Assignment 8.3.4

Notes:

Computer Graphics Lab 9:
Section Views in 3-D and 2-D

In Computer Graphics Lab 9, you will learn how to make section views from solid models. In each exercise, you will build a 3-D solid model of a part. You will then use a "Display Section View" function in SolidWorks that allows you to temporarily remove part of the solid model (e.g. the front half) to visualize the internal features of the 3-D part. You will open a Title Block in SolidWorks, and drag and drop the solid model into the Title Block. SolidWorks automatically will then project three orthographic views (front, top, and right side) of the part. You can then use a function in SolidWorks that allows you to create a section drawing view of the object.

VIEWING 3-D SECTION VIEWS

The section view of a 3-D solid model can be displayed by accessing the **View** pull down menu, then select **Display** and **Section View** as shown in Figure 9-1. When you select, the "Section View" item a menu appears on the screen as shown in Figure 9-2. With this menu, you can select the cutting plane (e.g. Front plane), the position of that cutting plane relative to the origin, and which side of the model to show. You

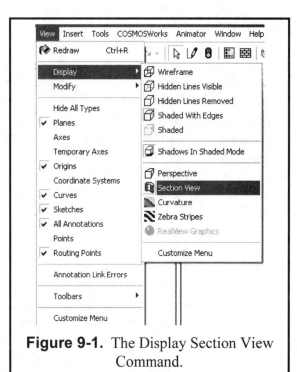

Figure 9-1. The Display Section View Command.

can then preview the 3-D section view of the model as shown in Figure 9-3. You can then return to the **View** pull down menu, select **Display** and deselect the **Section View** command to re-display the full 3-D solid model image.

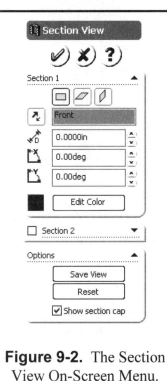

Figure 9-2. The Section View On-Screen Menu.

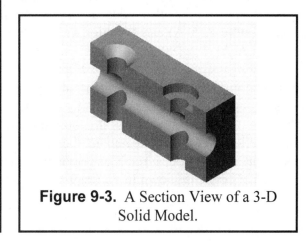

Figure 9-3. A Section View of a 3-D Solid Model.

CREATING 2-D SECTION VIEWS ON A DRAWING SHEET

A 2-D section view of a model can be created in a drawing file. First you must open a **TITLE BLOCK (INCHES or METRIC).drwdot** file. You start with the title block and then "drag and drop" the 3-D solid model onto the drawing sheet. SolidWorks is designed to automatically make a three-view orthographic layout of the model once it is dropped onto the sheet. This then becomes the starting point for making a detailed engineering drawing. From here, you can add centerlines, dimensions, notes, and title block information. One other thing you can do is to make a section view on the drawing.

You first decide which view will be the source for a section view projection. For example, the top view could be the source for projecting a full section in the front view. Select the Front view and **Delete** it. **Sketch** a **Line** that represents the cutting plane line on this source view. Then select the **Insert** pull-down menu, select **Drawing View** and then **Section**, as shown in Figure 9-4.

A dynamic section view now appears on the screen that you can move away from, but aligned with, the source view. For example, if the source view is the top view, then the front section view would be aligned vertically with the top view. Since SolidWorks cannot anticipate which side of the source view you want to project from, you have the option to "Flip Direction" of the section view. SolidWorks also adds a labeled cutting plane line (e.g. A-A) and a section view title (e.g. Section A-A).

For example, the solid model part of Figure 9-3 was dropped into a drawing sheet. A line was drawn across the full width of the top view, and a full section view was created in the front view using the above procedure. The resultant drawing for this example is shown in Figure 9-5.

Figure 9-4. Inserting A Section View on a Drawing Sheet.

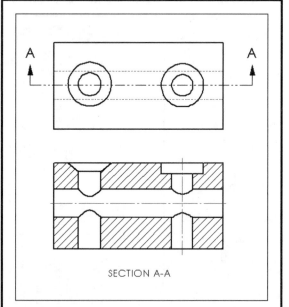

SECTION A-A

Figure 9-5. Creating a Labeled Section View on a 2-D Drawing Sheet.

Exercise 9.1: ROD BASE SECTION VIEWS

In this Exercise 9.1, you will build a solid model of the Rod Base using SolidWorks commands that you have learned in previous labs. You will display a 3-D section view of the model to visualize the internal features of the model. Next you will "drag and drop" the model onto a drawing sheet and then create a 2-D section view of the part. To get started, you will first build the solid model part.

BUILDING THE ROD BASE

Open your **ANSI-INCHES.prtdot** in SolidWorks. Immediately **SAVE AS – ROD BASE.sldprt**. Select the **Front** plane and start a new **Sketch**. Draw a vertical **Centerline** through the origin about 2 inches high from the origin. Sketch the given profile in Figure 9-6 using the **Line** tool. Apply the given dimension values using the **Dimension** tool. This will be "Sketch1" for the part.

Select the **Revolve Base** feature icon and revolve the profile into a solid using a **360** degrees angle. This forms the base part as suggested by Figure 9-7.

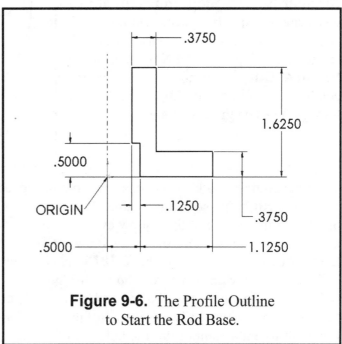

Figure 9-6. The Profile Outline to Start the Rod Base.

Now add a **Chamfer** design feature to the *top inner edge* of the through hole. Use a **Distance-Distance** parameter definition, with both distance values being **0.125** inches. Next add three **Fillet** design features to the following edges.

1. *Top outer edge* of the upright cylinder.
2. *Intersection edge* between the upright cylinder and the base plate.
3. *Top outer edge* of the base plate.

Use a common fillet radius of **0.0625** inches. When you are finished with the fillets, your part should look like Figure 9-7.

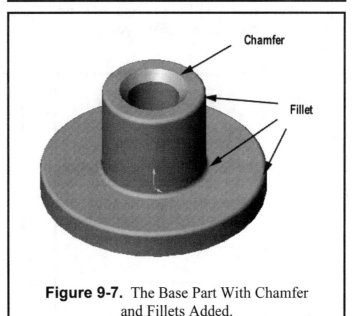

Figure 9-7. The Base Part With Chamfer and Fillets Added.

Now click on the top surface of the base plate of the Rod Base (it should turn *green*). Also chose a **Top** view orientation and select the **Sketch** icon. Sketch a **Circle** on this base plate surface and align it with the origin. **Dimension** its diameter to be **0.3125** inches and its distance from the origin to be **1.1825** inches. Now use the **Circular Sketch Step and Repeat** tool to create **4** equally spaced circles (total angle = 360) along this base plate, as suggested in Figure 9-8. Now execute an **Extrude Cut** command and use an end condition of **Through All** to create four through holes on the base plate.

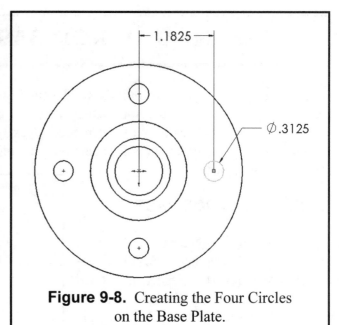

Figure 9-8. Creating the Four Circles on the Base Plate.

The final feature to add is the small pinhole that goes through one side of the upright cylinder. Select the **Right** plane in the Feature Manager and a **Right** view orientation. *Note:* The right plane is in the middle of the hollow cylinder, so you are not actually sketching on any surface of the part. Now in the **Sketch** mode, draw a **Circle** on this right plane, aligned with the origin. **Dimension** its diameter to be **0.1875** inches and its distance from the top surface of the cylinder to be **0.325** inches, as shown in Figure 9-9. Now **Extrude Cut** the hole through the right side of the cylinder wall using an **Up to Surface** end condition in "Direction 1," where the "up to" surface selected is the outer surface of the upright cylinder. *Note*: You could also just use a **Blind** end condition for the hole with the distance being around **1.50** inches. Either way, your model of the Rod Base is complete and it should look like Figure 9-10 in an **Isometric** view. At this point you can **Save** your part in your designated folder and name it **ROD BASE**.

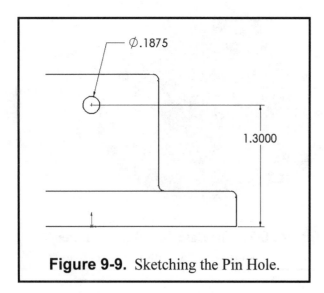

Figure 9-9. Sketching the Pin Hole.

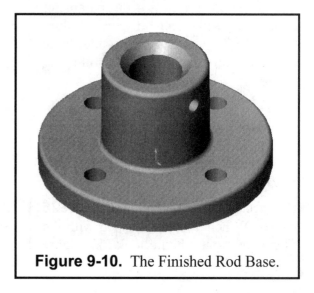

Figure 9-10. The Finished Rod Base.

MAKING A 3-D SECTION VIEW OF THE ROD BASE

You will now make a 3-D section view of the Rod Base model. First select the cutting plane by clicking the **Front** plane in the Feature Manager. Next pull down **View**, select **Display**, and then select **Section View**. The "Section View" on-screen menu now appears (refer back to Figure 9-2). Leave the "Section Position" at **0.0000** inches (middle of model), check (√) **on** the "Flip the Side to View," and then press the **Display** button on the menu. Notice the preview arrow pointing in the back direction on the model, which is the correct direction for the section view. So then click **OK** to close the menu. You should now have a 3-D full section view of the Rod Base showing a cut-away view of the part, as shown in Figure 9-11.

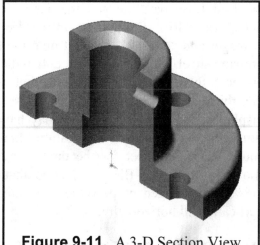

Figure 9-11. A 3-D Section View of the Rod Base.

If instructed to do so, obtain a document of this 3-D section view. Using **Insert Annotations**, add a **Note** with your name and class data. Then **Print** a shaded hardcopy of the 3-D Rod Base model for submission. Now return to the **View** pull down menu, re-select **Display**, and then re-select **Section View** again to turn **off** the 3-D section view, or select the Section View icon. *Do not* **Close** your solid model file yet, because you will need it for the next phase of this exercise; however, **SAVE** your solid as **ROD BASE.sldprt**.

INSERTING THE ROD BASE ON A TITLE BLOCK

At this point you will make a three-view layout of your model on a Title Block sheet. Open the file **TITLEBLOCK-INCHES.drwdot** from your folder and immediately **SAVE AS – ROD BASE.slddrw**.

Before you start the projection, there are some general settings that you need to make. Pull down **Tools** and select **Options**. Click the **Drawings, Display Type** tab. Check the dot (•) on the "Hidden lines visible" option and check the dot (•) on the tangent edges "Removed" option as shown in Figure 9-12. Next click the **Drawings, Area Hatch** tab. Select the **ANSI31** (Iron Brick Stone) "Pattern" option. Set the "Scale" to **1.000** and the Angle" to **0** degrees, as shown in Figure 9-13. Also go to **Document Properties, Line Font, Section Line** and change the thickness to **Thick**.

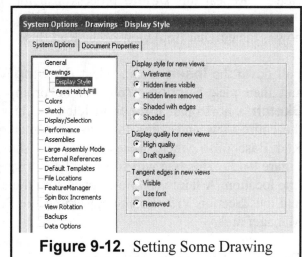

Figure 9-12. Setting Some Drawing Display Options.

Now pull down **Window** and select **Tile Vertically**. You now can see the two files: the Rod Base part file and the Title Block. Select the "Rod Base" part in its Feature Manager and "drag and drop" it onto the new drawing sheet. SolidWorks will automatically project a three-view orthographic layout using the third angle projection you just set, as displayed in Figure 9-14. You may have to right click on Sheet 1 in the Feature Manager and select Edit Sheet for the three views to show on the Title Block. Notice that the views are arranged properly, and are aligned vertically and horizontally.

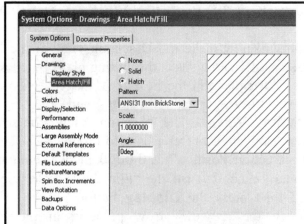

Figure 9-13. Setting Some Hatch Pattern Options.

MAKING A 2-D SECTION VIEW OF THE ROD BASE

You will only keep the top circular view of the rod base and use it as the source view to insert a full section view. You will not need to access the Rod Base model file anymore, so *maximize* the Title Block sheet by clicking its box in the upper right corner. Right mouse click (**RMB**) on the border of the front view border. On the pop-up menu, select **Delete**. Then, on the on-screen menu, answer **Yes** to the question "*Do you really want to delete this view*?" Repeat this **Delete** process also for the right side view. The only view remaining now is the circular (top) view of the Rod Base.

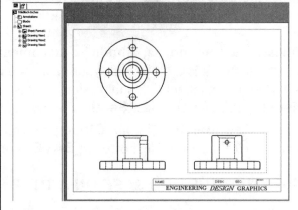

Figure 9-14. The Three Views of the Rod Base.

Pull down the **Insert** menu, select **Drawing View**, and then pick **Section**. You will be prompted to **Sketch** a horizontal **Line** from left to right across the entire view and going through the center of the Rod Base (also where the *origin* is) as shown in Figure 9-15. This line will serve as the cutting plane line location. A faint view now appears on the screen and the "Section View" menu appears in the Feature Manager area.

Drag this faint view down below the top view. Notice the vertical alignment between the two views is maintained as you move the section view. Also a cutting plane line labeled **A-A** appears where you drew the last line.

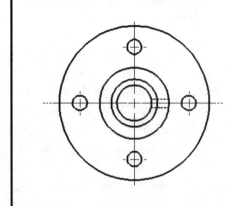

Figure 9-15. Drawing a Line for the Cutting Plane in the Top View.

9-6

Find a good position and click the **LMB** to fix the section view in that position. You now have a drawing with a section view that is labeled **Section A-A**, as indicated in Figure 9-17. If the arrows are pointing downward, check the box in the menu that will flip direction. Also, turn off the hidden lines in the Section view.

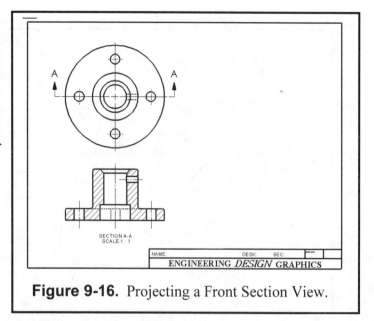

Figure 9-16. Projecting a Front Section View.

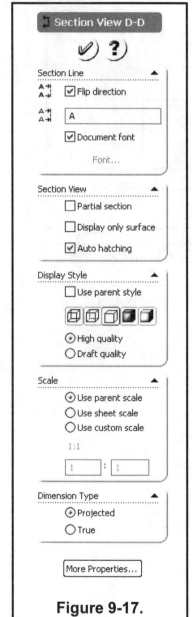

Figure 9-17.

The section view drawing may not be perfect. For example, the centerlines may not be showing. Select **INSERT, Annotations. Centerline**. You may want to increase the font size of the "Section A-A" label to **18 point**. Now reinsert the right side view. Select **INSERT Drawing view – Projected view**. Activate the section view and you will see a frame following the cursor as you move it toward the right of the section view. When you reach the desire location, click the left mouse button to position the view. This ensures that the right side view lines up with the section view. Also insert **Drawing view - Model – Isometric** with a custom scale of 1:2 in the upper right hand corner of the sheet. **Delete** the Center Marks for the four small holes in the top view. **Draw** a circle – centered at the origin with the radius to the center of one of the small holes. Immediately **right click** on the circle just drawn and change the **Properties** to **Construction**. See Figure 9-19 for an example of the finished drawing. Use **Insert**, **Annotations**, and **Note** to add a **ROD BASE** title and **SCALE 1:1** to the drawing as shown in Figure 9-18. Use caps, **Arial** font for all the labels. Use **20 point** font for the "Rod Base" title and **12 point** font for all the other annotations.

When you are finished you should **Save** your drawing file as **ROD BASE.slddrw** in your designated folder (*note*: its extension is now **.slddrw**). A finished section view drawing, with title block and pictorial, is shown in Figure 9-18 in a **Print Preview**. Then **Print** a hard copy of the drawing to submit to your instructor.

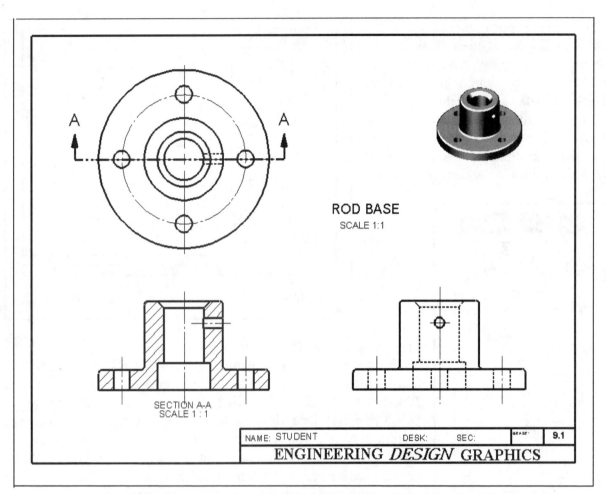

ROD BASE
SCALE 1:1

SECTION A-A
SCALE 1 : 1

NAME: STUDENT   DESK: SEC: GRADE: 9.1

ENGINEERING *DESIGN* GRAPHICS

Figure 9-18. The Finished Section View Drawing of the Rod Base.

Exercise 9.2: TENSION CABLE BRACKET
Section Views

In this Exercise 9.2, you will build a solid model of the Tension Cable Bracket using SolidWorks commands that you have learned in previous labs. You will display a 3-D section view of the model to visualize the internal features of the model. Next you will "drag and drop" the model onto a drawing sheet and then create a 2-D section view of the part. To get started, you will first build the solid model part.

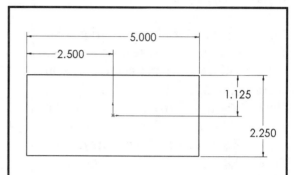

Figure 9-19. The Initial Outline to Start the Part.

BUILDING THE TENSION CABLE BRACKET

Open your **ANSI-INCHES.prtdot** in SolidWorks. Immediately **SAVE AS – TENSION CABLE BRACKET.sldprt**. Select the **Top** plane and start a new **Sketch**. Draw a **Rectangle** centered at the origin as indicated in Figure 9-19. Apply the given dimension values using the **Dimension** tool. This will be "Sketch1" for the part. Select the **Extrude Base** feature icon and extrude it **0.250** inches upward from the plane. This is the base plate.

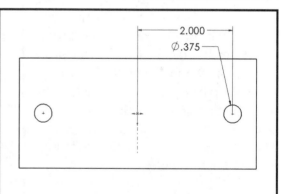

Figure 9-20. Sketching the Two Plate Holes.

Now click on the top surface of this base plate (it turns green). **Sketch** the right side **Circle** on the top plate and **Dimension** it as shown in Figure 9-20. Add a horizontal relationship between the hole and the origin. Draw a vertical **Centerline** and **Mirror** the circle to the left side. Next **Extrude Cut** the holes **Through All** with a **Taper** angle of **15** degrees, as suggested in Figure 9-21. This results in the two base plate tapered holes.

Now return to the top surface of the base plate and start another **Sketch** on it. Draw another **Circle**, centered at the *origin* and with a *diameter* of **1.750** inches. Execute an **Extrude Boss** command with the following data:

    "Direction 1" (up)   = **Blind 0.875** inches
    "Direction 2" (down)= **Blind 0.875** inches

You now have bosses going in each direction.

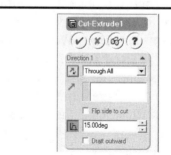

Figure 9-21. The Data for the Holes.

Now click on the top surface of the top boss (it turns green) and **Sketch** a **Circle** on it. Center the circle at the *origin* and give it a *diameter* of **1.000** inches. Next **Extrude Cut** the hole **Through All** with a **Taper** angle of **7.5** degrees. This makes a big tapered hole through the part as shown as a wireframe in Figure 9-22.

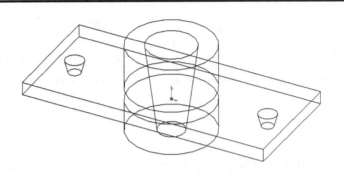

Figure 9-22. Wireframe Model of Cable Bracket at This Stage in the Building Process.

You will now add some triangular supports to the boss feature. These will be offset from the center, so you first need to add a new sketching plane. Click on the **Front** plane in the Feature Manager. Pull down **Insert**, select **Reference Geometry**, and then select **Plane**. Make the new **Plane1** a distance **0.750** inches from and in front of the Front plane, and then click the (√) button. The new Plane1 is now added to the Feature Manager. Click on this **Plane1** and make a **Sketch**. Sketch three **Lines** that form a triangle and **Dimension** them as shown in Figure 9-23. Draw a vertical **Centerline** through the origin, holding down the CTRL key select the three lines, and then select **Mirror**. This gives you a mirrored image of the triangle.

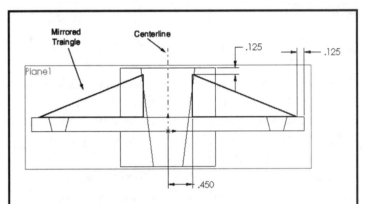

Figure 9-23. Sketching and Mirroring a Triangular Support on Plane1

Now execute an **Extrude-Boss** for this sketch, using a **Blind** distance of **0.250** inches towards the direction of the origin (into the object). You now have two triangular supports on the front side of the object. While holding down the CTRL button select the **Front** plane and the last extrusion in the Feature Manager and select the **Mirror Feature** icon, then click the (√) button. You now have a part as shown in Figure 9-24.

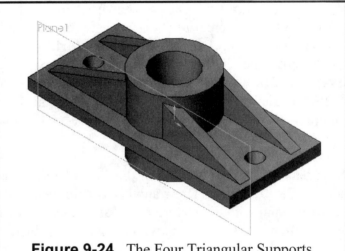

Figure 9-24. The Four Triangular Supports Added.

You now can complete the Tension Cable Bracket by adding some design features. First add a **Chamfer** feature to the inner hole edge on top of the upright boss. Define the chamfer with a **Distance-Distance** parameter that have both distances equal to **0.125** inches. Next add **Fillet** features to a number of edges. Make them all to have a uniform *radius* of **0.0825** inches. Pick the following edges to fillet with this command:

- Outer top edge of upright boss.
- All intersections of the upright boss with the base plate, both above and below the base plate.
- The top outer edges of the base plate.
- The top edges of the four triangular supports.
- The vertical edges of the rectangular base

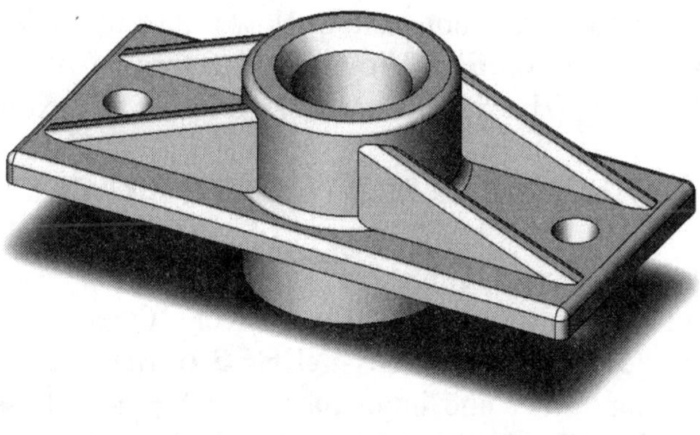

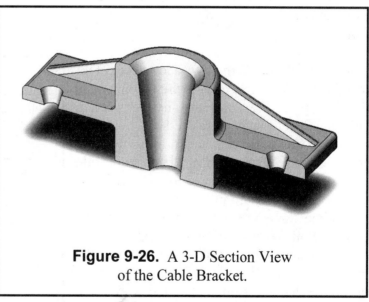

Figure 9-25. The Finished Tension Cable Bracket after Adding the Chamfer and Fillets.

When you are finished, you will have a finished part as shown in Figure 9-25 in a **Trimetric** view. At this point you may wish to **Save** your part in your designated folder and name it **TENSION CABLE BRACKET.sldprt**

MAKING A 3-D SECTION VIEW OF THE TENSION CABLE BRACKET

You will now make a 3-D section view of the Cable Bracket model. First select the cutting plane by clicking the **Front** plane in the Feature Manager. Next pull down **View**, select **Display**, and then select **Section View**. The "Section View" on-screen menu now appears (refer back to Figure 9-2). Leave the "Section Position" at **0.000** inches (middle of model), check (√) **on** the "Flip the Side to View," and then press the **Display** button on the menu. Notice the preview arrow pointing in the back direction on the model, which is

Figure 9-26. A 3-D Section View of the Cable Bracket.

the correct direction for the section view. Then click **OK** to close the menu. You should now have a 3-D full section view of the Cable Bracket showing a cut-away view of the part, as shown in Figure 9-26.

If instructed to do so, obtain a document of this 3-D section view. Using **Insert Annotations**, add a **Note** with your name and class data. Then **Print** a shaded hardcopy of the 3-D Cable Bracket model for submission. Now return to the **View** pull down menu, re-select **Display**, and then re-select **Section View** again to turn **off** the 3-D section view. *Do not* **Close** your solid model file yet, because you will need it for the next phase of this exercise.

INSERTING THE CABLE TENSION BRACKET ON A TITLE SHEET

At this point you will make a three-view layout of your model on a Title Block sheet. Open the file **TITLEBLOCK-INCHES.drwdot** from your folder and immediately **SAVE AS – CABLE TENSION BRACKET.slddrw..**

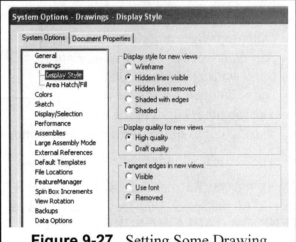

Before you start the projection, there are some settings that you need to make. Pull down **Tools** and select **Options**. Click the **Drawings**, **Display Style** tab. Check the dot (•) on the "Hidden lines visible" option and check the dot (•) on the tangent edges "Removed" option as shown in Figure 9-27. Next click the **Drawings**, **Area Hatch/Fill** tab. Select the **ANSI31** (Iron Brick Stone) "Pattern" option. Set the "Scale" to **1.000** and the Angle" to **0** degrees. Also go to **Document Properties, Line Font, Section Line** and change the thickness to **Thick**.

Figure 9-27. Setting Some Drawing Display Options.

Now pull down **Window** and select **Tile Vertically**. You now can see the two files: the Bracket part file and the newly created Drawing Sheet file. Now select the "Tension Cable Bracket" part in its Feature Manager and "drag and drop" it onto the title block sheet. You may have to right click on sheet 1 in the Feature manager and Edit Sheet to get the three views to appear on the title Block. SolidWorks will automatically project a three-view orthographic layout, using the third angle projection you just set, as displayed in Figure 9-28. Notice that the views are arranged properly and are aligned. *Note:* If the three views do not come in as a full 1:1 scale, return to **Sheet1 Properties** and reset the scale.

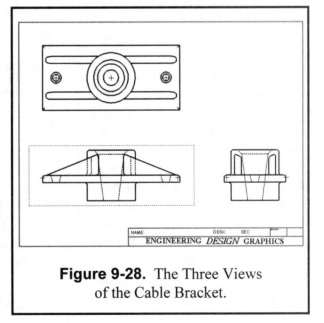

Figure 9-28. The Three Views of the Cable Bracket.

MAKING A 2-D SECTION VIEW OF THE CABLE BRACKET

You will only need the Title Block Sheet file now, so *maximize* it by clicking its box in the upper right corner. You will only keep the top view and use it as the source view to insert a full section front view. Right mouse click (**RMB**) on the border of the front view. On the pop-up menu, select **Delete**. Then, on the on-screen menu, answer **Yes** to the question "*Do you really want to delete this view?*" Repeat this **Delete** process also for the right side view. The only view remaining now is the top view of the Cable Bracket.

Select the Section Icon Figure 9-29 and draw a horizontal **Line** from left to right across the entire view and going through the center of the Cable Bracket (This also happens to be through the *origin*) as shown in Figure 9-30. This line will serve as the cutting plane line location. *Note*: If it does not appear that the line goes through the middle of model, you can use the *select* icon and *move* the line to the right position.

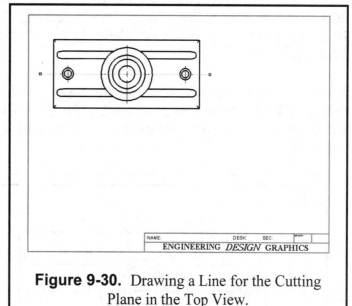

Figure 9-29. Section View Icon

Figure 9-30. Drawing a Line for the Cutting Plane in the Top View.

Drag this faint view down below the top view. Notice the vertical alignment between the two views is maintained as you move the section view. Also a cutting plane line labeled **A-A** appears where you drew the last line. The cutting plane arrows will point in the correct direction as you drag the section view into position. Find a good position and click the **LMB** to fix the section view in that position. You now have a drawing with a section view that is labeled **Section A-A**, as indicated in Figure 9-31.

The section view drawing may not be perfect. For example, the centerlines in the section view may

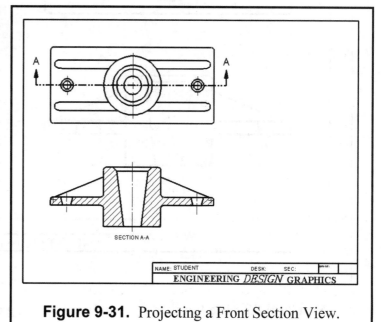

Figure 9-31. Projecting a Front Section View.

be missing. You can **Select – Insert, Annotations, Centerlines** to insert them. You can add circular centerlines in the top view by pulling down **Insert**, **Annotations**, and select **Center Mark**. Then click on each perimeter of the three circular features to add the center marks (i.e. centerlines). You may want to increase the font size of the "Section A-A" label to **18 point**.

Next activate the section view and select **Insert – Drawing View – Projected view**. Move the cursor to the right of the section view and when it is in the desired position, click the **RMB**. Repeat the process and insert an isometric model view with a custom scale of 1:3.

Use **Insert**, **Annotations**, and **Note** to add a **TENSION CABLE BRACKET** title and **SCALE 1:1** to the drawing as shown in Figure 9-32. Use *caps*, **Arial** font for all the labels. Use **20-point** font for the "Tension Cable Bracket" title and **12-point** font for all the other annotations.

When you are finished you should **Save** your drawing file as **TENSION CABLE BRACKET.slddrw** in your designated folder. A finished section view drawing, with title block and pictorial, is shown in Figure 9-33. **Print** a hard copy of the drawing to submit to your instructor.

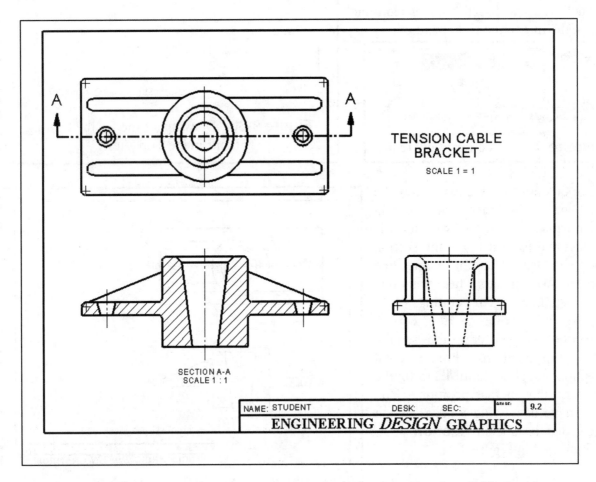

Figure 9-32. The Finished Section View Drawing of the Tension Cable Bracket.

Exercise 9.3: MILLING END ADAPTER
Section Views

In this Exercise 9.3, you will build a solid model of the Milling End Adapter using SolidWorks commands that you have learned in previous labs. You will display a 3-D section view of the model to visualize the internal features of the model. Next you will "drag and drop" the model onto a drawing sheet and then create a 2-D section view of the part. To get started, you will first build the solid model part.

BUILDING THE MILLING END ADAPTER

Open your **ANSI-INCHES.prtdot** in SolidWorks. Immediately **SAVE AS – MILLING END ADAPTER.sldprt**. Also set the "Major Grid Spacing" to **1** inch and "Minor Lines per Major" to **16**. Make sure the "Display Grid" is also set to **on**. Select the **Front** plane and start a new **Sketch**. Draw a horizontal **Centerline** through the origin about 3 inches long and centered at the origin. Sketch the given profile in Figure 9-33 using the **Line** tool. Follow the grid pattern in the figure in accordance with the previous settings to make your sketch profile.

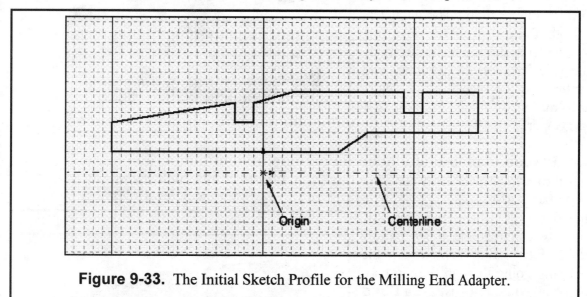

Figure 9-33. The Initial Sketch Profile for the Milling End Adapter.

Select the **Revolve Base** feature icon and revolve the profile into a solid using a **360** degrees angle. This forms the base part. Now add two **Chamfer** design features to the end edges of the part. Use a **Distance-Distance** parameter definition, with both distance values being **0.0625** inches. At this stage, you should have a revolved solid part with the ends chamfered, as shown in Figure 9-34 in a **Trimetric** view.

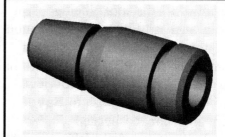

Figure 9-34. The Revolved Part with Chamfers.

You now need to create two screw holes on the round outer surfaces of the Milling End Adapter. SolidWorks needs a flat plane to sketch on, so first select the **Top** plane in the Feature Manager. Next pull down **Insert**, select **Reference Geometry**, and then **Plane**. The "Plane" menu appears. Key-in the plane distance of **0.5000** inches *above* the Top plane as indicated in Figure 9-35. Then click the green (√) mark to close the menu.

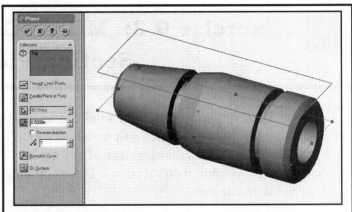

Figure 9-35. Inserting the Reference Plane.

You now have a "Plane1" in the Feature Manager tree structure. Click on that **Plane1** and enter the **Sketch** mode. Also select a **Top** view orientation to better see the Plane1 sketch plane. Sketch two **Circles** on the plane and **Dimension** them as shown in Figure 9-36. The diameters are both **0.1250** inches. The first circle center is **0.2500** inches from the right side end of the Milling End Adapter, and the second circle center is **0.3750** inches to the left of the first circle center.

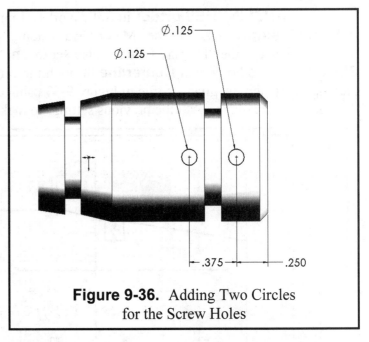

Figure 9-36. Adding Two Circles for the Screw Holes

Now **Extrude Cut** the two holes down through the cylinder wall using an **Up to Surface** end condition in "Direction 1," where the "up to" surface selected is the *inner* hollow surface of the shaft. This results in the holes only going through the top part. *Note*: You could also just use a **Blind** end condition for the holes with the downward distance being around **0.500** inches. Either way, your model of the Milling End Adapter is complete and it should look like Figure 9-37 in a **Trimetric** view. At this point you may wish to **Save** your part in your designated folder and name it **MILLING END ADAPTER.sldprt**.

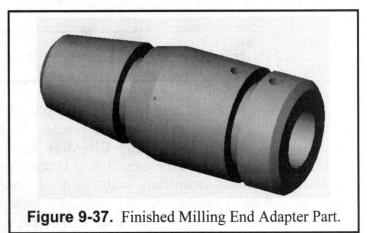

Figure 9-37. Finished Milling End Adapter Part.

MAKING A 3-D SECTION VIEW OF THE MILLING END ADAPTER

You will now make a 3-D section view of the Milling End Adapter model. First select the cutting plane by clicking the **Front** plane in the Feature Manager. Next pull down **View**, select **Display**, and then select **Section View**. The "Section View" on-screen menu now appears (refer back to Figure 9-2). Leave the "Section Position" at **0.0000** inches (middle of model), check (√) **on** the "Flip the Side to View," and then press the **Display** button on the menu. Notice the preview arrow pointing in the back direction on the model, which is the correct direction for

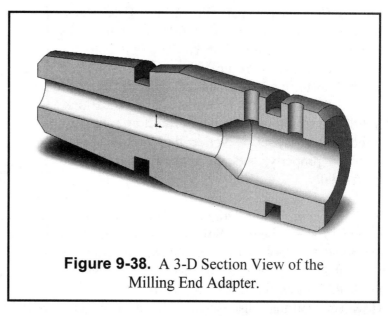

Figure 9-38. A 3-D Section View of the Milling End Adapter.

the section view. So then click **OK** to close the menu. You should now have a 3-D full section view of the Milling End Adapter showing a cut-away view of the part, as shown in Figure 9-38.

If instructed to do so, obtain a document of this 3-D section view. Using **Insert Annotations**, add a **Note** with your name and class data. Then **Print** a shaded hardcopy of the 3-D model for submission to your instructor. Now return to the **View** pull down menu, re-select **Display**, and then re-select **Section View** again to turn **off** the 3-D section view, or select the Section icon

. _Do not_ **Close** your solid model file yet, because you will need it for the next phase of this exercise.

INSERTING THE MILLING END ADAPTER ONTO A TITLE BLOCK

At this point you will make a three-view layout of your model on a Title Block sheet. Open the file **TITLEBLOCK-INCHES.drwdot** from your folder and immediately **SAVE AS – MILLING END ADAPTER.slddrw..**

Before you start the projection, there are some general settings that you need to make. Pull down **Tools** and select **Options**. Click the **Drawings**, **Display Type** tab. Check the dot (•) on the "Hidden lines visible" option and check the dot (•) on the tangent edges "Removed" option as shown in Figure 9-39. Next click the **Drawings**, **Area Hatch** tab. Select the **Brass** "Pattern" option. Set the "Scale" to **1.000** and the Angle" to **45** degrees, as shown in Figure 9-40.

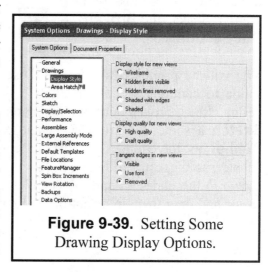

Figure 9-39. Setting Some Drawing Display Options.

Now pull down **Window** and select **Tile Vertically**. You now can see the two files: the Milling End Adapter part file and the Title Block. Now select the "Milling End Adapter" part in its Feature Manager and "drag and drop" it onto the new drawing sheet. You may have to right click on Sheet 1 in the Feature Manager and Edit Sheet to get the three views to appear on the Title Block. SolidWorks will automatically project a three-view orthographic layout.. Notice that the views are arranged properly, and are aligned vertically and horizontally.

Now *maximize* your Drawing Sheet file to full screen to see it better. SolidWorks automatically projected a three-view orthographic layout using the third angle projection. Notice that the views are arranged properly, and are correctly aligned. However, you may discover that the drawing scale is too small for this application. So return to **Sheet1, Properties** menu and set the "Scale" to **2:1** to get a bigger layout like the one shown Figure 9-41. You may also activate the views and change the custom scale of the view in the Feature Manger column.

MAKING A 2-D SECTION VIEW OF THE END ADAPTER

For this application, you will use all three views to make a layout and will show the front view with a broken-out section. Select the **Broken-Out Section** icon.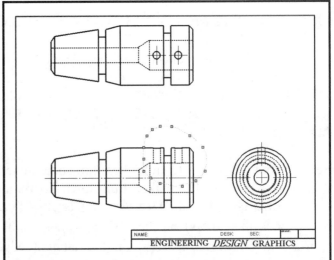

You will be prompted to "draw a closed spline to continue section creation." To define the broken-out section area, **Sketch** a somewhat arbitrarily enclosed **Spline** on the front view of the end adapter, as suggested in Figure 9-42. You can *grab* the nodes around the completed spline and drag them in or out of the loop to set your area until it is acceptable.

Figure 9-40. Setting Some Hatch Pattern Options.

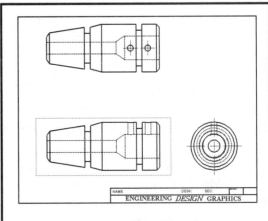

Figure 9-41. The Three Views of the End Adapter, Using a 2:1 Scale.

Figure 9-42. Sketching An Enclosed Spline on the Front View for the Broken-Out Section View.

In the "Broken-out Section" menu in the Feature Manager area, as shown in Figure 9-43. check on (√) the **Preview** box. You now get a preview of the cutting plane in both the top and right side views, including view direction arrows. On the "Broken-out Section" menu, key in the "Distance" for the cutting plane to be **0.5000** inches, which is right through the middle of the end adapter. Then click the green (√) button to close it.

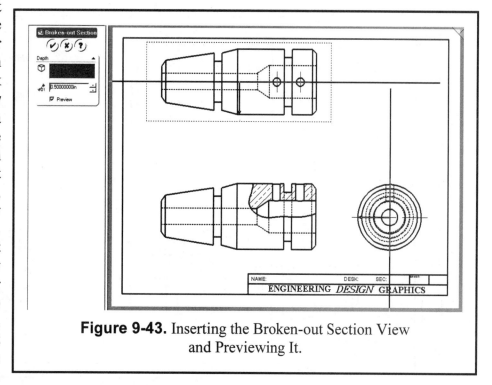

Figure 9-43. Inserting the Broken-out Section View and Previewing It.

Note: You can use a **Rectangle** instead of a Spline in this **Broken-out Section** command to make a *Half Section View* of a part using this same approach.

You now have a Broken-Out Section view of the Milling End Adapter in the front view, and also top and right side views, as suggested in the final Figure 9-44. However, it may not be a perfect drawing. **Insert – Annotations - Centerlines** in the front and top views if they are missing. You can **Insert**, **Annotations**, and select **Center Mark**. Then click on the perimeter of the circular features to add center marks (i.e. centerlines) to circular views. **Insert a small isometric model view in the upper right hand corner.** You may want to add a label below the front view that says **BROKEN-OUT SECTION** using **14**-point font size.

Use **Insert**, **Annotations**, and **Note** to add the **MILLING END ADAPTER** title and **SCALE 2:1** to the drawing as shown in Figure 9-44. Use *caps*, **Arial** font for all the labels, **20-point** font for the "Milling End Adapter" title, and **12-point** font for the other annotations.

When you are finished you should **Save** your drawing file as **MILLING END ADAPTER.slddrw** in your designated folder (note: its extension is now **.slddrw**). A finished broken-out section view drawing, with title block and border, is shown in Figure 9-44 in a **Print Preview**. Then **Print** a hard copy of the drawing to submit to your instructor.

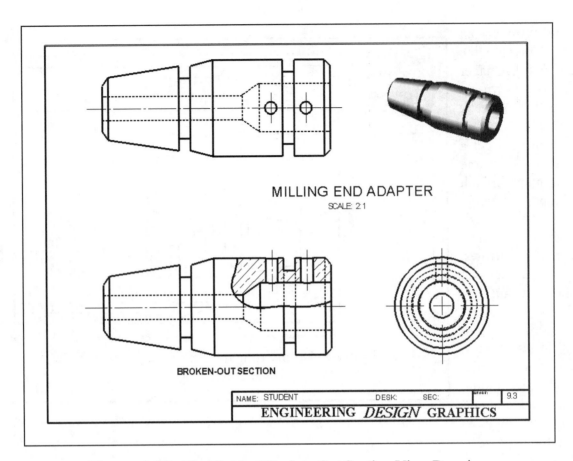

MILLING END ADAPTER
SCALE: 2:1

BROKEN-OUT SECTION

NAME: STUDENT   DESK: SEC: SHEET: 9.3

ENGINEERING *DESIGN* GRAPHICS

Figure 9-44. The Finished Broken-Out Section View Drawing.

In Exercise 9.4, you will build the three parts of the Plastic Revolving Ball assembly using SolidWorks commands that you have learned in previous labs. You will display a 3-D section view of the model to visualize the internal features of the model. Next you will "drag and drop" the assembly model onto a title block and then create a 2-D section view of the assembly. To get started, build the solid model of each part and then create an assembly of the three parts

Building the Ball

Open **ANSI-INCHES.prtdot** from your folder. Immediately **SAVE AS – PLASTIC BALL.sldprt**. Select the **Material Icon** (Figure 9-45) in the Feature Manager. Expand the **Plastics** option and select **PE High Density** and de-select the **"Use Material Color"**. Select the **Front** plane and start a new sketch. Draw a horizontal **Centerline** through the **Origin**. **Sketch** the given profile in Figure 9-46 and apply the given dimensions.

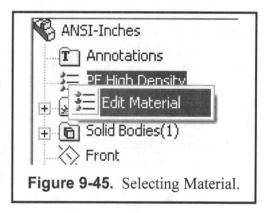

Figure 9-45. Selecting Material.

Select the **Revolve Base** feature icon and revolve the profile into a solid using a **360**-degree angle. This creates the Plastic Ball.   Your object should look like Figure 9-47. You can change the shading **Color** to **Blue**, and then **Save** your first part as **PLASTIC BALL.sldprt**.

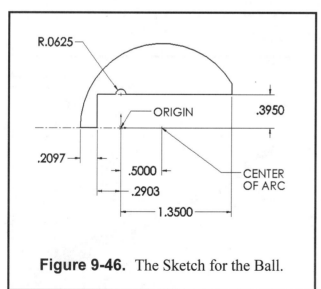

Figure 9-46. The Sketch for the Ball.

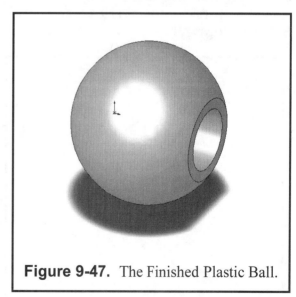

Figure 9-47. The Finished Plastic Ball.

Building the Steel Shaft

Open **ANSI-INCHES.prtdot** from your folder.Immediately **SAVE AS – STEEL SHAFT.sldprt.**. Select the **Material Icon** (Figure 9-48) in the Feature Manager. Expand the **Steel** option and select **AISI 1020** and de-select the **"Use Material Color"**. Select the **Front** plane and start a new sketch. Draw a horizontal **Centerline** through the **Origin**. **Sketch** the given profile in Figure 9-49 and apply the given dimensions.

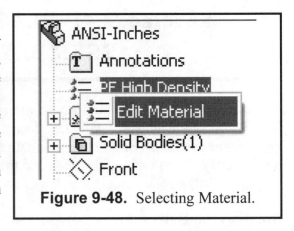

Figure 9-48. Selecting Material.

Select the Revolve Base Feature icon and **Revolve** the profile into a solid using a **360**-degree angle. This creates the Steel Shaft. Select the small end of the shaft and start a new sketch. **Sketch** the **Hexagon** as shown in Figure 9-50 and do a **Cut Extrude - Blind** of **0.25** inches. Add a **0.0375**-inch **Chamfer** on both ends of the shaft. Your object should look like Figure 9-51. Change the shading **Color** to **Silver**, and then **Save** your second part as **STEEL SHAFT.sldprt**.

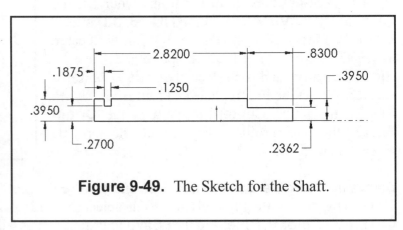

Figure 9-49. The Sketch for the Shaft.

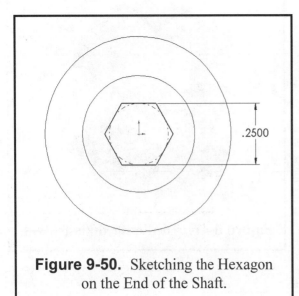

Figure 9-50. Sketching the Hexagon on the End of the Shaft.

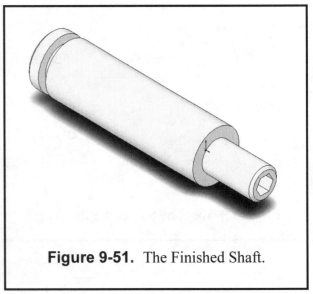

Figure 9-51. The Finished Shaft.

Building the Snap Ring

Open **ANSI-INCHES.prtdot** from your folder. Immediately **SAVE AS – SNAP RING.sldprt**. Select the **Material Icon** (Figure 9-52) in the Feature Manager. Expand the **Steel** option and select **Alloy Steel** and de-select the **"Use Material Color"**. Select the **Front** plane and start a new sketch. Draw a horizontal **Centerline** through the **Origin**. **Sketch** the given profile in Figure 9-53 and apply the given dimensions. **Constrain** the sketch so it is centered above the origin.

Select the Revolve Base Feature icon and **Revolve** the profile into a solid using a **360**-degree angle. This creates the Snap Ring.

Select the right plane and start a new sketch. **Sketch** the 2-D profile as shown in Figure 9-54 and do a **Cut Extrude – Through all in both directions.**

Your object should look like Figure 9-55. Change the shading **Color** to **Golden Yellow**, and then **Save** your third part as **SNAP RING.sldprt.**

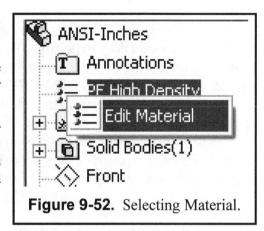

Figure 9-52. Selecting Material.

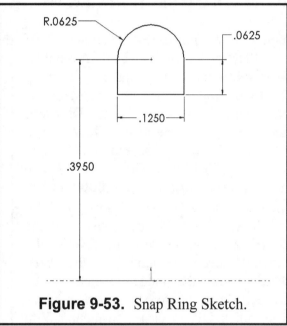

Figure 9-53. Snap Ring Sketch.

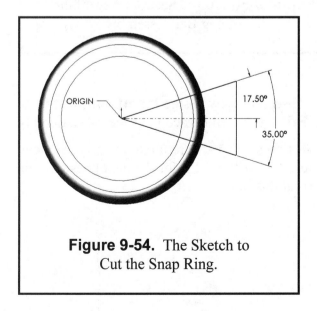

Figure 9-54. The Sketch to Cut the Snap Ring.

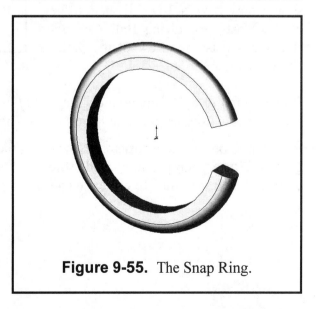

Figure 9-55. The Snap Ring.

Building the Assembly

With the three part files open, go to **File** and select **New, Assembly**. In the pull-down menu "Windows" select **Tile Vertically**. First drag the Snap-Ring to the **Origin** (When you see a double set of arrows) of the Assembly as the base part. Next select the Steel-Shaft and drag it into the assembly **BUT NOT TO THE ORIGIN**. Add the following **Mates** to the parts. The steel shaft should be **Concentric** with the snap-ring for the first mate and then make one of the vertical surfaces of the snap ring and the corresponding vertical surface of the ring groove of the shaft to be **Coincident**. This will position the snap ring in the groove of the steel shaft. When this is completed, drag the Plastic-Revolving Ball to the **Origin** (Take the cursor arrow to the origin. When you see a double set of arrows, release the mouse button) of the Assembly. **Save** the assembly to your folder as **PLASTIC REVOLVING BALL.sldasm**.

MAKING A 3-D SECTION VIEW OF THE PLASTIC REVOLVING BALL ASSEMBLY

You will now make a 3-D section view of the Plastic Revolving Ball Assembly. First select the cutting plane by clicking the **Front** plane in the Feature Manager. Next pull down **View**, select **Display**, and then select **Section View**. The "Section View" on-screen menu now appears (refer back to Figure 9-2). Leave the "Section Position" at **0.0000** inches (middle of model), check (√) **on** the "Flip the Side to View," and then press the **Display** button on the menu. Notice the preview arrow pointing in the back direction on the model, which is the correct direction for the section view. Then click **OK** to close the menu. You should now have a 3-D full section view of the Plastic Revolving Ball Assembly, showing a cut-away view of the part, as shown in Figure 9-56.

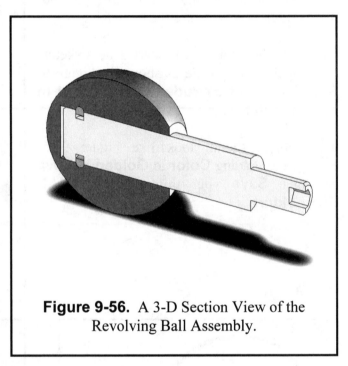

Figure 9-56. A 3-D Section View of the Revolving Ball Assembly.

If instructed to do so, obtain a document of this 3-D section view Using **Insert Annotations**, add a **Note** with your name and class data. Then **Print** a shaded hardcopy of the 3-D assembly for submission to your instructor. Now select the Section icon 🔳 to return to the original view. *Do not* **Close** your assembly model file yet, because you will need it for the next phase of this exercise. You may want to close the individual parts at this time.

INSERTING THE REVOLVING BALL ASSEMBLY ONTO A TITLE BLOCK

Before you start the projection, there are some settings that you need to make. Pull down **Tools** and select **Options**. Click the **Drawings**, **Display Type** tab. Check the dot (•) on the "Hidden lines visible" option and check the dot (•) on the tangent edges "Removed" option as shown in Figure 9-57.

Go to **Tools Options** and **select Document Properties.** Change the **Line Font** for **Section Line** to **Phantom** and **Thick**. See Figure 9-58.

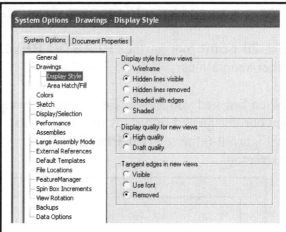

Figure 9-57. Setting Some Drawing Display Options.

Go to the pull down **Window** and select **Tile Vertically**. You now can see the two files: the Revolving Ball Assembly and the Title Block. Select the "Revolving Ball Assembly" in the Feature Manager and "drag and drop" it onto the title block sheet. SolidWorks will automatically project a three-view orthographic layout using the third angle projection you just set. Notice that the views are arranged properly, and are aligned vertically and horizontally.

At this time you can maximize the drawing sheet so you can see things more clearly. Move the views so they are properly spaced and positioned on your sheet.

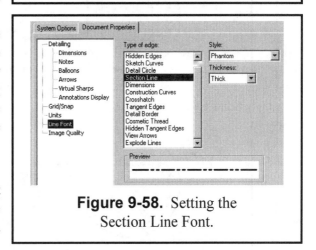

Figure 9-58. Setting the Section Line Font.

Right Click and **Delete** the front view and the right side view. In place of the front view you will create a full section view.

Select the Section Icon Figure 9-59. Draw a line through the center of the assembly and place the section view where the front view used to be. The arrows of the cutting plane line should be pointing upward. Once the section view is placed you will notice that the section lines may not be at different angles and the scale of the section lines is not appropriate. If you **Right Click** on the section lines a window appears that lets you edit the **Crosshatch Properties**. Make changes in the Hatch Pattern Scale and the Hatch Pattern Angle to change the density of the Hatch and their directions. Next activate the section view and go to **Insert - Drawing View – Projected View** to replace the right side view that was deleted earlier. You will notice that centerlines are missing in the right side view. Select **Insert,**

Figure 9-59. Section View Icon.

Annotations, Center Mark. SolidWorks will prompt you to "select a circular edge for center mark insertion." Select the largest circle in the right side view and the centerline will be added. **Insert a small isometric model view in the upper right hand corner.**

Use **20 point** font for the "**PLASTIC REVOLVING BALL**" title and **12 point** font for all the other annotations.

When finished you should **Save** your drawing file as **PLASTIC REVOLVING BALL. slddrw** in your designated folder. A finished section view drawing, with title block and border, is shown in Figure 9-60 in a **Print Preview**. Then **Print** a hard copy of the drawing to submit to your instructor.

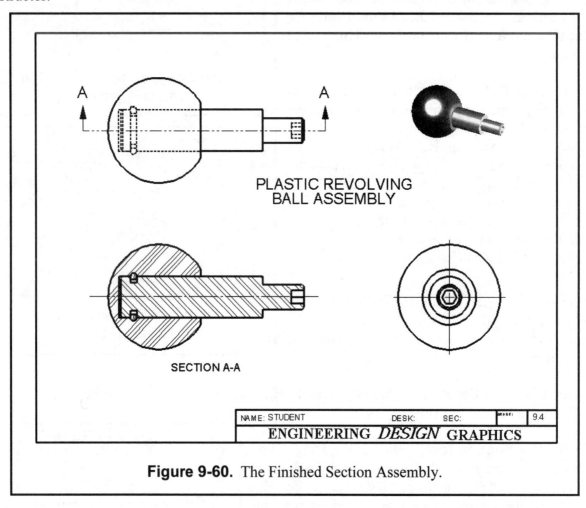

PLASTIC REVOLVING
BALL ASSEMBLY

SECTION A-A

| NAME: STUDENT | | DESK: | SEC: | | 9.4 |

ENGINEERING *DESIGN* GRAPHICS

Figure 9-60. The Finished Section Assembly.

SUPPLEMENTARY EXERCISE 9-5
CLAMPING BLOCK

Build a full size solid model of the figure below. Insert it on a Title Block and Provide a Full Section in the place of the front view. Insert a small pictorial of the object in the upper right hand corner of the sheet. Provide the proper Titles, Scales and other pertinent notes.

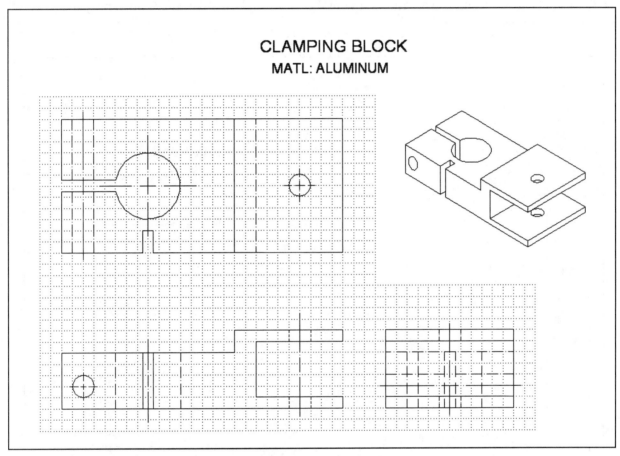

CLAMPING BLOCK
MATL: ALUMINUM

ASSUME THE GRID DIVISIONS TO BE 3 mm

SUPPLEMENTARY EXERCISE 9-6
TWO WAY BENCH BLOCK

Build a full size solid model of the figure below. Insert it on a Title Block. After deleting the front and the right side view, Draw an offset line through the two counterbored holes and the center hole. Next go to Insert – Drawing View – Section View and place it where the front view used to be. Continue by Inserting – Drawing View – Projected view to replace the right side view. Finally insert a small Isometric View in the upper right hand corner and supply the Title and Scale as in previous exercises.

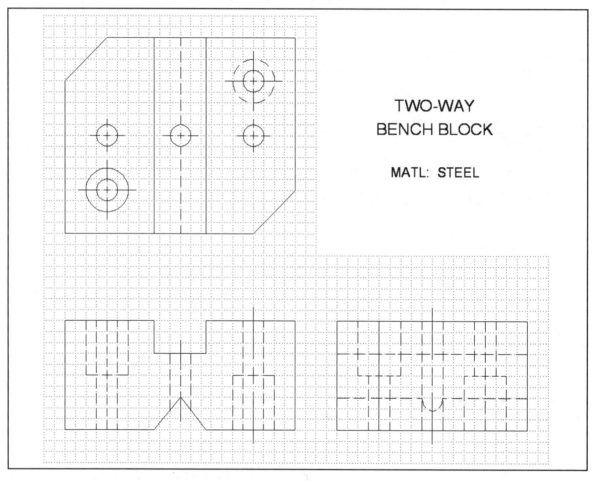

TWO-WAY
BENCH BLOCK

MATL: STEEL

ASSUME THE GRID DIVISIONS TO BE 0.125 INCHES.

Build a full size solid model of the figure below. Insert it on a Title Block. After deleting the front and the right side view, Draw an offset line through one of the small holes on the left end, then through the slot with the two holes in the center and through one of the slots on the right hand end. Next go to Insert – Drawing View – Section View and place it where the front view used to be. Continue by Inserting – Drawing View – Projected view to replace the right side view. Finally insert a small Isometric View in the upper right hand corner and supply the Title and Scale as in previous exercises.

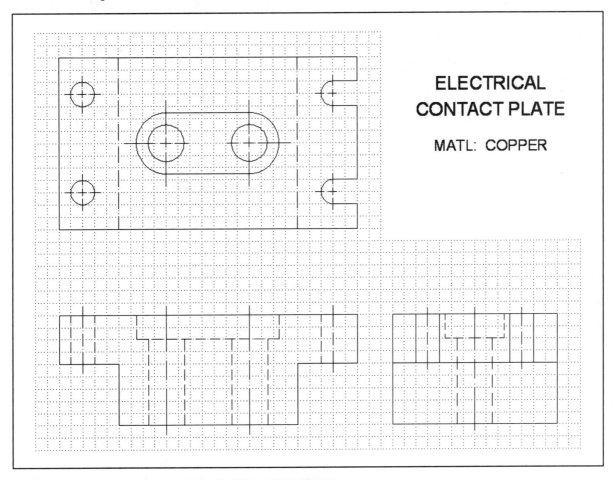

ELECTRICAL
CONTACT PLATE

MATL: COPPER

ASSUME THE GRID DIVISIONS TO BE 0.125 INCHES

SUPPLEMENTARY EXERCISE 9-8   DISC ASSEMBLY

Build full sized solid models of the **Disk Assembly Pieces** below. Build a fully constrained
Assembly of the parts and insert it on a Title Block. Provide a Full Section in the place of the
front view. Provide the proper Titles, Scales and other pertinent notes.

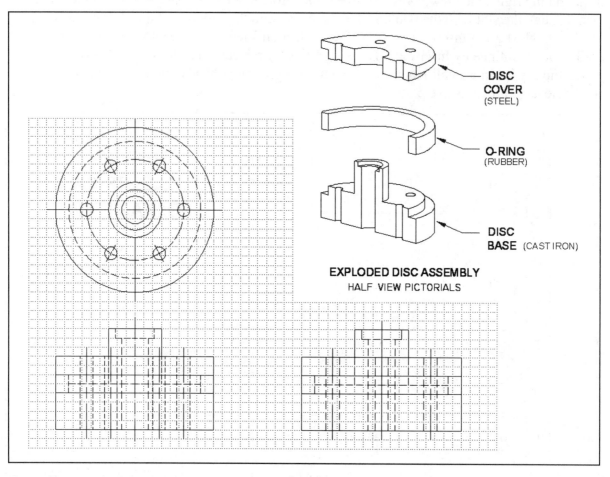

DISC
COVER
(STEEL)

O-RING
(RUBBER)

DISC
BASE (CAST IRON)

EXPLODED DISC ASSEMBLY
HALF VIEW PICTORIALS

ASSUME THE GRID DIVISIONS TO BE 0.25 INCHES.

Computer Graphics Lab 10: Generating and Dimensioning Three-View Drawings

In this Computer Graphics Lab 10, you will learn how to project three-view orthographic drawings from solid models. In each exercise, you will build a 3-D solid model of a part. You will then use a projection function in SolidWorks to make a three-view (front, top, and right side) drawing of the part. You will completely dimension the drawing using SolidWorks commands. You will finish the drawing by adding centerlines, annotations, and a title block. The following introduction will get you oriented to making a drawing using SolidWorks.

INSERTING A DRAWING SHEET FOR THE PROJECTION

You start the three-view layout of your model on a Title Block drawing sheet. You pull down **File**, select **Open**, and select the **TITLEBLOCK-INCHES.drwdot** Drawing Sheet that was made earlier. The Drawing Sheet is now on the screen as shown in Figure 10-1.

If you did not set up these parameters in Unit 1 follow these instructions. In the Feature Manager tree, the new **Sheet1** label will appear. If you right mouse click (**RMB**) on that label, the sheet **Properties** menu appears as shown in Figure 10-2. Here you can set the drawing sheet "Scale" and "Type of projection" to be used for the drawing. Usually you will use a "Scale" of **1:1**. Also, since the U.S. standard is *third angle projection*,. You will normally check the dot (•) on the "Third angle" menu item.

SETTING THE DRAWING SHEET DISPLAY TYPE

Before you start the projection, there are some general drawing sheet settings that you need to set. In the **Tools** pull down menu, you can select the **Options** menu to get all the tab settings for your file. Several of them are pertinent to drawing projections. If you click on the **Drawings**, **Display Type** tab, you can

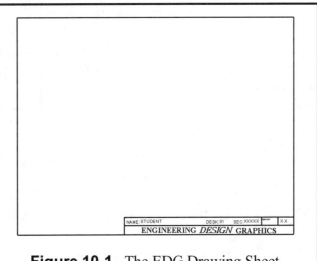

Figure 10-1. The EDG Drawing Sheet.

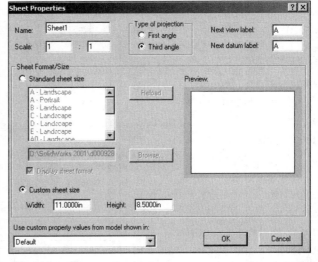

Figure 10-2. The Drawing Sheet Setup Menu.

set the projection line options, such as dot (•) **on** the "Hidden lines visible" option and dot (•) **on** the "Tangent Edges Removed" option as shown in Figure 10-3.

PROJECTING THE THREE VIEWS

When you have both your model and drawing sheet active, you can pull down **Window** and select **Tile Vertically**. Here you can see the two files: the part file and the newly created blank Drawing Sheet file. You would next select the "Part" label in its Feature Manager and "drag and drop" it onto the new drawing sheet. *Note:* You might have to right mouse click (**RMB**) on **Sheet1** in the Feature Manager, and select **Edit Sheet**. SolidWorks will automatically project a three-view orthographic layout using the

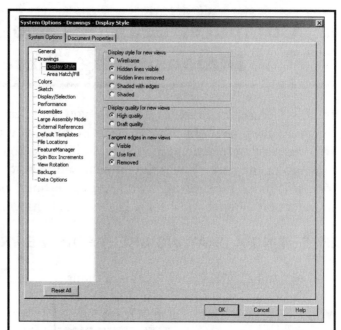

Figure 10-3. Setting the Drawing Sheet Default Display Types for the Projection.

scale and third angle projection that was earlier set. It is really quite easy and fast. Figure 10-4 is an example of such a three-view projection. Notice that the three views are arranged properly, and are aligned both vertically and horizontally. You can move them around on the sheet and this alignment will remain intact.

SETTING THE DIMENSIONING VARIABLES

You may first want to set some of the dimensioning parameters using the pull-down **Tools**, **Options** selection. There you can select the **Document Properties** tab and select the **Dimension** menu. This opens the menu, as shown in Figure 10-5. Here you can set the dimension parameters such as having a parenthesis around a dimension and whether to have the dimension arrows inside or outside the extension lines. These settings will depend on the application and will be set later in the specific exercises for this Computer Graphics Lab 10.

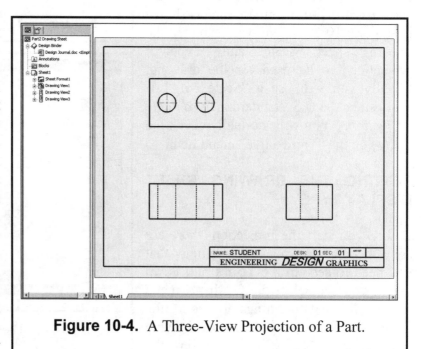

Figure 10-4. A Three-View Projection of a Part.

There is a tab for **Annotations Font** on the Document Properties menu (see Figure 10-5). Click on it, then click **Dimension** and the **Choose Font** menu appears as shown in Figure 10-6. Here you can set the dimension **Font**, **Font Style**, and **Height** (in either units or points).

DIMENSIONING THE DRAWING

You can now use the **Dimension** sketch tool to add the dimensions to your three views. You can also use the **Centerline** sketch tool to add any missing centerlines. An example three-view drawing, with dimensions and centerlines added, is shown in Figure 10-7.

INSERT A SHADED PICTORIAL

You can move the cursor over the drawing sheet and right click the mouse (**RMB**). A pop-up menu appears as shown in Figure 10-8. One of the selections allows you to insert a **Drawing View** of various types, such as **Model**. If you select this option, you can insert a pictorial view of the part. To facilitate this, a "Model View" menu appears in the design tree area.

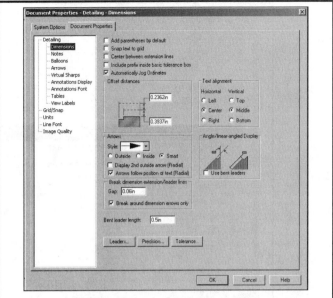

Figure 10-5. The Dimension Variables Menu.

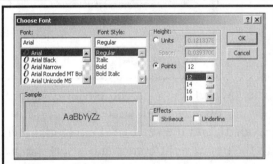

Figure 10-6. The Choose Font Menu.

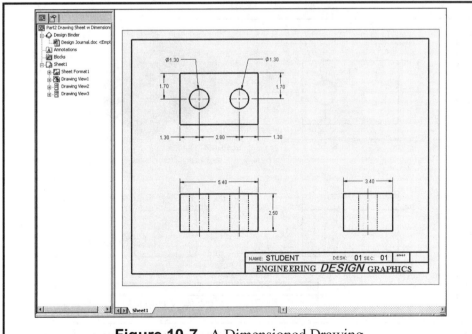

Figure 10-7. A Dimensioned Drawing.

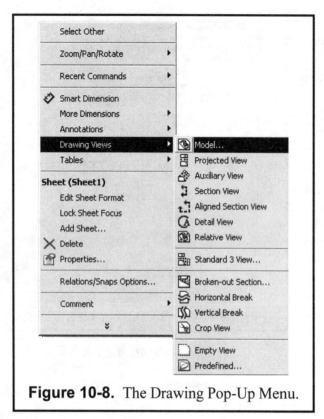

Figure 10-8. The Drawing Pop-Up Menu.

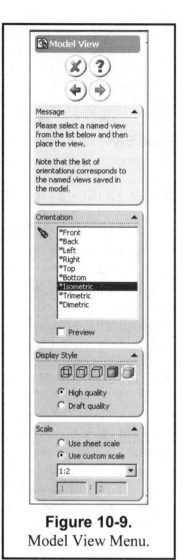

Figure 10-9.
Model View Menu.

The "Model View" menu is shown in Figure 10-9. Here you can set the display orientation (e.g. Isometric), the display style (e.g. Shaded), and the scale of the pictorial. Then move the cursor over to the upper right corner and insert the pictorial. The drawing can now be finished by **Insert**, **Annotations**, **Note**, as shown in Figure 10-10.

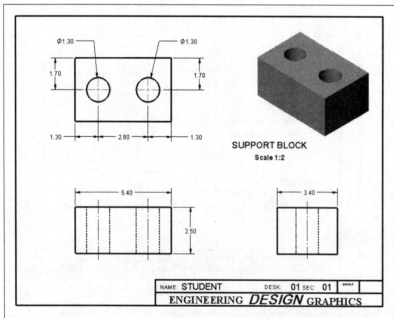

Figure 10-10. The Finished Drawing with a Pictorial and Annotations Inserted.

Exercise 10.1: GUIDE BLOCK Drawing

In Exercise 10.1, you will build a solid model of the Guide Block using SolidWorks commands that you have learned in previous labs. Next you will "drag and drop" the model onto a drawing sheet and then create a three-view orthographic drawing of the part. You will add dimensions and complete the drawing with annotations and a title block.

BUILDING THE GUIDE BLOCK SOLID MODEL

Open **ANSI-INCHES.prtdot** and immediately **SAVE AS – GUIDE BLOCK.slddrw**. . Select the **Top** plane and use a **Top** view orientation. Use **Inch** "Units" to **2** decimal places. In the **Sketch** mode, use the **Line** tool to draw the outline as shown in Figure 10-11. Use the **Dimension** tool to apply the given dimensions. Then **Extrude** the profile *upward* from the plane using a **Blind** end condition of **0.75** inches.

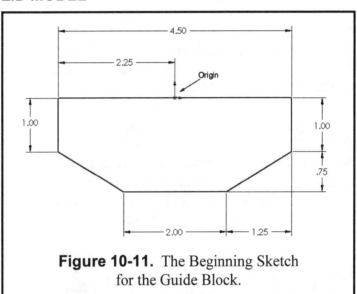

Figure 10-11. The Beginning Sketch for the Guide Block.

Change to a **Back** view orientation and click on the back surface of the model (it turns green). **Sketch** a **Rectangle** and **Dimension** it as shown in Figure 10-12. Draw a vertical **Centerline** through the origin and **Mirror** the rectangle to the other side. Then in an **Isometric** view, **Extrude** this Sketch2 *forward* using a **Blind** end condition of **1.00** inches.

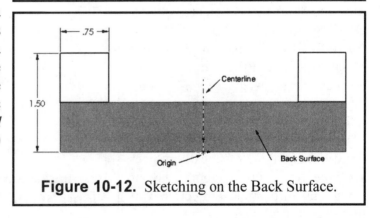

Figure 10-12. Sketching on the Back Surface.

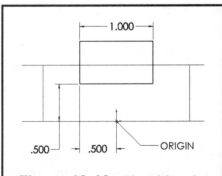

Figure 10-13. Sketching the Slot on the Front Surface.

The final feature for the Guide Block is a guide slot that goes all the way through from front to back. In a **Front** view orientation, click on the *middle* front upright surface (it turns green). **Sketch** a **Rectangle** and **Dimension** it as shown in Figure 10-13. Then **Extrude Cut** the sketch using a **Through All** condition in the *backward* direction.

The Guide Block solid model is now complete, as shown in Figure 10-14 in a **Trimetric** view. You may now wish to **Save** your part as **GUIDE BLOCK.sldprt** in your designated folder, but *do not Close* your file. You can now make a three-view projection.

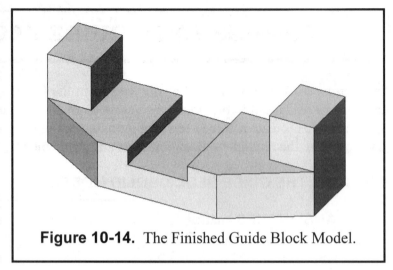

Figure 10-14. The Finished Guide Block Model.

PROJECTING THREE VIEWS

Pull down **File** and select the **TITLEBLOCK-INCHES.drwdot** Drawing Sheet. Immediately **Save as GUIDE BLOCK.slddrw**.

Before you start the projection, there are some other general drawing sheet settings that you need to make (refer back to Figure 10-3). Pull down the **Tools** menu and select **Options**. Click the **System Options – Drawings – Display Type** tab. Check the dot (●) on the "Hidden lines visible" option and check the dot (●) on the tangent edges "Removed" option. While under the Systems Options, Click on **Colors – System Colors select Drawings, Hidden Model Edges** and change the color to **Black**.

Now pull down **Window** and select **Tile Vertically**. You now can see the two files: the Guide Block part file and the newly created blank Drawing Sheet file. Now select the "GUIDE BLOCK" part in its Feature Manager and "drag and drop" it onto the new drawing sheet. *Note:* You might have to right mouse click (**RMB**) on **Sheet1** in the Feature Manager, and select **Edit Sheet**. SolidWorks will automatically project a three-view orthographic layout using the third angle projection you just set, as displayed in Figure 10-15 after *maximizing* it. Notice that the

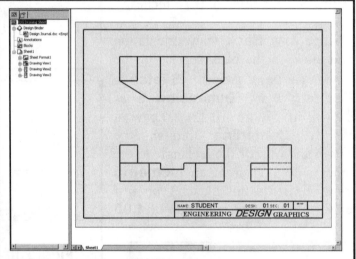

Figure 10-15. Projecting Three Views of the Guide Block onto a Drawing Sheet.

views are arranged properly, and are aligned vertically and horizontally.

SETTING THE DIMENSION VARIABLES

You are now ready to start dimensioning the Guide Block. But first you should set some general dimensioning variables. Pull-down **Tools**, and select **Options**. Then pick the **Document Properties** tab and select the **Dimensions** menu. This opens the menu, as shown earlier in Figure 10-5. Click **off** the "Add parentheses by default" variable so that the dimensions do not have parentheses around them. Next select the **Annotations Font** tab on the **Document Properties** menu. Click **Dimension** and the "Choose Font" menu appears (see Figure 10-6). Here you can set the following values:

> Font = **Arial**
> Font Style = **Regular**
> Height = **12 Points**

Then click **OK** twice to close the "Dimension" menu.

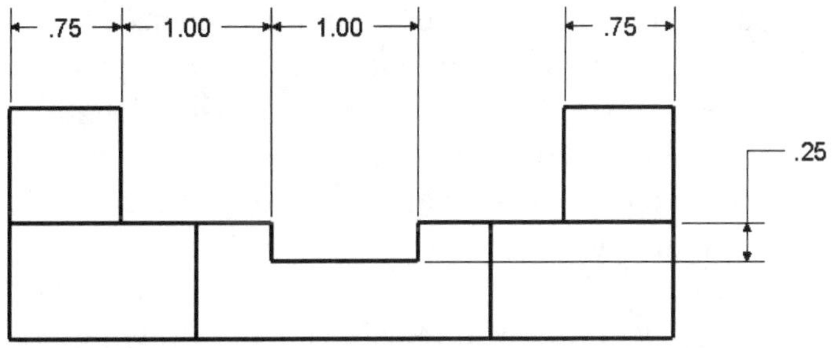

DIMENSIONING THE DRAWING

You will start dimensioning the front orthographic view. Click on the **Front** view and a gray border appears around it. You can **Move** the border over to the right a little to make room for the dimensions if needed. Now click the **Dimension** tool icon and start picking the edges to dimension. Start with the left upright width, and drag the **0.75** value outside and to the left of the dimension line, as shown in Figure 10-16.

Continue dimensioning some more widths (**1.00**, **1.00**, and **0.75**) as shown in Figure 10-16. Next dimension the **0.25** height of the slot. You can move this 0.25 height value outside the dimension line, but the arrows are still crowded inside the extension lines. So right mouse click (**RMB**) over the 0.25 value and select **Properties**. The "Dimension Properties" menu appears on the screen, as shown in Figure 10-17. Here you can override the general document settings. So click the dot (•) for Arrows **Outside** on the menu, so that the arrowheads for the 0.25 value will be outside the extension lines. Then click **OK** to close the menu. _Note:_ You can also activate the dimension in the edit mode so there are green dots on the arrows. Click on these green dots and the arrows will move to the outside.

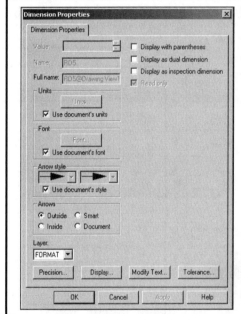

Figure 10-16. Dimensioning the Front View.

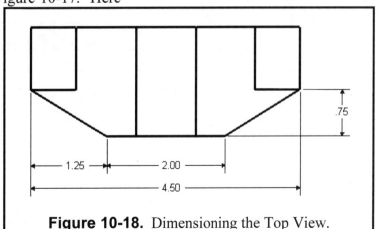

Figure 10-17. Dimension Properties Menu.

Figure 10-18. Dimensioning the Top View.

Now click on the **Top** orthographic view border, and **Move** it up and away from the front view, if needed, to make more room for the dimensions. Now **Dimension** the given values as indicated in Figure 10-18. In this case, you can pick the end *points* or *corner*s for the length of the dimension (instead of picking an actual line length). Use the **RMB Properties** approach to change the default dimension settings, if needed. Next complete the **Dimensions** on the **Right Side** orthographic view on your own (*hint*: there are three missing dimensions on the right side view, see Figure 10-19).

Now right click the mouse (**RMB**) on the drawing sheet and the pop-up menu (Figure 10-8) appears. Select **Drawing View,** then **Model**. On the "Model View" menu (Figure 10-9) select **Isometric** orientation, **Shaded** style, and **Scale** of **1:2**. Move the cursor to the upper right corner and insert the pictorial. Finish the drawing with **Insert, Annotations, Note** for adding a **GUIDE BLOCK** label and a **SCALE 1:1**. Use appropriate font style and height. Your drawing should now be complete, as suggested in Figure 10-19. Now **Save** your drawing and name it **GUIDE BLOCK.slddrw**. Then **Print** a hard copy to submit to your instructor.

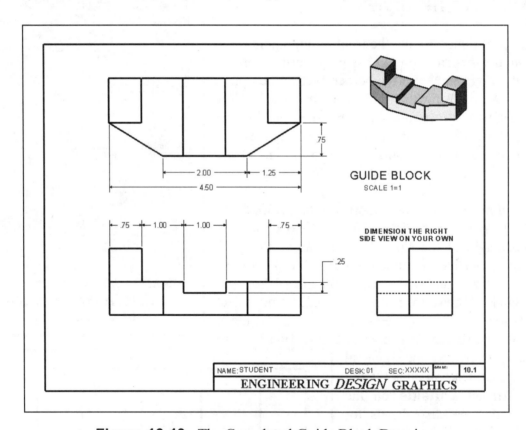

Figure 10-19. The Completed Guide Block Drawing.

Exercise 10.2: PIPE JOINT Drawing

In this Exercise 10.2, you will build a solid model of the Pipe Joint using SolidWorks commands that you have learned in previous labs. This exercise will be executed using millimeter units. Next you will "drag and drop" the model onto a drawing sheet and then create a three-view (top front and right side) orthographic drawing of the part. You will add dimensions and complete the drawing with centerlines, annotations, and a small pictorial on a title block.

BUILDING THE PIPE JOINT SOLID MODEL

Open the **ANSI-METRIC.prtdot**. Do a **Save As PIPE JOINT.sdlprt**. Select the **Top** plane and use a **Top** view orientation. In the **Sketch** mode, use the **Circle** tool to draw two circles as shown in Figure 10-20. The first circle is centered at the origin the other circle is to the right. **Dimension** the *diameters* as shown (φ**56** mm and φ**28** mm). **Dimension** the two circles **48** mm apart. Now **Add** a **Horizontal Relation** to the centers of the two circles so that they are aligned. Next draw two **Lines** that are approximately tangent to both circles on top and bottom as shown in Figure 10-20. Then **Add** a **Tangent Relation** to the circle and line in *four places* as shown. Also add a vertical **Centerline** that goes through the origin and extends beyond the big circle's perimeter.

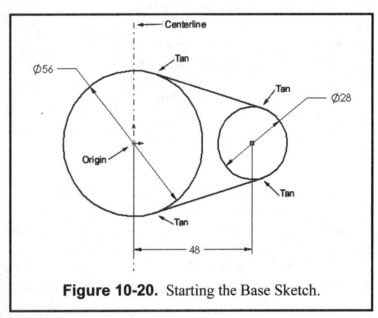

Figure 10-20. Starting the Base Sketch.

Now use the **Trim** tool to eliminate the left side of the small circle. Next **Trim** the left side of the large circle where it intersects the centerline. Then **Trim** the right side of the big circle where it is tangent to the top and bottom lines, leaving just two small pieces of the original big circle.

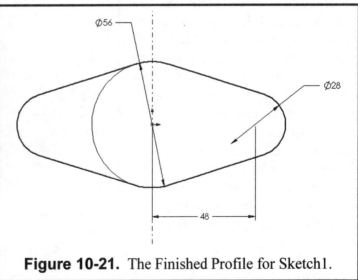

Figure 10-21. The Finished Profile for Sketch1.

Now **Mirror** the remaining sketch (there are five pieces) about the vertical centerline to get the finished Sketch1 profile as shown in Figure 10-21.

Now **Extrude** this Sketch1 *upward* using a **Blind** end condition of **16** mm. This yields the base plate for the Pipe Joint, as suggested in Figure 10-22.

Click on the top surface of this base plate (it turns green) and **Sketch** a **Circle** on the right end. This new circle should have a *diameter* of **12** mm and should have a **Concentric Relation** with the outer round edge of the base plate. Repeat this **12** mm **Circle** on the other side and also add a **Concentric Relation** with the other outer round edge. Then **Extrude Cut** this Sketch2 *downward* **Through All** to make two bolt holes on each end of the base plate, as shown in Figure 10-22.

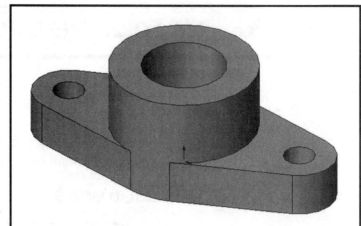

Figure 10-22. The Pipe Joint Model After:
a. The Base Plate is Extruded Upward,
b. The Side Bolt Holes are Cut Through,
c. The Big Center Boss is Added, and
d. The Hole is Cut through the Boss and Base.

Return to the top surface of this base plate (it turns green) and **Sketch** a **Circle** centered above the *origin* and with a *diameter* of **56** mm (same as the previous big circle of Figure 10-20). Then **Extrude Boss** this new circle *upward* to a **Blind** distance of **24** mm. Finally, click on the top surface of this new Boss and **Sketch** a **Circle** centered above the *origin* and with a *diameter* of **32** mm. Then **Extrude Cut** this circle *downward* **Through All** to make a large hole that goes all the way through the boss and base plate. Your part should now look like Figure 10.22.

The final step to complete the Pipe Joint is to add fillets to some edges. Select the **Fillet** feature icon and then, one-by-one, click the following lines: the tangent edges on the top of the base plate (4 places), the rounded ends on the top of the base plate (2 places), and the intersection edges of the boss with the top of the base plate (2 places). Set the fillet *radius* to **3** mm and then click the check mark (√) to close the "Fillet" menu. The Pipe Joint model is now finished, as shown in Figure 10-23 in a **Trimetric** view. You may now wish to **Save** your part as **PIPE JOINT.sldprt** in your designated folder, but *do not Close* your file. You can now make a three-view projection.

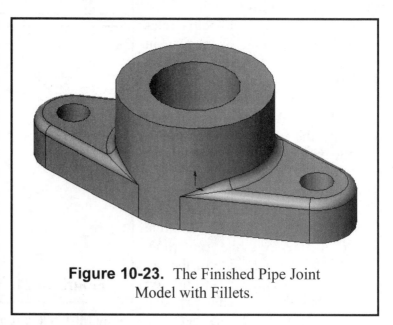

Figure 10-23. The Finished Pipe Joint Model with Fillets.

PROJECTING THREE VIEWS

Now **Open** your **TITLEBLOCK-METRIC.drwdot**. Go to **Save AS** and save this sheet as **PIPE JOINT.slddrw.**

Before you start the projection, there are some other general drawing sheet settings that you need to make (refer back to Figure 10-3). Pull down the **Tools** menu and select **Options**. Click the **System Options – Drawings - Display Type** tab. Check the dot (•) on the "Hidden lines visible" option and check the dot (•) on the tangent edges "Removed" option. While under the Systems Options, Click on **Colors – System Colors select Drawings, Hidden Model Edges** and change the color to **Black**. Also, on the **Document Properties**, **Detailing** tab, set "Dimensioning Standard" to **ANSI**. Click **OK** to close the menu.

Now pull down **Window** and select **Tile Vertically**. You now can see the two files: the PIPE JOINT part file and the newly created blank Drawing Sheet file. Now select the "Pipe Joint" part in its Feature Manager and "drag and drop" it onto the new drawing sheet. *Note:* You might have to right mouse click (**RMB**) on **Sheet1** in the Feature Manager, and select **Edit Sheet.** SolidWorks will automatically project a three-view orthographic layout using the third angle projection you just set, as displayed in Figure 10-24 after *maximizing* it. Notice that the views are arranged properly, and are aligned vertically and horizontally.

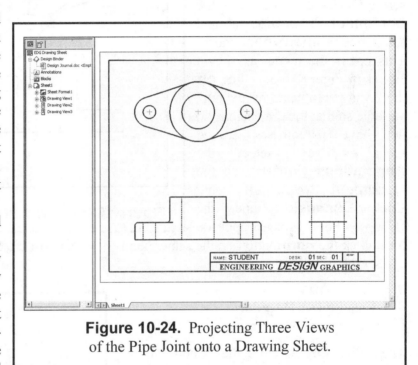

Figure 10-24. Projecting Three Views of the Pipe Joint onto a Drawing Sheet.

This is a simple part and the right side view is not needed. So move your cursor over the right side view and click on it to activate its border (it should highlight green). Right mouse click (**RMB**) on this green border and a pop-up menu appears at the cursor position. Select the option **Delete** and a second menu now appears, as shown in Figure 10-25. The menu asks you "*Do you really want to delete this*" and you should select **Yes**. You now have deleted the right side view and this frees some room on the sheet for all the dimensions.

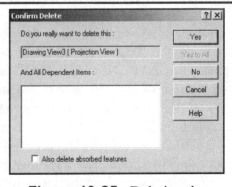

Figure 10-25. Deleting the Right Side View.

This now leaves the remaining two views (front and top) as full scale, as shown in Figure 10-26. You can **Move** the views over a little to the right by clicking on the **Front** view border and dragging it. You can Move the Top view a little upward to allow more room for the dimensions around it.

SETTING THE DIMENSION VARIABLES

You are now ready to start dimensioning the PIPE JOINT model. But first you should set some general dimensioning variables. Pull-down **Tools**, and select **Options**. Then pick the **Document Properties** tab and select the **Dimensions** menu. This opens the menu, as shown earlier in Figure 10-5. Click **off** the "Add parentheses by default" variable so that the dimensions do not have parentheses around them. Next select the **Annotations Font** tab on the **Document Properties** menu. Click **Dimension** and the "Choose Font" menu appears.

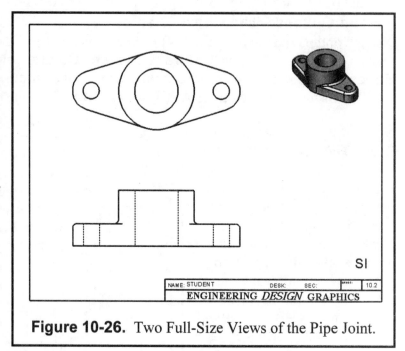

Figure 10-26. Two Full-Size Views of the Pipe Joint.

Next click the **Font** button on the same menu. The "Choose Font" pop menu appears. Here you can set the following values:

Font = **Arial**
Font Style = **Regular**
Height = **12 Points**.

Then click **OK** to close the "Choose Font" menu..

DIMENSIONING THE DRAWING

You will start dimensioning the top view. Click on the **Top** view and a gray border appears around it. Now click the **Dimension** tool icon. Pick the *diameter* of the small bolt hole on the right side and drag the φ**12** value outside the object and position it as shown in Figure 10-27. Next pick the rounded end and drag the **R14** *radius* over as shown in Figure 10-27. When you place these two dimensions a text box appears to the left of the screen

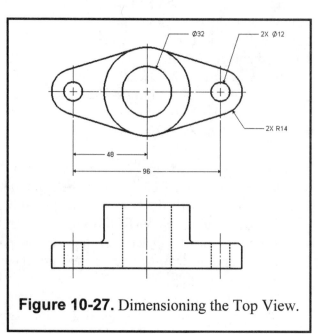

Figure 10-27. Dimensioning the Top View.

10-12

labeled **TEXT DIMENSION**. You can add the text for **2 Holes** and **2 Places** to the dimensions as shown Figure 10-27.

Next dimension the φ**32** *diameter* of the through hole on top of the boss. *Recall:* If the dimension arrowhead styles are not the way you want them, you can always right mouse click (**RMB**) over the dimension value and select **Properties**. Then use the "Dimension Properties" menu to set your arrowhead style (see earlier Figure 10-17), or activate the dimension in the edit mode so there are green dots on the arrows. Click on these green dots and the arrows will move to the other option. Finally, dimension the **48 mm** distance from the center of the boss to the center of a bolt hole and then one **96mm** dimension between the centers of the bolt holes. This finishes the dimensioning of the Top View as shown in Figure 10-27.

You will next dimension the front view. Click on the **Front** view and a gray border appears around it. Now click the **Dimension** tool icon. The diameter of the large boss appears in the top view, but dimensioning standards require that you dimension it in the cylindrical view. So pick the length of the boss (that represents its diameter) in the front view and drag the **56** mm value to an appropriate position. This is a diameter value, but the φ symbol does not automatically appear as it did earlier for the top view diameters. You can add this symbol. Right mouse click (**RMB**)

over the 56 dimension value and select **Properties**. Then in the "Dimension Properties" menu (see earlier Figure 10-17), select the **Modify Text** button. The "Modify Text of Dimension" menu appears as shown in Figure 10-28. Now click on the **Add Symbol** button and a new "Symbols" menu appears on the screen as shown in Figure 10-29. Select the **Diameter** symbol option, and then click **OK** to close the menu. This returns you to the "Modify Text of Dimension" menu where you can see the new φ symbol appear in front of the **56** value in the "Preview" box (see Figure 10-28). Then click **OK** twice to return to the drawing.

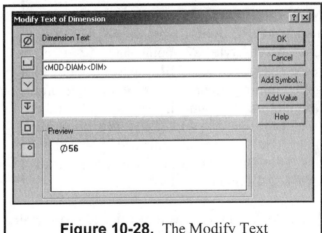

Figure 10-28. The Modify Text of Dimension Menu.

Finally apply the two height **Dimensions** on the right side of the front view. These two dimensions may require some skill. First select the *top right corner* of the boss length. A dimension may quickly pop up with just this one selection, but disregard it. Next pick the *top surface* of the base plate, and the correct **24** mm height dimension should now appear. Drag it over to an appropriate place on the drawing. Return and pick the *top right corner* of the boss

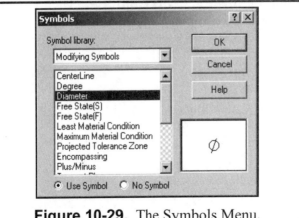

Figure 10-29. The Symbols Menu.

length, and this time select the *bottom surface* of the base plate. The correct **40** mm height dimension should now appear. Drag it over to an appropriate place on the drawing. The front view dimensioning is now complete as shown in Figure 10-30.

You now need to add some centerlines in both the top and front views. Use **Insert, Annotations, Centerline** and click on the box around the front view. The centerlines will be added automatically. You can use **Insert, Annotations** and **Center Mark** to get the centerlines in the top view. Select the two arcs on the ends and the large circle in the center.

Now add a shaded pictorial image to the drawing. Right click the mouse (**RMB**) on the drawing sheet and the pop-up menu (Figure 10-8) appears. Select **Drawing View,** then **Model.** On the "Model View" menu (Figure 10-9) select **Isometric** orientation, **Shaded** style, and **Scale** of **1:2.** Move the cursor to the upper right corner and insert the pictorial.

Next use **Insert, Annotations, Note** for adding a **PIPE JOINT** label and **SCALE 1:1.** Use **Arial** style **22** point and **12** point respectively. Add the **SI** (metric) symbol in the bottom right corner. Use **Arial** style and **36** point for this symbol. Also add a note for fillets and rounds: **ALL F&R: R3** using **12** point **Arial.** Add your name and class data to this Title Block Drawing Sheet using **Arial** style and **12** point.

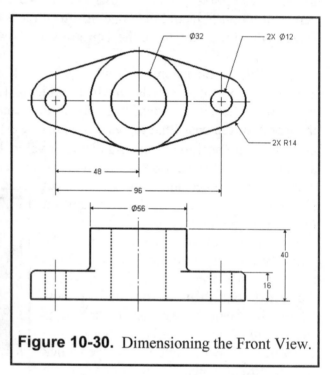

Figure 10-30. Dimensioning the Front View.

Note: You can move the dimensioned views over a little to the left if you need more room on the right side of the drawing sheet for all these annotations. Just pick the border of the front view (it turns green) and **Move** it. The top view will automatically follow since it is aligned with it. Your drawing should now be complete, as suggested in Figure 10-31. Now **Save** your drawing and name it **PIPE JOINT.slddrw.** Then **Print** a hard copy to submit to your instructor before you leave the computer lab.

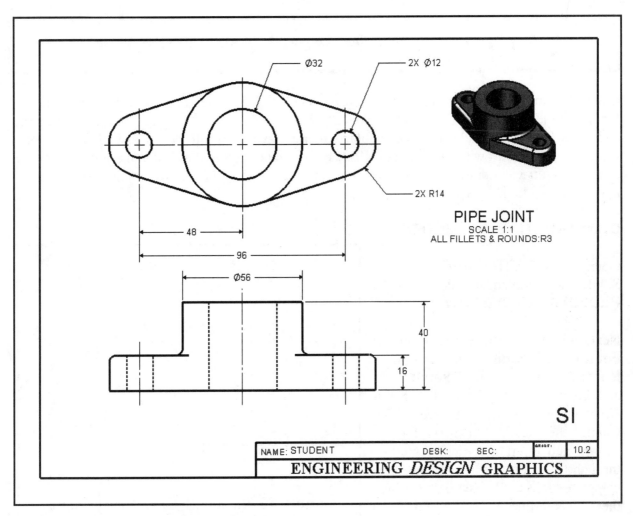

Ø32   2X Ø12

2X R14

PIPE JOINT
SCALE 1:1
ALL FILLETS & ROUNDS:R3

48

96

Ø56

40

16

SI

NAME: STUDENT	DESK:	SEC:	GRADE:	10.2
ENGINEERING *DESIGN* GRAPHICS				

Figure 10-31. The Finished Pipe Joint Drawing.

Exercise 10.3 Pedestal Base Drawing

Quite often in mechanical design, features such as holes are repeated in a regular circular pattern. Examples include flanged pipe joints, inspection cover plates, portal bezels, motor end housings, and many others. Circular and rectangular patterns have been introduced in earlier exercises; here, we create a part with multiple bolt circle patterns and discuss dimensioning practices for the part in a multi-view drawing. You will create a Pedestal Base typical of a stage in a precision manufacturing tool.

CONSTRUCTING THE MODEL

Open **ANSI-METRIC.prtdot**. file in Solidworks. Immediately do a Save As **PEDESTAL BASE.sldprt**.

Next, select the **Front Plane** in the **Feature Manager** and choose a **Normal** view. Enter the **Sketch** mode and create the sketch for the **Base Revolve**, as shown in Figure 10-32. Control the sketch with dimensions as shown, and insert a vertical centerline through the origin. When the profile is complete, select all line segments and the centerline and go to **Insert/Base/Revolve**. Then accept the default condition in the dialog box, which is to create a **360-degree** revolve. Select √ to complete this step. The resulting part will look like Figure 10-33 when viewed in **Trimetric** mode.

Next create the circular hole patterns in the pedestal base. There are two primary methods for doing this; you could use the **Insert/Feature/Hole Wizard** to both specify and place the base hole in each pattern, or you can use a sketch in the appropriate plane as the basis for an **Insert/Cut Extrude** to create the holes. The **Hole Wizard** is well suited to more complex features such as counterbored holes (see the next

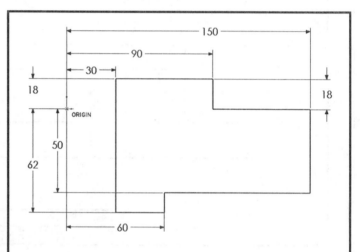

Figure 10-32. Sketch for creating the Base Revolve.

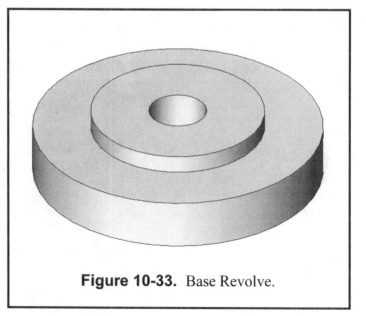

Figure 10-33. Base Revolve.

Exercise 10.4), so you will use a **Cut Extrude** in this exercise. You should feel comfortable using either method once Lab 10 is completed.

Select the outer top surface of the **Part**, choose a **Normal** view, and enter the **Sketch** mode. Use two lines and a circle as construction elements, placed and dimensioned as shown in Figure 10-34. Use these features and the dimension tool to locate two circles in the sketch, sized at φ**18** mm and φ**8** mm, as shown. Next, use the **Tools, Sketch Tools, Circular Step and Repeat** tool to create eight total instances of each size hole, by designating the **Radius** as **120 mm**, the **X** and **Y** coordinates of the center to be **0,0**, and the **Total Angle** as **360 Degrees**. Accept these values and the repeated holes in each circular pattern will appear as in Figure 10-34 (they will also be pre-viewed before you close the dialog box).

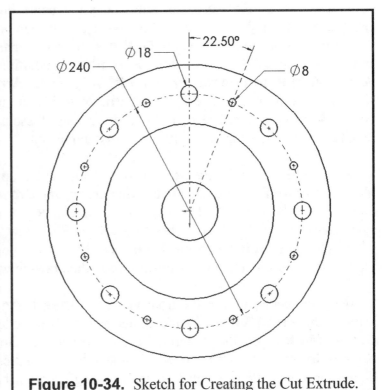

Figure 10-34. Sketch for Creating the Cut Extrude.

Next, delete the φ240 construction circle and all their associated dimensions. Finally, while still in the **Sketch** mode, go to **Insert/ Cut/Extrude** and choose the **Through All** method. Select √ to complete the model, which should look like Figure 10-35 in the **Trimetric** mode. Save your part **File** as **PEDESTAL BASE.sldprt**.

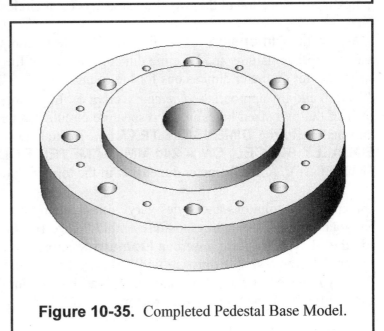

Figure 10-35. Completed Pedestal Base Model.

CREATING THE DRAWING

Now **Open** your **TITLEBLOCK-METRIC.drwdot** drawing sheet and **Save** the new file to the same directory as the **Part** file, with the same name but a different extension - **Pedestal Base.slddrw** (they are of different file types so they can be named the same). There are several formatting options to make. Go to **Options** and set the parameters for **Units, Decimal** places, and **Grid** as you did earlier for the **Part** file. In addition, go to **Options/Dimensions** and *deselect* **Add Parentheses by Default**. Also, under **Arrows** select a closed and filled arrow style with the following sizes: **H = 2 mm, W = 4 mm**, and **L = 8 mm**. Finally under **Font** choose **Arial** type with size equal to **12** pt. Accept these changes; there may be more tweaking required later depending on existing default parameters.

View both files in **Tile Vertical** mode. Drag and drop the top-level icon in the **Feature Manager** of the **Part** file into the drawing area of the **Drawing** file, and the standard three-view drawing will be created. Because the Front and Right Side views are identical due to the symmetry of the pedestal base, **Delete** the Right Side view by selecting its viewport. Next under **View**, choose **Display Hidden Lines Visible**. Now you can select both the Front and Top views and move them to be well positioned in the drawing window. (See Figure 10-36).

To place the centerlines in the front view, use **Insert, Annotations** and **Centerline**. Next, activate the **Front View** and the centerlines will be added. Use **Insert, Annotations** and **Center Mark** to get the centerline in the top view as shown in Figure 10-36. Also place an *angled* **Centerline** as shown with respect to the vertical centerline in the top view—this dimensioned centerline establishes the "clocking" relationship between the two circular bolt hole patterns. Also in the top view, add a circular construction line (styled as a **Centerline**) indicating the location of the two circular arrays (bolt circles).

Now, use the **Dimension** tool in the drawing file to completely dimension the drawing. First, use appropriate datums and baseline dimensions to size the front view profile. Also in this view add the outer diameter dimensions for the round features—use the **Modify** box in the dimension dialog to add the appropriate *diameter symbol* ϕ. In the top view, insert diameter dimensions for each of the two sized holes in the respective circular patterns, and each time add the additional information in the **DIMENSION TEXT** box to include the specification of **EIGHT HOLES, EQUALLY SPACED, ON A 240 MM DIAMETER BOLT CIRCLE** (see the notation used in Figure 10-36). Add a diameter dimension in the top view for the inner through hole as well.

Dimensioning solutions and styles vary with company practices and drawing standards applied, but your completed drawing should resemble Figure 10-36. Since it is a metric drawing, you can add the **SI** symbol. Also, insert an **Isometric** pictorial in the upper right corner of the drawing. In general even a simple drawing will include a border and title block; this is left to the student. When you have done any necessary modifications to your dimension properties, **Save** all work and **Print** a hard copy for your instructor.

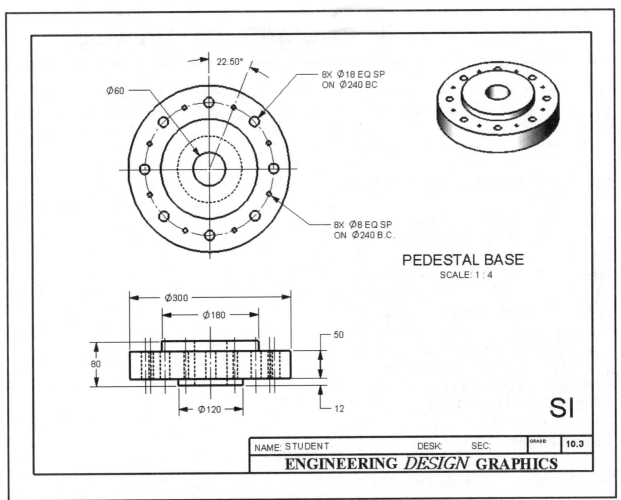

22.50°

Ø60

8X Ø18 EQ SP
ON Ø240 BC

8X Ø8 EQ SP
ON Ø240 B.C.

PEDESTAL BASE
SCALE: 1 : 4

Ø300

Ø180

50

80

Ø120

12

SI

NAME: STUDENT   DESK: SEC: GRADE   10.3

ENGINEERING *DESIGN* GRAPHICS

Figure 10-36. Dimensioned Drawing of the Pedestal Base.

Exercise 10.4: TOOLING PAD Drawing

In Exercise 10.4, you will build a solid model of the Tooling Pad using SolidWorks commands that you have learned in previous labs. Next you will "drag and drop" the model onto a drawing sheet and then create a three-view orthographic drawing of the part. You will add dimensions and complete the drawing with annotations on a title block.

BUILDING THE TOOLING PAD MODEL

Open **ANSI-INCHES.prtdot** and Save As – **TOOLING PAD.sldprt**.

Select the **Top** plane and use a **Top** view orientation. In the **Sketch** mode, use the **Rectangle** tool to draw the outline as shown in Figure 10-37. Use the **Dimension** tool to apply the given dimensions. Then **Extrude** the profile *upward* from the plane using a **Blind** end condition of **0.725** inches.

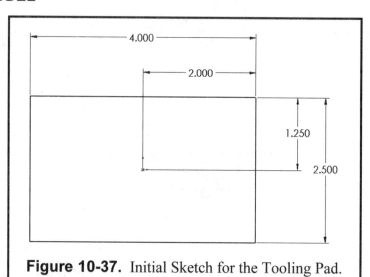

Figure 10-37. Initial Sketch for the Tooling Pad.

Adding a Hole

Now you will use the Hole Wizard to place some holes on the Tooling Pad. Click on the top surface of the base part (it turns *green*) and then pull down **Insert, Features, Hole**, and then **Wizard**. The "Hole Definition" menu appears, as indicated in Figure 10-38. Click on the "Hole" tab and make the following settings:

    Standard = **Ansi Inch**
    Hole Depth = **Through All**
    Hole Diameter = **0.375 in**

Then click the **Next** button. This brings you to the second stage of the Wizard as shown in Figure 10-39. It will display a faint image of a circle and ask you to use the **Dimension** tool to locate the center of the faint hole that appears. Apply the two locating dimensions as shown in Figure 10-39 and then click the **Finish** button on the pop-up menu.

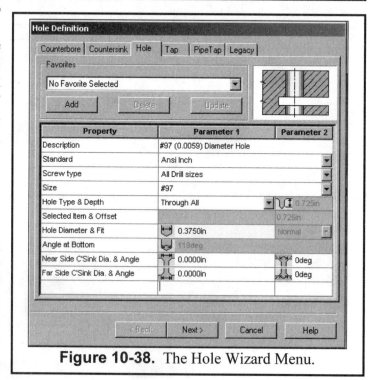

Figure 10-38. The Hole Wizard Menu.

Repeat this "Hole Wizard" process to locate two more holes on the base plate. The **diameter** of the two holes should be the same value (**0.375** in) and they should be **0.650** inches horizontally and vertically from the diagonal corners (*upper right* and *lower left*) of the base plate. They should go **through all**. (See later Figure 10-41).

Adding a Counterbore

Now you will add a counterbore hole

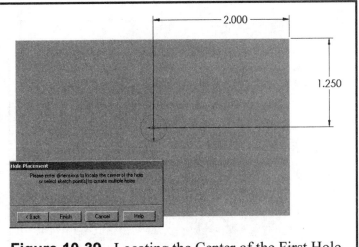

Figure 10-39. Locating the Center of the First Hole.

using the same "Hole Wizard." Click on the top surface of the base part (it turns *green*). Pull down **Insert, Features, Hole**, and then **Wizard**. The "Hole Definition" menu appears, as indicated in Figure 10-40. Click on the "Counterbore" tab and make the following settings:

> Standard = **Ansi Inch**
> End Condition = **Through All**
> Hole Diameter = **0.375 in**
> C'Bore Diameter = **0.875 in**
> C'Bore Depth = **0.250 in**

Then click the **Next** button. This brings you to the second stage of the Wizard as shown in Figure 10-41. It will display a faint image of a counterbore and ask you to use the **Dimension** tool to locate the center of the faint counterbore hole that appears. Apply the two locating dimensions as shown in Figure 10-

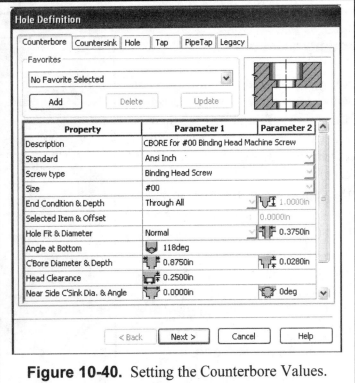

Figure 10-40. Setting the Counterbore Values.

41 and then click the **Finish** button on the pop-up menu. Basically, the counterbore is **0.750** inches vertically and horizontally from the *upper left corner* of the base plate.

You can now finish the top surface by adding an identical counterbore on the diagonal (*lower right*) corner, **0.750** inches vertically and horizontally from it. Use the same data as indicated above for the counterbore values. You now have a preliminary solid model, as indicated in Figure 10-42.

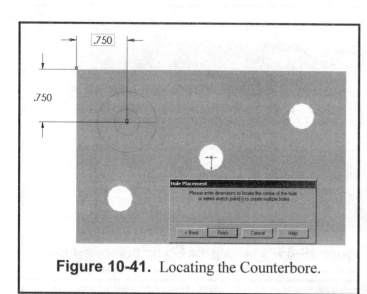

Figure 10-41. Locating the Counterbore.

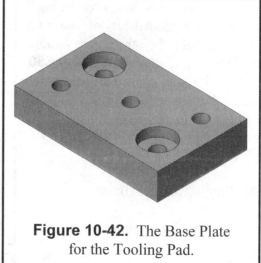

Figure 10-42. The Base Plate for the Tooling Pad.

Adding a Countersink

Now you will add a countersink hole using the same "Hole Wizard." Click on the front surface of the base part (it turns *green*). Pull down **Insert, Features, Hole**, and then **Wizard**. The "Hole Definition" menu appears, as indicated in Figure 10-43. Click on the "Countersink" tab and make the following settings:

Standard = **Ansi Inch**
End Condition = **Up to Surface***
Hole Diameter = **0.25 in**
Angle at Bottom = **180 deg**
C'Sink Diameter = **0.50 in**
C'Sink Angle = **90 deg.**

*For the "End Condition" setting, click the *inner surface* of the small middle through hole.

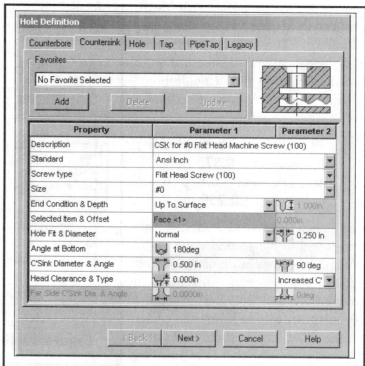

Figure 10-43. Setting the Countersink Values.

Click the **Next** button. This brings you to the second stage of the Wizard. It will display a faint image of a countersink and ask you to use the **Dimension** tool to locate the center of the faint counterbore hole that appears. Apply two locating dimensions to locate it on the front surface: *horizontal* from the left edge = **2.00** inches, *vertical* from the top edge = **0.325** inches. Then click the **Finish** button on the pop-up menu to apply the countersink.

An **Isometric** view of the model at this stage is shown in Figure 10-44.

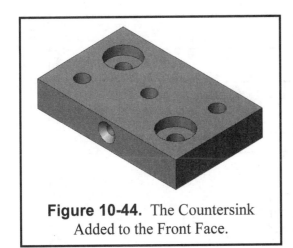

Figure 10-44. The Countersink Added to the Front Face.

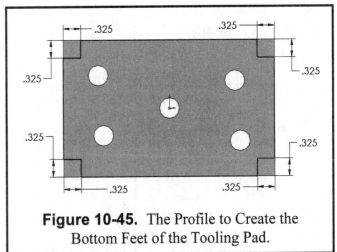

Figure 10-45. The Profile to Create the Bottom Feet of the Tooling Pad.

Adding the Base Feet

Switch to a **Bottom** view to add the four corner feet to the Tooling Pad. Use the **Sketch** tools to draw the profile as shown in Figure 10-45. You could use a **Convert** command to get the outer edges, add four small **Rectangles** in the four corners, and then use **Trim** to cut away some lines. Then add the **0.325 Dimensions** on the feet. Next **Extrude** a **Cut** that is **0.100** inches **Blind** into the model. The finished model is now shown in Figure 10-46 in a **Trimetric** view. Use the **Rotate** button to view your various features of the finished model, if you wish.

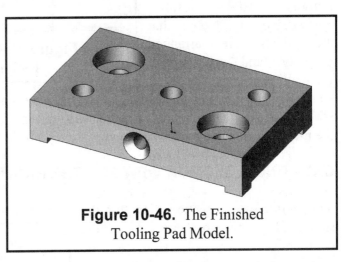

Figure 10-46. The Finished Tooling Pad Model.

Then **Save** it as **TOOLING PAD.sldprt** in your designated folder, but *do not Close* your file. You can now make a three-view projection.

PROJECTING THREE VIEWS

Pull down **File** and select the **TITLEBLOCK-INCHES** Drawing Sheet. Immediately **SAVE AS TOOLING PAD.slddrw**

Before you start the projection, there are some other general drawing sheet settings to make (refer back to Figure 10-3). Pull down the **Tools** menu and select **Options**. Click the **System Options – Drawings - Display Type** tab. Check the dot (•) on the "Hidden lines visible" option and check the dot (•) on the tangent edges "Removed" option. While under the **Systems Options**, click on **Colors – System Colors** select **Drawings, Hidden Model Edges** and change the color to **Black**. Also, on the **Document Properties**, **Detailing** tab, set "Dimensioning Standard" to **ANSI**. Click **OK** to close the menu.

Now pull down **Window** and select **Tile Vertically**. You now can see the two files: the Tooling Pad part file and the newly created blank Drawing Sheet file. Now select the "Tooling Pad" part in its Feature Manager and "drag and drop" it onto the new drawing sheet. SolidWorks will automatically project a three-view orthographic layout using the third angle projection, as displayed in Figure 10-47 (after *maximizing* it). Notice that the views are arranged properly, and are aligned vertically and horizontally. *If*

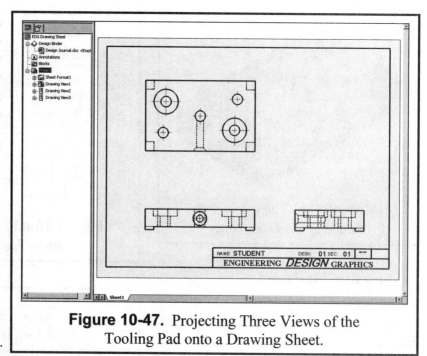

Figure 10-47. Projecting Three Views of the Tooling Pad onto a Drawing Sheet.

your projection results in a smaller than full-size scale, then return to the Feature Manager tree, **RMB Sheet1**, and select the **Properties** option. Set the "Scale" back to **1:1,** and then close the menu. You can also **Move** the views over a little to the center them on the sheet.

CREATING A SECTION VIEW FOR THE RIGHT SIDE

You will create a section view for the right side view to better show the countersink hole. First delete the existing right side view. Move your cursor over the right side view and click on it to activate its border (it should highlight green). Right mouse click (**RMB**) on this green border and a pop-up menu appears at the cursor position. Select the option **Delete** and then delete it.

Next **Sketch** a vertical **Line** right through the middle of the front view, making sure you cut through the center of the countersink diameter. Pull down **Insert**, select **Drawing View**, and then **Section**. Move the new section view

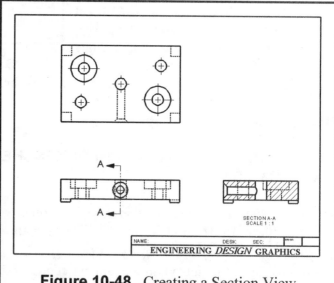

Figure 10-48. Creating a Section View of the Tooling Pad.

over to the right side of the front view and position it as shown in Figure 10-48. Also notice the **Section A-A** cutting plane line and label. Now turn off the hidden lines in the section view.

ADDING CENTERLINES

The drawing may not be perfect. For example, the centerlines in the views may be missing or incomplete. So **INSERT, ANNOTATIONS, Centerline** and activate each of the view to automatically add the centerlines in the top and front views. Now **Insert, Annotations**, and select **Center Mark**. Then click on each perimeter of the circular features to add the center marks (i.e. centerlines).

SETTING THE DIMENSION VARIABLES

You are now ready to start dimensioning the Tooling Pad drawing. But first set some general dimensioning variables. Pull-down **Tools**, and select **Options**. Then pick the **Document Properties** tab and select the **Dimensions** menu. This opens the menu, as shown earlier in Figure 10-5. Click **off** the "Add parentheses by default" variable so that the dimensions do not have parentheses around them. Next click the **Annotations Font, Dimension** option on the same menu. The "Choose Font" pop menu appears, as shown earlier in Figure 10-6. Here you can set the following values:

Font = **Arial**
Font Style = **Regular**
Height = **12 Points**.

Then click **OK** to close the "Choose Font" menu. Next click on the **Units** tab and set the units to **3** decimal place **Inches**, then click **OK** to close the menu.

DIMENSIONING THE DRAWING

You will start dimensioning the top view. Click on the **Top** view and a gray border appears around it. Now click the **Dimension** tool icon. Pick the *diameter* of the small hole in the upper right corner and drag the φ.375 value outside the object and position it as shown later in Figure 10-50. Below it, add an **Annotations Note**: **3 HOLES THRU** to cover the other two small holes. Use the same font type and size for these notes as used for the dimensions.

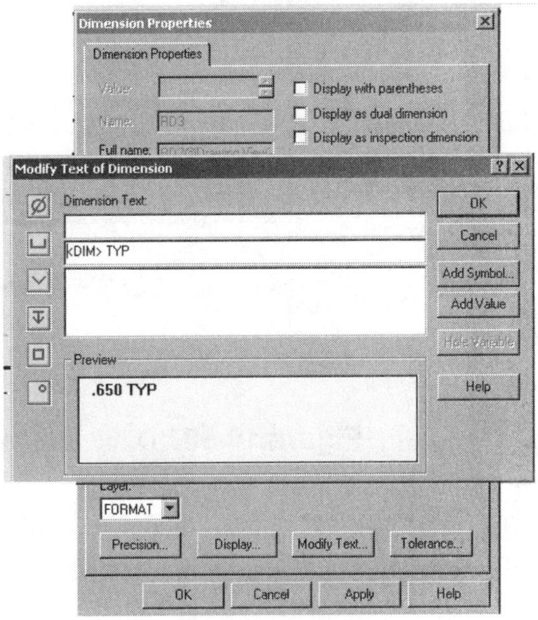

Figure 10-49. Modifying Dimension Text.

Next **Dimension** the position of the hole relative to the upper right corner (**0.650** in both directions). Add the note **TYP** after each of the dimensions. This can be done by doing a **RMB** over the dimension value and then select **Properties**. In the "Dimension Properties" menu, select the **Modify Text** button. The "Modify Text of Dimension" menu appears as shown in Figure 10-49. Now type in **TYP** after the <DIM> to add this note to the dimension value. Then click **OK** twice to close the menus.

Now dimension the counterbore. Click the **Dimension** tool icon and pick the *outer diameter* of the large counterbore in the upper left corner. Drag the ϕ**.875** value outside the object and position it as shown in Figure 10-50. Notice that the method of dimensioning a counterbore is to call out the small thru hole first. So repeat the previous "Modify Text of Dimension" process (see Figure 10-49) to change the dimension value to: ϕ**.375, THRU.** Now below it, add the rest of the call out using an **Annotations Note**:

2X ⌀.375 THRU
⊔ ⌀.875 ⊽.25

The symbol <MOD-DIAM> just adds the ϕ symbol in front of the **0.875** diameter for the counterbore. Now complete the linear dimensions of the top view as suggested by Figure 10-50. You can **Dimension** the **2.500** depth and the **4.000** width. You can position the counterbore as **0.750 TYP** from the bottom right corner in both directions. You can position the small center hole several ways, one of which is depicted below.

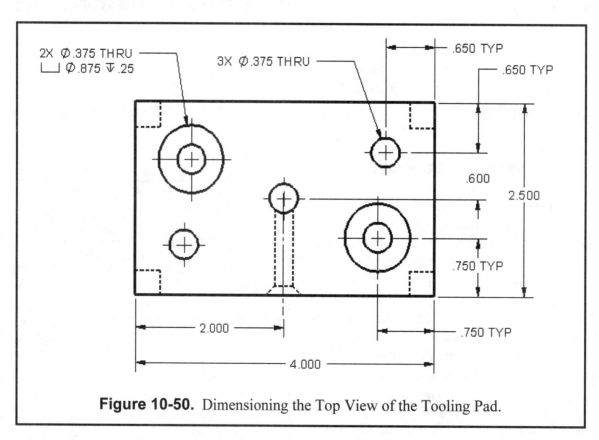

Figure 10-50. Dimensioning the Top View of the Tooling Pad.

Now start your dimensioning on the front view. Make a call out for the countersink using a similar technique as the counterbore. Make the note as follows:

⌀.250 ⊽1.25
⌵ ⌀.500 X 90°

Complete the exercise by adding the remaining linear dimensions to the front and right side section view, as suggested by the finished drawing in Figure 10-51. Use your choice of style.

Now right click the mouse (**RMB**) on the drawing sheet and the pop-up menu (see earlier Figure 10-8) appears. Select **Drawing View,** then **Model**. On the "Model View" menu (see earlier Figure 10-9) select **Isometric** orientation, **Shaded** style, and an arbitrary user defined **Scale** of **1:1.75** Move the cursor to the upper right corner and insert the pictorial.

Next use **Insert, Annotations, Note** for adding a **TOOLING PAD** label and **SCALE 1:1**. Use **Arial** style **22** point and **12** point respectively. Add your name and class data inside the title block using **Arial** style and **12** point. Your drawing should now be complete, as shown in Figure 10-51. Now **Save** your drawing and name it **Tooling Pad**. Then **Print** a hard copy to submit to your instructor before you leave the computer lab.

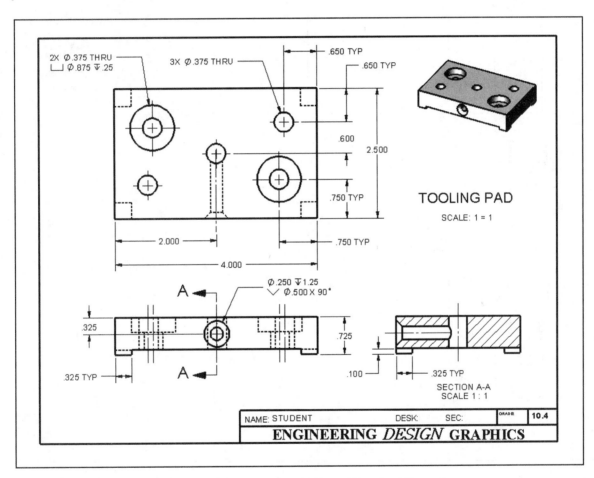

Figure 10-51. The Finished Tooling Pad Drawing.

SUPPLEMENTARY EXERCISE 10-5 PILLOW BLOCK

Build a full size solid model of the figure below. Insert it on a Title Block and Dimension it. Insert a small pictorial of the object in the upper right hand corner of the sheet. Provide the proper Titles, Scales and other pertinent notes.

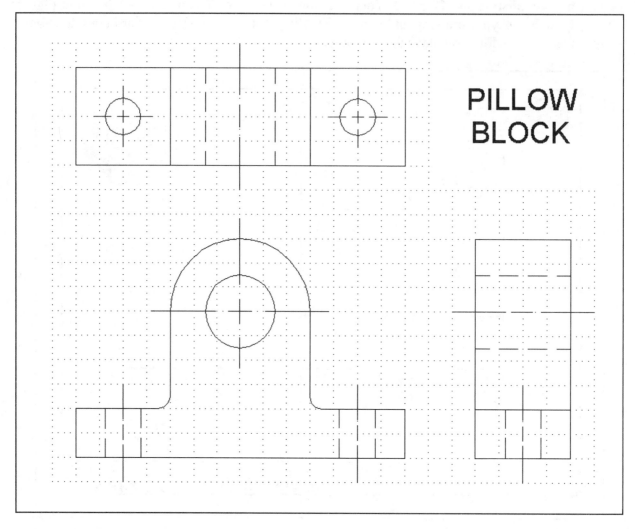

PILLOW BLOCK

ASSUME THE GRID DIVISIONS TO BE 5 mm

Build a full size solid model of the figure below. Insert it on a Title Block. Dimension the drawing according to standards learn doing the exercises in Unit 10. Finally insert a small Isometric View in the upper right hand corner. Provide the proper Titles, Scales and other pertinent notes.

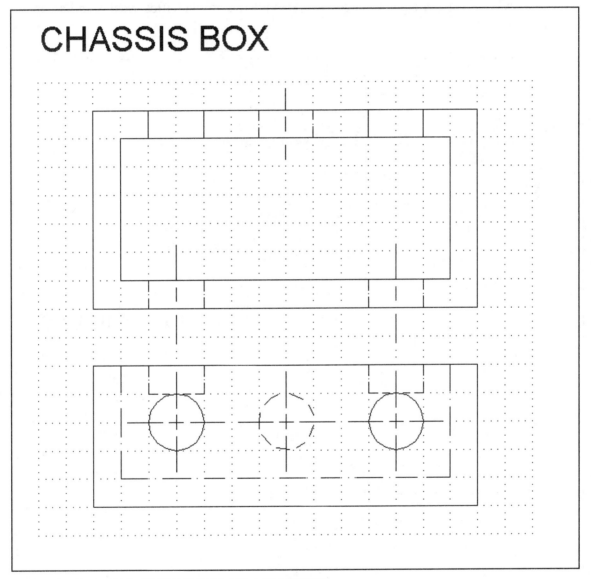

CHASSIS BOX

ASSUME THE GRID DIVISIONS TO BE 0.50 INCHES.

SUPPLEMENTARY EXERCISE 10-7 COLUMN BASE

Build a full size solid model of the **COLUMN BASE** below. Insert it on a Title Block. After deleting the front and the right side view, Draw a horizontal line through center of the top view. Next go to Insert – Drawing View – Section View and place it where the front view used to be. Dimension the drawing according to the standards learned in Unit 10. Finally insert a small Isometric View in the upper right hand corner. Provide the proper Titles, Scales and other pertinent notes.

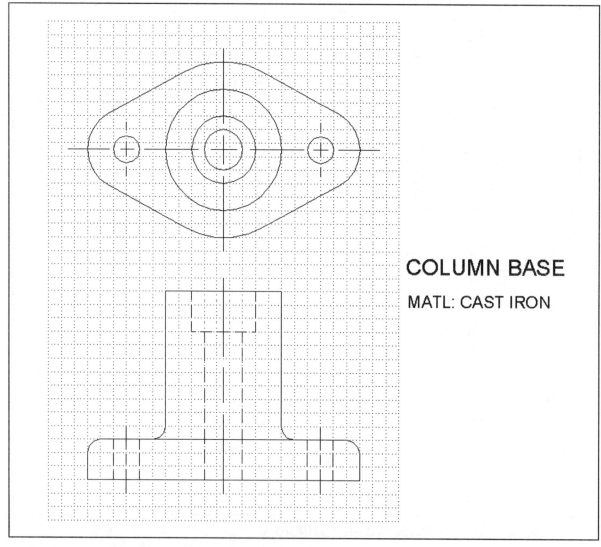

COLUMN BASE

MATL: CAST IRON

ASSUME THE GRID DIVISIONS TO BE 0.25 INCHES

SUPPLEMENTARY EXERCISE 10-8 VALVE HOUSING

Build full sized solid models of the **VALVE HOUSING** below. After deleting the front and the right side view, Draw a horizontal line through center of the top view. Next go to Insert – Drawing View – Section View and place it where the front view used to be. Also Insert – Drawing View – Projected View to replace the Right Side view. Dimension the drawing according to the standards learned in Unit 10. Finally insert a small Isometric View in the upper right hand corner. Provide the proper Titles, Scales and other pertinent notes.

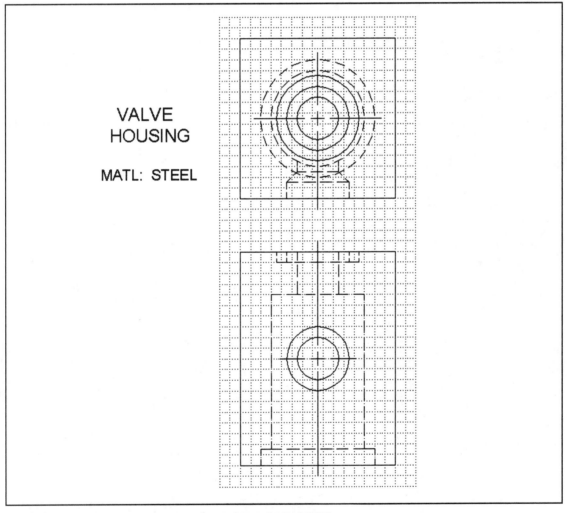

VALVE
HOUSING

MATL: STEEL

ASSUME THE GRID DIVISIONS TO BE 0.25 INCHES.

Notes:

Notes:

Notes:

Notes:

Notes:

Notes:

Notes: